# Beyond Binaries

# Beyond Binaries

## Trans Identities in Contemporary Culture

Edited by
Mike Perez, Rachel Friedman,
and John C. Lamothe

LEXINGTON BOOKS
*Lanham • Boulder • New York • London*

Published by Lexington Books
An imprint of The Rowman & Littlefield Publishing Group, Inc.
4501 Forbes Boulevard, Suite 200, Lanham, Maryland 20706
www.rowman.com

6 Tinworth Street, London SE11 5AL, United Kingdom

ISBN 9781498593656 (cloth)
ISBN 9781498593670 (pbk)

British Library Cataloguing in Publication Information Available

**Library of Congress Control Number: 2020949700**

*Mike dedicates their work on this book to the unceasingly fabulous memory and activism of Marsha P. Johnson.*

*Rachel dedicates her work on this book to her Domestic Partner, Martin D. Garcia, and her cats, Monty and Romeo.*

*John dedicates his work on this book to the Trans community and all those fighting for human equality.*

# Contents

# Introduction

## Rachel Friedman, Mike Perez, and John C. Lamothe

Globally, a growing awareness of transgender issues has intensified in recent years, especially after the high-profile media examples of Chaz Bono and Caitlyn Jenner, the formidable career ascension of Laverne Cox, and the multimedia achievements of Jazz Jennings, both as author and reality television star. This rising awareness has caused activism both for and against the transgender community and compels us to question many of the binaries that permeate popular culture. Few issues question borders and transcend boundaries in such an important manner as current transgender concerns, and although there has been scholarly attention on trans communities, there has been less attention given to the intersection of trans identities and broader contemporary culture in an interdisciplinary context.

This collected work will explore numerous aspects of trans identity from a scholarly perspective while at the same time using *trans* as a lens to investigate cultural practices and constructions. It will be multidisciplinary and well researched, but also accessible to a non-scholarly audience. The book will be organized in three major sections roughly corresponding to the past, present, and future of the transgender presence and movement.

What exists within and beyond the binaries that were, upon a time, never questioned or examined, especially as expressed through a transgender lens and in popular culture? In shaping this book and guiding contributors, we were particularly interested in projects that question or redefine gender and transgender identities beyond the expectations of binary codes, be it language, media portrayals, and historical considerations, such as but not limited to the following: transgender presences in cinema, music, and culture both past and present, not to mention that which is rapidly developing as this book is taking shape (such as the assembling of the largest transgender cast actually portraying trans characters in the Summer 2018 FX mini-series *Pose*);

fashion perspectives; international perspectives; social media representations of trans identities, as well as the active and ubiquitous presence of trans identities in video games, even if they are textual (such as the character of Aech, Parzival's best friend online in the virtual world of OASIS, in Ernest Cline's *Ready Player One*). Cline's character falls prey to a pattern often found in trans media portrayals (although his is a technologically savvy example, and a welcome one insofar that a queer woman of color is directing her male avatar of Aech as role-playing in more ways than one)—the pattern of the transgender "reveal" or betrayal of transgender identity as being commiserate with biological gender only. In looking beyond binaries, we strive to locate and analyze such "outings" as the false transphobic system they inherently uphold and perpetuate, both in cultures and in lives.

Thus, this anthology will address a trans-continuum and historicity as one way in to contextualize the significant iterations of transgender across multimedia platforms. A starting point for such a timeline will be tentative at best, as the transgender presence in certain modes of media—especially religious texts and cultures—can go back hundreds, if not thousands, of years. The visibility of transgender individuals is not based in a "reveal" (that awkward noun created in American popular culture usage by Fox Network's short-lived reality makeover show *The Swan*); on the contrary, the transgender presence has thrived beyond binaries for more years than are currently being disclosed as the daily revelation they actually are.

Regarding the transgender "reveal," even a popular example such as the American reality show *RuPaul's Drag Race* falls prey to the cliché of the transgender "reveal" in its earlier seasons, somewhat reflecting transphobic expectations prevalent in aspects of even cis-normative gay male homosocial culture, culminating in the season 9 presence (and subsequent first runner-up status) of the show's first transgender contestant, Peppermint, who identified as transgender from the season's beginning. That transgender identities have always coexisted with the large, diverse, and consistently evolving world of drag performance not only in the United States reinforces a concept integral to this anthology: that there has always been at work and as a daily fact, transgender contributions to not only divergent countercultures or sub-cultures but culture itself as we both know and do not know it.

To expand upon the concept of "rapidly developing presences in culture"—other chapters in our anthology also aim to rectify this idea somewhat in presenting an active trans continuum. Several chapters of the anthology concern themselves with the present, or the "now" as reflected by transgender concerns and identities being formed faster than the book itself can keep up (or so it seems); other chapters address the future identities that might be expressed by transgender men and women, who may be referred to, according to their preference, as simply "men" or "women" very soon, alongside nonbinary conforming individuals who, for the first time, have the option of choosing in a fluid way their individual gender truths beyond the confinement or linguistic tyranny of set pronouns. As if gender is rarely simple and not predicated on just one reductive choice, one surgery, one revelation fixed in time.

This book is dedicated to the historical and developing genres of transgender media and their ongoing visibility and elucidation in the face of ignorance and violence, always keeping in mind scholar Susan Stryker's reminder that different media iterations and genres are integral to this process, as "the English word 'gender' is derived from *genre*, meaning kind or type" (Stryker 11).

This edited volume is unique in that it collects international voices as well as those from the American academic dialogue currently interested in transgender concerns and iterations. Authorship includes scholars who identify as not only transgender but gender-fluid and non-gender conforming from an international perspective as well. *Beyond Binaries* is the first transgender media anthology on the international level that also aims for a larger readership and usability beyond academia. We are particularly qualified to write and edit the volume because of our allegiance with the transgender communities we support and promote on the academic level as well as the many authors (Kate Bornstein, Susan Stryker, Janet Mock, Riki Wilchins, and Pat Califia, to name a few) whom we have studied and taught in our own humanities or communications courses at Embry-Riddle Aeronautical University in Daytona Beach, Florida.

*Chapter 1*

# TransForming Society?

## *Examining the Pros and Cons of the Trans Celebrity Spokesperson*

### J. Michael Ryan

Recent years have seen the emergence of a growing number of trans celebrities including reality television stars (Caitlyn Jenner, Jazz Jennings), actors (Ian Harvie, Chaz Bono), actresses (Candis Cayne, Laverne Cox, Indya Moore), fashion models (Andreja Pejic, Laith Ashley, Aydian Dowling), directors (Yance Ford, Lana and Lilly Wachowski), authors (Janet Mock, Jenny Boylan), and professional athletes (Harrison Browne, Balian Buschbaum). Alongside this rise in media attention to trans lives, the political world has also seen a sharp increase in debates around trans-related issues such as bathroom bills (Schilt and Westbrook, 2015), service in the military (Yerke, 2020), and gender identity laws (Ryan, 2018). The academic world has also seen growing attention to trans issues with the development of specialized journals (*Transgender Studies Quarterly*), edited volumes (*Trans Lives in a Globalizing World: Rights, Identities, and Politics* [Ryan, 2020]), award-winning compendiums (*The Transgender Studies Reader* [Stryker and Whittle, 2006]), and even a Chair in Transgender Studies (University of Victoria) devoted specifically to investigating trans lives and issues. Some have even argued that we are now at a "transgender tipping point" highlighting the rapid growth in awareness of, and social advances made by, transgender people (Steinmetz, 2014).

One of the more notable aspects of the growing attention to trans lives is the extent to which trans people themselves have been in the lead of growing awareness. Celebrities like Laverne Cox, Chaz Bono, and Caitlyn Jenner have become increasingly well-known pop culture figures. Conchita Wurst became a household name throughout much of Europe after winning the Eurovision Song Contest in 2014. Political figures like Chelsea Manning

1

have continued to showcase the multidimensional nature of being trans. And even everyday individuals—like Jazz Jennings—have become spokespeople for their own community. Rather than simply being talked about, trans individuals are now doing the talking.

Sociologist Erving Goffman (1963) spoke about the role of "spokespeople" in representing stigmatized minorities. In discussing the role of these spokespeople, he noted that "they appear as 'speakers' before various audiences of the 'normals' and of the stigmatized; they present the case for the stigmatized and, when they themselves are natives of the group, provide a living model of fully-normal achievement, being heroes of adjustment who are subject to public awards for proving that an individual of this kind can be a good person" (24–25). It should be noted that being a spokesperson is not necessarily something that is chosen by individuals who fill the role, but rather something that can be forced upon them. This is especially true in the contemporary age where celebrities have taken increasingly prominent roles in the broader culture, including expectations to also serve as political figures who speak out on behalf of particular people and issues. As Goffman notes, "It might be added that once a person with a particular stigma attains high occupational, political, or financial position . . . a new career is likely to be thrust upon him, that of representing his category. He finds himself too eminent to avoid being presented by his own as an instance of them" (26). The point remains, however, that once such a position is either achieved or ascribed, it becomes a powerful platform fraught with responsibility.

Spokespeople can have a number of positive influences on the communities they represent. Empowered with a platform, they have the ability to draw attention to issues and to advocate for greater rights and decreased stigma for their population. The spokesperson can also become the sole source of information about a particular stigmatized group for a public who is not otherwise knowledgeable about them or their daily lives. Christopher Reeve brought awareness to peoples with disabilities, Marlee Matlin to people who are hard of hearing, and Chris Burke introduced millions to the lives of people with Down syndrome. The power of the spokesperson is the ability to speak and, more importantly, to be heard.

When a minority group has a particularly negative stigma attached, spokespeople can also become exceptions to a rule. At the same time that Matthew Shepard was being tied to a fence post, Elton John was selling millions of records (even Trump now exhibits some fascination with Elton John while rolling back transgender rights in the United States [Richards, 2018]) and while record numbers of Black men are landing in prison, Oprah need only mention a book for it to become a best seller. Thus, it is important not to confuse allowing, or even embracing, a certain stigma found in the rich and famous with acceptance of such a stigma in daily life. As Meyerowitz (2015) notes, "Transgendered people, especially poorer ones, are still fired from their jobs, ejected from their homes, abused on the streets and in prison, ostracized and sometimes murdered, while Caitlyn Jenner enjoys the trappings of celebrity" (Politico website).

Since spokespeople are often used to represent groups with which the average person has little to no personal contact, they face the unfair responsibility of representing that group. As Hart (2000) noted, people who have no, or limited, contact with a minority group are more likely to rely on the media when forming their opinions of that group. Ironically, however, as it is usually high levels of fame, power, and/or money required to reach such a position, these spokespeople are rarely representative of the larger populations they are intended to represent. As Goffman (1963) notes, "Instead of leaning on their crutch, they get to play golf with it, ceasing, in terms of social participation, of being representative of the people they represent" (27). Thus, while bringing attention to a stigmatized group, spokespeople might not necessarily be bringing attention to stigmatized issues of that group.

This chapter begins by examining the rise of trans celebrities as trans spokespersons. These celebrities have done a great deal to advance awareness of trans lives among the general public but, at the same time, have also come to act as spokespeople for an entire community, one of which they are arguably not representative. An examination will then be made of the often vast differences between the lived experiences of these celebrities and those of the general trans population. An argument will be made that while trans celebrity spokespeople are beneficial in fostering greater acceptance of trans individuals and bringing awareness to certain critical issues, when taken as representative spokespeople for an entire population, they can also serve to deflect attention away from the critical issues facing that population. As Gamson (1998) notes, "As we make ourselves visible, do those among us with less status get to speak just as anyone else (increasing the risk of further stigma as the price for democratic diversity) or do the more acceptable get the upper hand (reproducing class and racial hierarchies as the price for gaining legitimacy)? Any path to visibility must face this question" (14). It is to answering that question that this chapter will now turn.

## THE RISE OF THE TRANS CELEBRITY

It is important to note that this chapter will focus on trans celebrity spokespeople and not just representations of trans people in popular culture. In other words, while media representations can, and do, also influence how a particular group is viewed by the general public, they do not themselves speak for that group in the same way that individuals do. In fact, with the case of trans issues, it is arguably the case that the rise of individual spokespeople, rather than simply media representations, has done much to reverse the sentiment toward trans individuals. While many earlier representations of trans people in the media portrayed them as depraved (*Silence of the Lambs*), deceptive (*The Crying Game*), or victims (*Boys Don't Cry*), all negative representations, the rise of the individual spokesperson has shifted that view to showing images of people who are wealthy, glamorous, and beloved.

The story of the rise of the trans celebrity has a defensible starting point with Christine Jorgensen. Although Jorgensen was not the first person to undergo gender-affirming surgery, she was the first person to gain fame for doing so. After undergoing a series of surgeries in Denmark during 1951 and 1952, Jorgensen later returned to the United States and became an almost overnight celebrity (Flinn, 2016). The *New York Daily Times* ran a front page story on Jorgensen on December 1, 1952, titled "Ex-GI Becomes Blonde Beauty" (a story that would become their top headline of the year, even overtaking the execution of the Rosenberg spies) doing much to push Jorgensen into not only the national spotlight, but the international one as well. Hailed as "once more famous than Marilyn Monroe" (Anderson-Minshall, 2017), Jorgensen became not just the first major trans celebrity, but one of the first major international celebrities as well. Jorgensen used her platform to not only gain celebrity for herself but also to advocate for trans people in general and to challenge society to see the differences between biological sex and social gender.

Although Jorgensen remained in the spotlight for many years, it was tennis star Renee Richards who would again be stealing headlines when she won her legal battle to compete in the 1977 U.S. Open as a woman. That case is still widely cited in contemporary battles over trans athletes participating in sex-segregated sports. Although Richards did little in the ways of advocacy, her position as a successful tennis player, and also as a successful medical doctor (she worked as an ophthalmologist both before and after her tennis career), provided a positive image of trans people to the often homophobic and transphobic world of sport.

Another milestone moment in the rise of trans celebrity was the public transitioning of Chaz Bono, son of superstars Sonny Bono and Cher. Chaz, who had already been out as a lesbian named Chastity, announced his transition in a series of widely publicized media events including a two-part Entertainment Tonight special in 2009 and a documentary about his transition, *Becoming Chaz*, that premiered at the Sundance Musical Festival in 2011 and later on the Oprah Winfrey Network. He has subsequently gone on to appear on *Dancing With the Stars* that same year and has become a regular on the hit *American Horror Story* anthology since 2016. Famous by birth, as well as in his own right, Chaz has used his celebrity status to serve as an advocate for trans rights, having worked with such high-profile organizations as the Human Rights Campaign (HRC) and the Gay and Lesbian Alliance Against Defamation (GLAAD) as well as working on the political campaign of Bill Clinton.

The last several years have seen a rapid increase in the number of trans-identified celebrities but perhaps the most well-accomplished trans celebrity to date is Laverne Cox. Cox has set a number of milestones for the trans community including being the first trans person to be nominated for an Emmy (for her work on the hit Netflix show *Orange is the New Black*), the first trans person to appear on the cover of *TIME* magazine as well as *Cosmopolitan* magazine, and the first trans person to win a Daytime Emmy as an executive producer. Her fame has also led to her being the first openly trans person to have a wax figure of themselves at Madame Tussauds. In addition to being arguably the most accomplished trans celebrity, Cox is also perhaps the most outspoken trans celebrity having committed herself to advocacy of LGBTQ+ since even before she became famous.

Caitlyn Jenner, although lacking many of the entertainment accolades of Cox, has been heralded as "the most famous transgender woman in history" (MSNBC, 2015). Having already lived a life of high-profile fame as both an Olympic gold medalist and member of the media-savvy Kardashian clan, Jenner has also found considerable fame as a trans woman. Since coming out in April 2015, Jenner has appeared on the cover of *Vanity Fair*, launched a reality TV show, *I am Cait*, and won the Arthur Ashe Courage Award at the ESPYS where she was introduced as "someone whose mission isn't to bring attention to herself, but the ones who truly need it" (ESPYS, 2015). Jenner's conservative political views, among other things, however, have often made her spokesperson status a source of great discomfort for many in the trans community (Brady, 2017; Serano, 2016).

## NOW YOU SEE ME: THE PROS OF TRANS CELEBRITY SPOKESPEOPLE

There is no doubt that trans people and trans issues have seen a meteoric rise in media appearance, both quantitatively and qualitatively, and that it has happened during an era when celebrity, more than expertise, has become the currency of advocacy and awareness. It is perhaps even arguable that celebrity, as opposed to critical academic or political knowledge, has become the primary fuel in the fight for awareness of trans people and their issues. In fact, Hirshfield (2015) found that both trans and cis individuals reported that they felt transgender celebrities were the main reason for the increased appearance of trans issues in the media. These celebrities, acting in the role of spokespeople, have had a positive impact on the trans community by drawing attention to the community itself, by drawing attention to certain issues facing the trans community, and by empowering members of the community.

Although LGBT has become a well-known acronym, it was only recently that the T began getting any attention of its own. In fact, there has been some debate about why the T has been included in the larger acronym at all given that L, G, and B all represent sexual minorities while T, although it can also represent individuals of a particular sexual minority, is more about representing a gender minority, and one which has its own distinctive set of issues. Arguably, one of the advantages of the rise of the trans celebrity has been a growing awareness to this distinction and the fact that T need not be LGB. Thus, for example, Li (2018) found that after Jenner's interview with Diane Sawyer, transgender-related stories appearing in the media were more likely to differentiate transgender issues from LGB issues and to also take in-depth approaches to report the stories.

Trans people receive less support from their families than their cisgender siblings (Factor and Rothblum, 2007). They are also less likely to have immediately accessible role models and are thus more likely to turn to celebrities as role models (Bird et al., 2012). Research has shown that the increased presence of LGBT individuals in the media has had a positive influence on LGBT youth (Grossman and D'Aguelli, 2004). For this reason, the ways those celebrities are not only portrayed, but also received, can have a particularly powerful effect on trans individuals and "the positive reception of a transgender celebrity may be especially important for transgender individuals' cultivation of their perceived acceptance and legitimacy in society" (Miller and Behm-Morawitz, 2017, p. 141).

A survey conducted by Trans Media Watch in 2010 found that 70 percent of the respondents felt that representations of transgender people in the media were negative while only 5 percent of the respondents considered images of transgender people in the media to be positive (Trans Media Watch, 2010). By 2017, only 48.5 percent felt that representations were negative and 71 percent felt that representations had become more positive in the last seven years (Liu, 2017). Further, 51 percent felt that media coverage had become more accurate in the past seven years (Liu, 2017). As Kermode (2015) notes, "Far more positive stories are being published or broadcast. Neutral stories are notably more respectful than they used to be. The accuracy of reporting has improved and a wider range of trans identities is represented" (Kermode, 2015). Increasingly positive representations of transgender people have been shown to have a positive effect on trans people themselves. Liu (2017) found that "positive media coverage made 62% of respondents feel happy, 55% feel included, and 46% feel both good about society and more able to talk about their gender identity" (website).

The emergence of trans celebrities, many of whom who have endeared themselves to the general public, has arguably been a large part of what has shaped the growing positive views of the transgender community at large (Day, 2015). The HRC conducted a poll in 2015 and found that 44 percent of likely voters had positive views of transgender people, and 25 percent felt negatively. The same poll conducted in 2017 found a rise in favorability in these numbers such that 47 percent of respondents saw transgender people in a favorable light while only 19 percent had an overall negative opinion (Murchison, 2017). The role of the trans celebrity, alongside other factors such as the growing probability of someone knowing a trans individual personally and the liberalizing attitudes toward the LGBT community, has no doubt played a significant role in how the trans community at large has come to be more positively viewed.

It is not just representations of a particular group in the media, but positive representations of that group that can most positively impact public opinion. Public opinion is also more likely to be positively swayed when someone announcing membership in a minority is an already beloved figure. Thus, "humanizing stories—such as Diane Sawyer's interview with Caitlyn Jenner—may play a role in cultivating favorable attitudes toward trans individuals and issues" (Miller and Behm-Morawitz, 2017, p. 143). As Bruce Jenner had already been a beloved icon of American sporting history and popular culture for decades, his announcement to "call me Caitlyn" was arguably more positively received than those of unknown individuals. For Jenner, it is not that she has become a trans celebrity so much as that she was a celebrity who became trans.

Janet Mock, author, editor, and television host, was one of the first trans celebrities to use her status to draw attention to the issues targeting the larger trans population. As she told *Elle* magazine, "As long as people are targeted because of their identities, our politics and our movement and our actions need to be just as targeted. We need to be exacting about who is most vulnerable, who is not being served. It's the poor, the incarcerated, the condemned, the feminine, the trans, the queer. It's the uneducated. That's what we need to center in our politics. And when we center our most vulnerable, we actually are a stronger society" (Kahn, 2016). Although highly immersed in the world of celebrity (she was previously a staff editor for *People* magazine and now hosts the show *So POPular!* on MSNBC), Mock understands the power that fame can have in drawing attention to critical issues and has used her own growing celebrity to do just that.

Laverne Cox (2016), much like Mock, notes that "For me, being in the media has been a powerful tool and a huge responsibility." Cox has used her platform as a celebrity to become one of the leading activists for trans rights in the world today. For example, upon learning of her Emmy nomination in

2016, she responded in a statement to *Huffington Post* "As I celebrate this day, I can't help but remember it is still a state of emergency for far too many trans people across this country right now. We need love, and support. We need public policy and our fellow citizens to value our lives and our humanity. Most of all we, ourselves need to value our lives" (Michelson, 2016). Indeed, Cox has taken advantage of nearly every public speaking opportunity to insist that these issues are not just about her as an individual, but are about a larger trans population, one that is in need of greater awareness, acceptance, and support.

Caitlyn Jenner has also been influential in using her fame to bring attention to trans issues. Through her reality television series, *I Am Cait*, Jenner allowed the public an insight into her own struggles and triumphs post-transition. In a review of the show for *TIME* magazine, James Poniewozik (2015) noted that "I Am Cait . . . is always conscious of its dual purpose: it's a personal story played out for an audience of millions, on behalf of a much larger community" (website). In addition to herself, Jenner also has a supporting cast of several well-known scholars, academics, and activists, including Jennifer Boylan and Kate Bornstein, to help bring an academic educational angle to the platform of reality television. More than just a ply for continued fame (as is arguably the case with her kin, the Kardashians), one gets the sense watching the show that Jenner is earnest is her desire to use her platform as a celebrity to become an advocate and an activist. As Andresen (2016) argues, "It remains difficult to say whether or not Jenner should be the trans community's spokesperson, but it is nevertheless true that her transition has created an enormous interest in and attention to the trans cause, and ultimately it seems fair to state that *visibility* is very important for the future" (46).

## AND NOW YOU DON'T: THE CONS OF
## TRANS CELEBRITY SPOKESPEOPLE

Thomas Beattie grabbed headlines in 2008 for becoming a "pregnant man" at the same time that a rise in transgender violence was being ignored. Caitlyn Jenner and Jazz Jennings have made headlines in recent years but reports indicating trans individuals' attempted suicide at more than twenty-five times the general population went unnoticed. Even in the 1950s as the Rosenbergs were being put to death as Soviet spies (a storyline all too familiar with contemporary headlines), Christine Jorgensen was the real headliner. Reality television stars have become some of the most powerful people in the world today (including U.S. president Donald Trump), Katy Perry's Twitter feed has more readers than any newspaper on the planet, and Twitter has become a means of disseminating public policy. There is no doubt that popular culture has increasingly become the currency of politics, activism, and social change—but at what cost?

Trans celebrities have done much to bring awareness of, and attention to, trans people. That said, they have also reinforced certain ideas of what it means to be trans and portrayed very particular images of trans lives (McIntyre, 2018). Using examples of some of the best known contemporary trans celebrities, Lovelock (2017a) argues that "In becoming legible as transgender through celebrity . . . Jenner and Jennings' media narratives have worked to confer recognisability to a highly limited model of transgender life, fraught with exclusions around race and gender normativity" (737) and that "under the aegis of social transformation, has worked to reaffirm highly normative understandings of gender, race and self-identity, and the relations of power which structure, and are structured by, these norms" (739). Indeed, it is debatable whether greater attention is being paid to trans peoples' lives or to the lives of certain trans people.

In many ways, the rise of the trans celebrity has fit an already established model of general celebrity in contemporary culture. Many trans celebrities either identify with, or have been molded into, a viewpoint that they were born "trapped in the wrong body." In this way, there is an argument that those trans people who have been allowed to become famous, have been granted the privilege because they fit the pre-existing notions of what it means to be trans. In other words, they are not rocking the boat. Lovelock (2017a) argues that "At a cultural moment in which the visibility of transgender celebrities appears greater than ever . . . through these figures, discourses and conventions of celebrity itself have been instrumental in producing and circulating a series of normative epistemologies on what it means to be transgender in the contemporary moment" (2017a, p. 751) and that "mainstream media representations of transgender people have historically employed, and continue to employ, various discursive strategies which render transgender identities coherent and, crucially, *consumable*, within normative frameworks of knowledge" (739). Thus, "for transgender identities, mainstream media offers a highly limiting frame of visibility, bringing gender mobility into legibility through readily consumable narratives which do not unsettle traditional understandings of gender and personhood" (743). In other words, the rise in the presence of the trans celebrity has been restricted to a certain kind of trans person, arguably one who fits the mold of expected conventions of what it means to be trans. Thus, although the presence of trans celebrities is very much on the rise, it is only a particular type of trans celebrity that has become visible—one that fits the pre-established notions, especially of the "wrong body narrative" (Lovelock, 2017b; Mock, 2012; Riggs et al., 2016).

Some of those who have become celebrity spokespeople for the trans community had already led lives of privilege and prestige. Caitlyn Jenner, for example, had already led a life as a famous, well-respected Olympic athlete, multimillionaire, white heterosexual-identified male, and one of the stars of the famous Kardashian family media enterprise. She has a reported net worth of more than $100 million and was esteemed for decades as "the pinnacle of human athleticism and masculinity" (Compton and Bridges, 2016, p. 84). Thus, although she now identifies in a minority position, she still does so with the privilege of whiteness and a life history of extreme celebrity, wealth, and social privilege.

That said, many of those who have since become celebrity spokespeople for the trans community did not spend their formative years in positions of relative power and privilege. Laverne Cox, for example, grew up in Mobile, Alabama as a racial minority and in a single female-headed household. She has been the self-reported victim of numerous acts of prejudice, discrimination, and even violence for much of her life. Hers, perhaps, is a story that more closely resembles that of the "typical" trans narrative in the United States today. That said, nearly all of those who have gone on to become spokespeople, regardless of their pre-celebrity lives, are now in positions of greater social and socioeconomic privilege than the majority of trans individuals. Cox, for example, now has a reported net worth of more than $2 million.

There is no doubt that the formative upbringing of an individual has a lasting impact on their perspective of the world. That said, most of these individuals are famous to the general public as they are *now*, not as they were *then* (Caitlyn Jenner and Chaz Bono being notable exceptions). This is an especially important point as the general public is likely to know (or at least to imagine) their current social positions rather than the (non-)privileged history of their life course. Thus, the image of the trans celebrity is in many ways comparable to those of other celebrities and in fewer ways comparable to those of the general trans population.

It should also be noted that many of those who have become trans spokespeople are noted for their beauty. There is little doubt that Janet Mock, Laverne Cox, Laith Ashley, and Jake Graf all fit very conventional standards of beauty. As Andresen (2016) notes, not recognizing beauty as privilege is harmful because, "it unintentionally fails to identify the core of discrimination and judgment against Trans people, which is ultimately rooted in how conformist (or not conformist) their new appearance is" (p. 18). This is not to say that that the majority of trans people are not also instantly recognizable as beautiful, but rather to say that, much like the majority of the population, it is doubtful that every member would be considered as such. The role of beauty should not be underestimated and, to date, nearly all trans celebrities could be widely considered as conventionally beautiful. As Lovelock (2017b) notes, "Trans women . . . are accepted *as women* so long as they adhere to the visual codes of female attractiveness" (680).

Perhaps the greatest harm of trans celebrity spokespeople is that they do not reflect the situation of the majority of the trans population. Indeed, increased representation does not equate to accurate representation. For example, the National Transgender Discrimination Survey (NTDS) reports a very different experience of the lives of trans individuals in the United States today. Key findings from their seminal report include the following:

- Discrimination was pervasive throughout the entire sample, yet **the combination of anti-transgender bias and persistent, structural racism was especially devastating.** People of color in general fare worse than white participants across the board, with African American transgender respondents faring far worse than all others in most areas examined.
- Respondents **lived in extreme poverty.** Our sample was nearly four times more likely to have a household income of less than $10,000/year compared to the general population.
- A staggering 41% of **respondents reported attempting suicide** compared to 1.6% of the general population, with rates rising for those who lost a job due to bias (55%), were harassed/bullied in school (51%), had low household income, or were the victim of physical assault (61%) or sexual assault (64%).

(Grant et al., 2011, p. 1 [bold in original])

As Hirschfield (working paper) notes, "[Caitlyn Jenner's] self-disclosure may have increased keyword frequencies for 'transgender,' but it did not translate to visibility for the general transgender community." Lourdes Ashley Hunter made similar comments in an interview about Jenner's coming out stating that "Her celebrity status is great for visibility, but it can and will be used as a distraction from the lived experiences of trans folk who continue to battle discrimination when accessing basic needs such as housing, employment, education and health care" (Grinberg, 2015).

So what does one do then? Ignore or condemn trans celebrities because they are not representative of the whole? Or accept their representations through a lens of privilege? Perhaps the debate is best summed up by Jen, one of the "supporting cast" of *I Am Cait* who in an episode called "The Road Trip part 1" notes the following:

We can support an individual trans person and celebrate their authenticity and their . . . their place for dignity and what they do with their privilege while still calling into question a system that makes this particular story the one that we finally listen to while we've been ignoring the stories of Black and Latina trans poor women, poor trans women. Cait's experience of coming out is singular. I . . . I don't think in history anyone has ever been so publicly welcomed. For most of us, coming out is a really kind of a terrifying, horrifying experience. And it's a little discomforting that everything Cait says is gonna receive far more attention than anything anyone else in the community will say, and she has relatively little experience in the community. So I think everyone is a little bit cautious." (*The Road Trip*)

Perhaps then, following Jen's advice, the best approach is to celebrate the increased visibility of certain types and particular individuals who are trans but to also be cautious to not assume that the battle for trans equality is anywhere near complete.

## CONCLUSION: THE ROLE OF THE TRANS CELEBRITY SPOKESPERSON

It should be remembered that few trans celebrities are asked to become role models. Minorities who are famous are often thrust into the position of spokesperson whether they want to be or not. And, for some, this role and their own minority status can sometimes overshadow the reasons they became famous in the first place. Laverne Cox is a talented actress whether or not she is trans. The Wachowski siblings are brilliant directors, whether they are working together as brothers or as sisters. And Laith Ashley is a gorgeous man, whether or not he was raised as a little girl. The talent behind the celebrity status should not be forgotten any more than the fact that celebrity is not merit for representation.

The lives of celebrities are often ones of glitz and glamor, of power and wealth, and of "respectable" people living the kinds of lives most of us only dream of. In this sense, the representation of trans celebrities in positions of privilege can be a good thing in that it presents a positive image. On the other hand, these images are not reflective of the lived struggles and realities of the general trans population and thus can not only a present a false image, but can leave people unaware or, perhaps worse yet, complacent in the struggle for trans equality. Thus, "The flip side of visibility—especially when it appears to be sudden, and media-driven—is vulnerability. Any mention of a 'tipping point' should come paired with the knee-buckling figures on the reported murders of transgender women, very often women of color who either were or assumed to be engaged in sex work. It should be heard also with their names read aloud" (Grant, 2016).

Gamson (1998) notes that "The desire to be recognized, affirmed, validated, and to lay the cultural groundwork for political change, in fact, are so strong they have tended to inhibit careful analysis of the dynamics of becoming visible" (p. 12). It is perhaps this more careful analysis that is still somewhat lacking in relation to the role of trans celebrity spokespeople (or the role of spokespeople for any minority group in general). Visibility is good, but social change is even better and it should not be forgotten that just because Caitlyn Jenner may have become, yet again, a national hero, the lived realities of most trans people remain one fraught with social, economic, and health disparities, increased levels of violence, and daily battles with discrimination. As Compton and Bridges (2016) point out, "The public celebration and recognition of transgender people is a start, but it has not yet been matched by achievements in gender equality and diversity" (p. 84). Let us hope those achievements are soon to come.

## REFERENCES

Anderson-Minshall, Jacob. 2017. "Don't Forget the Long, Proud History of Transgender Activism," *The Advocate*, June 6, 2017. https://www.advocate.com/advocate50/2017/5/01/these-trans-revolutionaires-are-unforgettable.

Andresen, Kristian Otterstad. 2016. "'TransJenner'—Exploring the Role of Caitlyn Jenner in I Am Cait; An Unsolicited Spokesperson for the Trans Community?" Master's thesis, University of Oslo.

Bernstein, Mary, Brenna Harvey, and Nancy A. Naples. 2018. "Marriage, the Final Frontier? Same Sex Marriage and the Future of the Lesbian and Gay Movement," *Sociological Forum* 33, no. 1, pp. 30–52.

Bird, Jason D.P., Lisa Kuhns, and Robert Garofalo. 2012. "The Impact of Role Models on Health Outcomes for Lesbian, Gay, Bissexual, and Transgender Youth," *Journal of Adolescent Health* 50, pp. 353–57.

Brady, Anita. 2017. "'Caitlyn Jenner "Likes" Ted Cruz but the Feeling May Not Be Mutual': Trans Pedagogy and I Am Cait," *European Journal of Cultural Studies* 20, no. 6, pp. 672–86.

Cavalcante, Andre. 2018. *Struggling for Ordinary: Media and Transgender Belonging in Everyday Life*. New York: New York University Press.

Compton, D'lane and Tristan Bridges. 2016. "#callmecaitlyn and Contemporary trans* Visibility," *Contexts* 15, no. 1, p. 84.

Cox, Laverne. 2016. "Cecile Richards," *Interview Magazine*. March 29, 2016. https://www.interviewmagazine.com/culture/cecile-richards#_.

Day, Elizabeth. 2015. "Lives Transformed: Do Famous Transgender People Help the Cause?" *The Guardian*, Sunday, August 23, 2015. https://www.theguardian.com/society/2015/aug/23/famous-transgender-help-the-cause-caitlyn-jenner-laverne-cox-kellie-maloney.

ESPYS. 2015. TV, ABC, July 15, 2015.

Factor, R.J. and E.D. Rothblum. 2007. "A Study of Transgender Adults and Their Non-Transgender Siblings on Demographic Characteristics, Social Support and Experiences of Violence," *Journal of LGBT Health Research*, 3, pp. 11–30.

Flinn, Celia M. 2016. "Sugar and Spice and Everything Nice: 'America's Original Transgender Sweetheart' and the Construction of Womanhood," *CMC Senior Theses* 1259. http://scholarship.claremont.edu/cmc_theses/1259.

Gamson, Joshua. 1998. "Publicity Traps: Television Talk Shows and Lesbian, Gay, Bisexual, and Transgender Visibility," *Sexualities* 1, no. 1, pp. 11–41.

Goffman, Erving. 1963. *Stigma: Notes on the Management of Spoiled Identity*. Englewood Cliffs, NJ: Prentice-Hall.

Grant, Jaime M., Lisa Mottet, Justin Edward Tanis, Jack Harrison, Jody Herman, and Mara Keisling. 2011. *Injustice at Every Turn: A Report of the National Transgender Discrimination Survey*. National Center for Transgender Equality.

Grant, Melissa Gira. 2016. "After the Transgender Tipping Point," *Pactific Standard*, February 16, 2016. https://psmag.com/news/after-the-transgender-tipping-point.

Grinberg, Emanuella. 2015. "Why Caitlyn Jenner's Transgender Experience Is Far from the Norm," July 15, 2015. CNN.com. https://edition.cnn.com/2015/06/03/living/caitlyn-jenner-transgender-reaction-feat/index.html.

Grossman, A.H. and A.R. D'Aguelli. 2004. "The Socialization of Lesbian, Gay, and Bisexual Youth: Celebrity and Personally Known Role Models," in E. Kennedy and A. Thornton (eds.), *Leisure, Media and Visual Culture: Representations and Contestations*. Eastbourne, UK: LSA Publications, pp. 83–105.

Hart, K.P.R. 2000. "Representing Gay Men on American Television," *Journal of Men's Studies* 9, pp. 59–79.

Hirshfield, Aiden. 2015. "Has Increased Media Representation and Celebrity Disclosure Impacted Views on Transgender Identity? A Survey of Transgender Individuals and How They are Seen by Others." Working Paper, pp. 1–22.

*I Am Cait*. Road Trip, Part 1 [Television series episode]. (2015, August 2). In *I Am Cait*. E!

Kahn, Mattie. 2016. "Janet Mock Is Here to Remind You Activism Doesn't Just Happen Every Four Years," *Elle Magazine*, December 5, 2016. https://www.elle.com/culture/movies-tv/news/a41218/janet-mock-trans-list-interview/.

Kermode, Jennie. 2015. "Transgender Issues in the media: 'Improving Picture, Still a Way to Go,'" September 28, 2015. BBC. http://www.bbc.co.uk/blogs/collegeofjournalism/entries/a324dfd7-e4fd-4352-b696-46f59d80267a.

Li, Minjie. 2018. "Intermedia Attribute Agenda Setting in the Context of Issue-Focused Media Events," *Journalism Practice* 12, no. 1, pp. 56–75.

Liu, Qiuling (in collaboration with On Road Media). 2017. "Breaking the Binary: Key Findings," http://www.allabouttrans.org.uk/wp-content/uploads/2017/06/Breaking-the-Binary-2017-Key-Findings.pdf.

Lovelock, Michael. 2017a. "I Am . . .": Caitlyn Jenner, Jazz Jennings and the Cultural Politics of Transgender Celebrity," *Feminist Media Studies* 17, no. 5, pp. 737–54.

———. 2017b. "Call Me Caitlyn: Making and Making over the 'Authentic' Transgender Body in Anglo-American Popular Culture," *Journal of Gender Studies* 26, no. 6, pp. 675–87.

McIntyre, Joanna. 2018. "'They're So Normal I Can't Stand It': I Am Jazz, I Am Cait, Transnormativity, and Trans Feminism," in *Orienting Feminism*, pp. 9–24. Cham: Palgrave Macmillan.

Michelson, Noah. 2016. "Laverne Cox Makes History with Emmy Nomination," *The Huffington Post*, February 2, 2016. https://www.huffingtonpost.com/2014/07/10/laverne-cox-emmy-nomination_n_5574608.html?guccounter=1.

Miller, Brandon and Elizabeth Behm-Morawitz. 2017. "Exploring Social Television, Opinion Leaders, and Twitter Audience Reactions to Diane Sawyer's Coming Out Interview with Caitlyn Jenner," *International Journal of Transgenderism* 18, no. 2, pp. 140–53.

Meyerowitz, Joanne. 2015. "America's Original Transgender Sweetheart," *POLITICO Magazine* June 16, 2015. https://www.politico.com/magazine/story/2015/06/caitlyn-jenner-was-not-americas-first-transgender-sweetheart-christine-jorgensen-1 19080_full.html.

Mock, Janet. 2012. "Trans in the Media: Unlearning the 'Trapped' Narrative and Taking Ownership of Our Bodies," *JanetMock.com*, July 9, 2012. http://janetmock.com/2012/07/09/josie-romero-dateline-transgender-trapped-body/.

MSNBC. 2015. "Transgender Reality, Post-Jenner," MSNBC, June 2, 2015. Archived from the original on March 4, 2016.

Murchison, Gabe. 2017. "New HRC Poll: Improving Favorability Toward Transgender People," March 31, 2017. https://www.hrc.org/blog/new-hrc-poll-improving-favorability-toward-transgender-people.

Poniewozick, James. 2015. "Review: I Am Cait Shows What It's Like to Come Out with the Kardashians," *TIME Magazine*, July 22, 2015. http://time.com/3967543/i-am-cait-review-caitlyn-jenner-e-reality-show/.

Richards, Chris. 2018. "Why Does President Trump Love Elton John?" *The Washington Post*, September 24, 2018. Available at: https://www.washingtonpost.com/lifestyle/style/why-does-president-trump-love-elton-john/2018/09/23/9c04bdb4-bf66-11e8-90c9-23f963eea204_story.html.

Riggs, Damien W., Chloe Colton, Clemence Due, and Clare Bartholomaeus. 2016. "Mundane Transphobia in Celebrity Big Brother UK," *Transgender and the Media* 1–40.

Ryan, J. Michael. 2018. "Gender Identity Laws: The Legal Status of Global Sex/Gender Identity Recognition," *LGBTQ Policy Journal, Vol VIII*. Cambridge, MA: Harvard Kennedy School, 3–16.

Ryan, J. Michael (ed.). 2020. *Trans Lives in a Globalizing World: Rights, Identities, and Politics*. London: Routledge.

Schilt, Kristen and Laruel Westbrook. 2015. "Bathroom Battlegrounds and Penis Panics," *Contexts* 14, no. 3, pp. 26–31.

Serano, Julia. 2016. "The Truth About Caitlyn Jenner's Politics," *TIME Magazine*, March 28, 2016. http://time.com/4268422/caitlyn-jenners-politics/.

Steinmetz, Katy. 2014. "The Transgender Tipping Point," *TIME Magazine*, May 29, 2014. http://time.com/135480/transgender-tipping-point/.

Stryker, Susan and Stephen Whittle (eds.). 2006. *The Transgender Studies Reader* (Vol. 1). Taylor & Francis.

Trans Media Watch. 2010. "How Transgender People Experience the Media," http://www.transmediawatch.org/Documents/How%20Transgender%20People%20Experience%20the%20Media.pdf.

Yerke, Adam. 2020. "Stronger Together: The Global Shift to Transgender-Inclusive Armed Forces," in J. Michael Ryan (ed.), *Trans Lives in a Global(izing) World: Rights, Identities, and Politics*. London: Routledge.

## Chapter 2

# Popular vs. Personal

## *Transgender Narratives in Public Media Culture*

### G. M. Mozer

Both online and offline, there is a significant disjunction between the way transgender people represent themselves and the ways they are represented in popular culture. In *A Queer Time and Place*, Jack Halberstam (2005) reminds us that "transgender lives often seem to attract enormous attention from biographers, filmmakers, talk show hosts, doctors, and journalists, all of whom are dedicated to forcing the transgender subject to make sense" (p. 54). While there are myriad films featuring or including trans people, it is television programs, specifically, that feature the most, and the most readily accessible, examples of that dedication to sense-making. Broadcast, cable, and streaming television programs that do include trans people often dissect trans experiences and organize images and stories of trans identity and embodiment into a "grand narrative," that is, one narrative taken to represent all or most transgender experiences. In this narrative, the transgender subject is cut, pasted, edited, retouched, and aired as an image of a binary medically modified figure. This common representation of transgender prioritizes science and medicine over interiority and affect, using physical "transformation" as a way of making the complexities of transgender identity "make sense" to mass audiences.

Trans communities formed online have their own strong opinions about televised depictions of trans lives. In one video posted to the YouTube channel "uppercaseCHASE1," Chase Ross, a sociologist and social media figure, interviews Amy Fox about her upcoming web series *The Switch*. Ross is also a transgender YouTuber, someone who invests time and resources into YouTube content creation to a degree that the platform itself becomes part of their professional identity. Ross urges his audience, a modest viewership of 160,000 regulars, to support Fox's series, as it is "a TV show with lots of trans people in it" (Ross, 2017, 0:45). Intercut with the interview are stills of select characters who, much to Chase's delight, "are *actually* trans, *and* played by trans people" (Ross, 2017, 0:53). Why is it so exciting to see a web series feature trans characters played by trans actors? Why do certain realms of the internet vibrate with discontent when a production casts someone who is not trans to play a transgender character in a film or TV show? Why does Ross express such an enthusiasm for trans productions, of trans people, by trans people, and for trans people? This particular interview with Fox is one example of a cornucopia of digital videos that address these questions, providing a concise answer: trans people want to be included in the conversations about their own public representation, and they do not just want to be the subjects of those conversations. They want to be heard.

## UNDERSTANDING TRANSGENDER

It is important to acknowledge the semiotic gap between what transgender represents to transgender individuals, including its academic and activist applications, and how transgender is used in media productions. Susan Stryker (2008) offers one of the most commonly used and productive understandings of transgender in *Transgender History*, using the word "to refer to people who move away from the gender they were assigned at birth, people who cross over (trans-) the boundaries constructed by their culture to define and contain that gender" (p. 1). This interpretation of the word emphasizes the Latinate root "trans-," indicative of motion away from something, rather than toward a fixed point of opposition. It thus includes people who move away from their assigned at birth gender, but does not pigeonhole them into a binary opposite. Stryker's understanding of transgender opens the term to include all those who trans-, that is move away from an assigned gender value. For example, one could be assigned male at birth and identify as transgender, without a mandate to also identify as a woman. As Stryker and other scholars argue, transgender acts as an umbrella term for many different types of gender identity and should not be understood to only indicate those who identify as female-to-male or male-to-female. Similarly, scholars such as Cressida J. Heyes and J. R. Latham (2018) remind us that many individuals identify as transgender, but do not seek out medical interventions. These are the perceptions of transgender that appear in many—but not all, iterations of trans self-representation, and these are the nuances of transgender that are absent from most—but not all, mainstream media conversations of transgender.

Perhaps because of the disjuncture between public images and personal understandings of their identity, more and more transgender individuals are claiming space for personal representation in public forums, and they are availing themselves of emerging media formats to do so. The most widely accessible example of new media trans self-representation, and the one that most directly corresponds to popular media representations of trans life, occurs on the free media platform YouTube. YouTube is a Google-owned website where users can create their own pages or "channels," upload personal media archives and video blogs (vlogs), and cultivate a public persona in online communities. Beyond sharing videos, users of the site can organize topical playlists, create special interest pages, and air live broadcasts. Unlike other social media platforms, such as Tumblr, Facebook, or Twitter, YouTube blurs the lines between artistic expression and commodity culture. Registered users can partner with companies to earn revenue through product promotions, gain significant income from ad revenue on videos that garner enough views, and review free products related to their channels' ethos.

## TRANSGENDER YOUTUBE COMMUNITIES

Its hybridization of commerce and creative culture makes YouTube a media format instrumental to queer self-articulation and the creation of digital support networks for the transgender community. Craig, McInroy, McCready, and Alaggia (2015) found that LGBTQ youth use online platforms for immediate reaction and response to the offline world, "finding empowerment and representation online" (p. 266). The world of YouTube offers accessible means of creative self-representation that allow trans individuals to explore and express their own ontological journeys, reactions, and opinions. The creative agency involved in filming, editing, and publishing an account of one's self serves as a digital outlet for individuals who may not have such agency in their immediate surroundings. Tobias Raun (2015) argues that vlogging in particular has become an affirming personal media practice for trans people because it allows them to visibly narrate their own lives and experiences in their own voices (Raun, 2015, p. 370). The trans autobiographies and voices on YouTube are indeed numerous and diverse, as trans-identified people of various abilities and backgrounds from around the world, ranging in age from fourteen to their late seventies, create a visible archive of their stories and thoughts. And while, as Raun notes, their videos can be personal and autobiographical, they are also communal: channels run by transgender collaborators post daily videos addressing trans-related topics, answering questions, organizing community meet-ups, and offering emotional support.

These digital YouTube communities predate both the breakout of transgender characters on television and YouTube's expansion into a multimillion-dollar industry. For instance, DominoAyeJae and ANF Jace, two of the earliest transgender YouTubers, joined the site in 2007 and 2008, respectively, before the introduction of ad revenue and more diverse profit lines for creators. Some of the more prolific transgender YouTubers, such as Skylar Kergil, Aydian Dowling, Jamie Raines, Ty Turner, and Chase Ross, first began posting regular transition updates, commentaries on social issues, and informative videos geared toward trans people and allies between 2009 and 2011. Other YouTubers, such as Kat Blaque (2010), Riley Dennis (2011), and Stef Sanjati (2012), appeared soon after, posting videos that feature less autobiography and more social commentary, moving the conversation about transgender topics away from the details of medical transition and toward issues such as what it means to be trans during the Trump presidency, navigating intersectional trans identity, and more. Along with these individual channels, collaborative groups such as FTMTranstastic (2010), My Genderation (2013), and Transcollab (2013) began video sharing programs with daily, or almost-daily, videos responding to viewer questions.

The aforementioned list is not exhaustive, but these creators, specifically, have transformed the social, commercial, and educational nature of YouTube. Transgender YouTubers who post videos frequently and regularly use the site as an intersectional communal anchor space, where the work surpasses personal and communal storytelling and information dissemination. Individual creators and group channels produce curated "101" videos modeled after introductory college classes and speaking to a range of intersectional topics. Others bring in experts or use their own experiences to answer "Q&A" videos about issues such as coming out, navigating the workplace, deciding on whether or not to take hormones or have surgery, finding local support, or communicating with family. Still others publish heavily researched lectures and videotaped podcasts on global and national issues affecting the trans and/ or LGBTQ community. Transgender creators also use YouTube to launch offline collaborations, including group meetings with their audiences, creative projects with one another, and, most significantly, forging communal ties that manifest as meet-ups at annual international transgender conferences, such as the Philly Trans Health conference. What began as a place for visible individual self-representation now functions as a digital hub of online and offline community, socialization, education, transaction, and support.

While YouTube creators tell their stories, build communities, educate, and support other trans people, television portrayals of transgender reach much larger audiences and thus do the necessary public work of advancing transgender visibility on a greater scale. A study, in which viewers were surveyed before and after exposure to transgender storylines on television, found that "exposure to transgender narratives reduced the influence of viewers' political ideology on their attitudes" about trans people (Gillig, Rosenthal, Murphy, and Folb, 2017, p. 1). Entertainment narratives of transgender positively impact viewers' attitudes toward transgender people and policies by fostering identification and empathy. When viewers identify with a character, even if that character is notably different from them, "they perceive the events happening to the character as if they were happening to themselves" (Gillig et al., 2017, p. 3). Television thus offers the opportunity to influence a majority about minority issues, in a way that yields demonstrably effective results.

According to media-monitoring organization GLAAD, "84 percent of Americans say they do not personally know someone who is transgender—which means they only learn about trans people through the images they see [through media]" (GLAAD, 2017, p. 26). This means that for the majority of Americans, the primary opportunity to encounter transgender people in any capacity occurs through television exposure. The accumulation of these exposures has quantifiable positive effects, too. Gillig et al. found that, for viewers starting out with negative attitudes or ideology toward transgender people, "the impact of political ideology on attitudes was reduced by approximate one-half for viewers who saw two or more transgender narratives" (p. 9). Mass media thus has a tremendous power to shape 'viewers' attitudes toward people from marginalized groups who they may not encounter in their everyday lives" (Gillig et al., 2017, p. 11). In terms of transgender representation specifically, television representations can both expose people to the idea of transgender and images of transgender individuals, and foster an empathetic identification that incites a change in attitudes toward or ideology about trans people.

Not all transgender narratives on television, however, are constructed in a way that portrays trans characters as realistic, empathetic, or relatable. Trans people are still parodied as a source of humor, disgust, or spectacle on television, particularly in comedy programs. These depictions take the shape of characters such as Carmen on *It's Always Sunny in Philadelphia* (McElhenney and Biermann, 2005), who, despite never using the word to describe herself, is more often than not referred to as "The Tranny"; Jeffrey Tambor's George Sr. on *Arrested Development* (Fortenberry and Hurwitz, 2006), who is dosed with estrogen and "becomes" a caricature of a woman; or *Weeds*'s Bruce, also known as "Dean's little girl [who has] got a dick now" (Trim and Kohan, 2012, 32:00). While these crude effigies are no longer the only images of transgender, they still dominate the canon of visible transgender characters on television, and thus still have the potential to influence viewers' opinions. Their impact must be taken seriously, as the number of transgender series regulars across broadcast, cable, and streaming television peaks at seventeen (GLAAD, 2017, p. 27). These representations span television genres. They occupy too much screen time to dismiss as one might dismiss *30 Rock*'s throwaway jokes about transgender identities and bodies.

Encouragingly, in the post-Chaz Bono and Caitlyn Jenner world of entertainment, offensive depictions of transgender people do constitute a smaller proportion of overall representation. Audiences can now expect serious television portrayals of transgender. More "realistic" representations of trans people feature a number of configurations of transgender life that construct a grand narrative of what transgender looks like. The content of inclusive trans-programming embraces and capitalizes on transgender topics, meshing much-needed representation with growing public fascination. These TV representations of transgender people share a number of distinctive characteristics that cohere into a totalizing narrative of trans experience. In the trajectory of this grand narrative, transgender identity is largely constructed around and defined by medical intervention, markedly binary gender presentation and identification, and a collapsed time frame of transition. This narrative, while profoundly important in terms of visibility and inclusion, creates an image of transgender that does not accurately represent the daily reality of many transgender people's lives.

Some television images of trans are particularly two-dimensional. In 2010, for example, *Degrassi*, a Canadian soap opera for teenagers, featured a transgender character in its rolling ensemble of high school characters. Adam Torres was an FTM teen, seeking hormone replacement therapy and gender confirmation surgery. Much of the story surrounding his identity emphasized his desire to begin hormone replacement therapy. The character was killed off before any other storylines could develop. While this depiction of a trans youth marked a stepping-stone for visibility, it unblinkingly reinforced the script that the primary technology of transgender life is medical: hormones and surgery.

Similarly, in the final season of *Glee*, Coach Bieste endures a rushed storyline, announcing in "Jagged Little Tapestry" (McCrane and Falchuk, 2015) that he always felt like a man and now would become one, then reappearing in "Transitioning" (Di Loreto and Hodgson, 2015) in the late stages of hormone therapy. In the space of a few episodes, Bieste undergoes a cinderella-esque transformation: acquiring and taking testosterone, developing facial hair and a deep voice, and undergoing a morphological alteration that in an actual human being would take up to five years—that is, five years providing every doctor, surgeon, insurance agent, and therapist expedited their paperwork. No mention is made of the social elements of transition, aside from hate crimes. Bieste's transition appears not only accelerated, but so abridged that the only visible elements are the touchstones of coming out, discrimination, medical transition, and eventually passing as his identified gender. Absent are the massive financial commitments, the negotiations of gender illegibility, the traumas of misgendering and microaggressions, the navigation of "second puberty," and the emotional work of being trans in both public and private spheres.

Other programs such as Showtime's *Shameless* (cable), MTV's *Faking It* (streaming), and ABC's *The Fosters* (broadcast), represent the transmasculine community through Elliot Fletcher, a transgender actor who portrays a trans character with a story arc (as opposed to a singular appearance) in each afore-mentioned program. Media culture has been criticized for giving the roles of trans characters to cisgender actors, but Fletcher's casting represents laudable and significant inclusivity. Fletcher, however, is years into hormone therapy, has had gender confirming surgery, and plays characters always easily read as male. In *Shameless*, Fletcher plays Ian Gallagher's boyfriend Trevor, a masculine activist with sideburns and facial hair to whom the Gallaghers refer as "the dude with the vag" (Rossum and Callaghan, 2016). At one point, Ian's brother, Lip, meeting Trevor for the first time, comments "you'd never be able to tell" (Rossum and Callaghan, 2016), confirming Trevor's gender presenta-tion, but simultaneously implying that the truly masculine must be void of legible femininity. This is not to say that portrayals of trans masculinity are wrong, but rather to suggest that in the state of current representation there exists an undercurrent of essentializing binary gender, even in progressive representations of trans figures.

Storylines like Adam's and Bieste's—and series regular characters like Trevor—do the much-needed work of positively depicting and normalizing trans characters across generations and asserting their legitimacy. For many viewers, these characters may be a first or only exposure to transgender nar-ratives, modeling what to expect from and how to treat real trans individuals. While providing necessary exposure, the television images of trans, however, compress the realities of transition, and overlook nonbinary forms of trans identity. Of the programs airing in the 2017–2018 season, GLAAD reported seventeen occurrences of transgender characters, only nine of whom were series regulars, making transgender representation constitute a mere 5 percent of LGBTQ representation overall (GLAAD, 2018, p. 26). This dearth of rep-resentation not only places great pressure on the shoulders of the transgender characters who are featured on broadcast, cable, and streaming television but also makes the task of analyzing and commenting on the collective effect of these images a much easier one, as many transgender YouTubers demonstrate through their responsive content.

Transgender content creators publicly respond to the images of themselves they see on television, turning stereotypical and reductive images of trans into anchor points for dialogue. Two transgender content creators in particular, Chase Ross and Aaron Ansuini, frequently respond to media depictions of trans characters, critiquing and destabilizing the metanarrative of transgender life that these characters represent. Ross, Ansuini, and other transgender individuals who make their narratives public on YouTube assert transgender identity as diverse, as complex, and above all as individual. These self-representations play a powerful role in "(re-)claiming a trans identity" (Raun, p.373). As Raun argues "Digital autobiographies can contribute to a correction of the hidden injuries of media power" (Raun, p. 373), which is precisely what the personal narratives of trans YouTubers do by refocusing trans narratives, documenting their own processes, and demonstrating that transgender identity is never-already a reification of binarism.

Chase Ross, as previously mentioned, is particularly active in this process. Ross has posted public videos to his YouTube channel for seven years, and in the process has accrued 10.5 million views, and a small following of about 200,000 subscribers. Along with fellow trans activist Aaron Ansuini, Ross has scripted, shot, edited, and produced over eighty hours of "You're so Brave," a video podcast on topics pertinent to the transgender community. Independently, he has produced over 500 hours of both scripted and extemporaneous content, addressing topics ranging from documentation of his personal transition to "information for the trans community and people on the outside who are curious or interested in learning how to be a better ally" (uppercaseCHASE1). Both independently and in his work with Ansuini, Ross voices concerns about misrepresentation of or lack of representation for transgender people in the media, frequently critiquing the flatness of the TV trans storylines and the overall lack of trans characters to whom he can relate.

Ross and Ansuini articulate many of their frustrations at the gap between how they identify and how they see themselves represented publicly when responding to the public coming out and subsequent reality show of Caitlyn Jenner. Jenner's status as a transgender woman and a celebrity very much in the public eye represents to these activists part of the dilemma of public narratives of trans visibility. Ross expresses his concerns in a 2016 video entitled *"positive" trans representation*. In "I'm not a fan" (FTMTranstastic, 2016, 1:27), he explains, "she [Jenner] just doesn't understand [the issues of the transgender community], she doesn't know, she didn't Google [. . .] or go on YouTube and learn about all these things" (FTMTranstastic, 2016, 1:39). He argues that along with a public presence comes responsibility to other members of one's marginalized community: transgender people of color, transmen, nonbinary folk, and transgender individuals who do not want or cannot access medical transition technologies (FTM- Transtastic, 2016). Ross's own filmed narratives are filled with the minutia of social and medical transition. His videos detail issues such as dysphoria, prosthetics, dealing with male pattern baldness, transphobia, the materiality of trans life outside of medical needs, and the gradual changes that happen when one takes testosterone for a decade.

In Caitlyn Jenner's public persona, a mainstream media representation of transgender, Ross identifies a narrative antithetical to his own. He observes Caitlyn Jenner:

> came out to the world and then disappeared for a couple of months and then BANG she came back as a beautiful woman—it gives the impression that surgery is an in-and-out kind of deal, like you go into the hospital and you have "The Surgery" which turns your body completely into "A Woman" and then you come out and you're just like . . . yeah, my life is good. It's not like that. (FTMTranstastic, 2016, 2:33)

In short, the accomplished athlete and hypermasculine celebrity Bruce Jenner vanishes from public view and the curvaceous, ultrafeminine Caitlyn Jenner emerges to fill the public void left behind. The process of transition itself, which Ross, Ansuini, and hundreds of other transgender individuals painstakingly document for years using YouTube and other public platforms, is effectively erased in this narrative. Transition appears as a simple step from one gender to another, facilitated by science, and, if one has enough money, bound to result in beautiful, binary-passing bodies. Ansuini laments the hyperfocus this kind of narrative draws to transgender bodies, wondering "why are you making my body into a spectacle? Why does that have to be a thing? You're othering us a lot by doing that" (*You're So Brave*, 2017, 46:50).

Transgender YouTubers also use the grand narrative in which transgender is reduced to what Amy Fox describes as "medical medical medical" (Ross, 2017, 1:55) to push back against medical-industrial definitions of transgender. FTMTranstastic contributors Kai and Aiden (names withheld) argue that, unlike the reality of life for many trans people, "the problem with trans visibility in the media is a lot of the trans people are cis-passing, and a lot of them are white, and they're always binary" (FTMTranstastic, 2016, 0:42). Like the fictional characters on television, the locus of trans identity in Jenner's public image is that of biomedical alteration to fit into an exacting model of binary gendered appearance. On one hand, that is how Caitlyn Jenner wants to express herself and experience her own body. Where that representation becomes problematic, however, is when it functions as a public paradigm for *all* trans women. Ross has argued that "there's one specific type of trans woman and that's how you have to be and that's problematic" (*You're So Brave*, 2016). Jenner seems to echo the doctrine of binary feminine uniformity for trans women when, in her 2015 *TIMES* interview, she asserts "it's much easier for a trans woman or a trans man who authentically kind of looks and plays the role. So what I call my presentation. I try to take that seriously. I think it puts people at ease. If you're out there and, to be honest with you, if you look like a man in a dress, it makes people uncomfortable" (Steinmetz,

2015). This moment emphasizes the expectations of a public transgender figure. A transwoman who is "out there," as Jenner says, in the public sphere,
must be under a tremendous amount of pressure to visibly demonstrate a
femininity that will not make people "uncomfortable," a femininity that reads
as morphologically female and not, as Jenner says, as a "man in a dress."

Several transgender women YouTubers concur with Ross, expressing
disappointment in the ways Jenner's transition was publicized. In the As/
Is channel's video about Jenner, one woman argues "there's no wrong way
to be trans." Another woman in the same video comments, "I was thrilled
[when Jenner first came out] because most of the media coverage is of people
in advanced stages in their transitions and I think that paints kind of a banal
picture of the experiences and interior and external struggles gender varying
people have" (*As/Is*, 2015, 2:04). As trans activist and YouTube educator Kat
Blaque notes, "when you're trans, you live in a world surrounded by people
who don't understand you . . . and ultimately believe that they have the
authority and ability to deconstruct and redefine your gender based on how
they feel about it" (Kat Blaque, 2015). Public coverage of Jenner's transition, however, has done little to express the interior and external struggles of
gender-varying people, and instead represents another exercise in deconstruc-
tion and redefinition of trans identity as something ultimately reducible to
repositioning in a rigid binary legitimized by medical interventions.

I believe trans YouTubers' responses to Jenner underscore two of the
main forms of erasure in publicized trans narratives. First, like other forms
of popular public media narratives, Jenner's transition represents a uniform
binarism which is not an accurate articulation or appropriate generalization
of transgender life. Second, the flurry of media around the newly minted
Jenner eclipses transgender temporality. The temporality of transgender life
is not a montage in which one's body and socialization change like a costume
between scenes. Transgender artists, writers, and filmmakers depict a side of
identity and becoming that is visible and slow, not the in-and-out rapid transformation that Ross finds so disingenuous. The ongoing self-representations
on YouTube include vlogging and other forms of digital autobiography in
the social technology of transition. YouTubers such as Ross, Kergil, Turner,
Dowling, Sanjati, Raines, Hardell, and numerous others publicize the steps
and struggles of trans lives over long periods of time. The temporality is a
crucial part of the narrative itself.

While Ross, Ansuini, and others use their reactions to Jenner to anchor
more extensive conversations, even more transgender YouTubers take up the
task of correcting the misconceptions of other publicized images of transgender. In these videos, a sense of transgender that prioritizes knowledge
of the self over the public script of transition emerges. On their channel,
Ash Hardell (2009) argues that some transgender individuals do not want

medical intervention, and that these people are no "less trans" for wanting to live their genders in the ways that make them comfortable (Hardell, 2017). Transgender is diverse and to identify as transgender does not mean one must also identify as one end of a gender binary. Speaking of their own struggle to publicly come out as both nonbinary and transgender, wishing to use gender-neutral pronouns and wanting to have surgery but not take hormones, Hardell says "transitioning, legally changing my name, altering my body, switching my pronouns, these things felt off-limits for me. Cuz (sic) that's only what binary trans people do" (Hardell, 2017, 2:24). Similarly, in an interview with trans activist, author, and musician Skylar Kergil, singer Ryan Cassata speaks about his decision to forego hormone replacement therapy in order to preserve his recognizable voice, a key part of his identity: "I've written like a hundred songs with this voice [. . .] I feel like if I went on [testosterone] I would lose this voice that I have now" (Kergil, 2016, 1:06). Aydian Dowling, discussing surgical intervention, comments "I know gender-fluid people who get it, a good chunk of female-to-male people get it. It's really open to anybody who wants it" (Dowling, 2017, 2:53). Dowling emphasizes that the deciding factor for surgery should be comfort, and whether or not intervention will make one more comfortable with one's body (Dowling, 2017, 2:40). While these examples are only a few of many accounts, they indicate the tone of transgender YouTube, wherein transition narratives may have hallmarks like months on testosterone or estrogen, or weeks before or after surgery. Ultimately, though, the ethos of transition in these narratives is a process of becoming more comfortable with oneself and one's gender identity.

Speaking directly to the disconnect between the images of trans on the television screen and the images of trans on the computer screen, Kat Blaque and Riley Dennis, both creators of informative and educational videos rather than autobiographical material, offer concrete solutions. The answer to the problems of transgender representation is simple: include trans people in the conversations about *how* trans people should be represented. Blaque, responding to *Transparent* among other programs, and exasperated with depictions of trans women as men who cross-dress, decries the image of "a man standing in front of a mirror crying with make up on his face" (Blaque, 2015, 1:54). To correct the misrepresentations she sees on television, Blaque calls for a more authentic depiction of trans life:

> It would literally be a story of someone who is a woman, but there are always these little things that they had to do, that would come up. [Things that] were almost inconsequential to the whole story, but they came up. It could be something like somebody's ID card saying the wrong gender. It could be something as simple as someone talking about their hormones. You don't need to create a narrative where the focus is on someone's trans identity. (Blaque, 2015, 3:30)

Transgender lives are, as Blaque argues, far more complex than even some of the better representations on television. Gender identity does not constitute a transgender person's entire identity. The kind of narrative Blaque calls for does not pigeonhole transgender characters, or actors, into one definitive category. By simply decentering trans identity, it presents transgender individuals as multifaceted people, who also happen to be transgender. Nick Adams, Director of GLAAD's Transgender and Media Representation division, echoes Blaque's sentiment, stating that GLAAD wants to see transgender character writing "moving beyond focusing solely on their trans identity and telling stories about them as whole human beings" (GLAAD, 2017, p. 27).

To facilitate such well-rounded transgender characters, Blaque argues that we need trans roles written by trans people (Blaque, 2015). Blaque argues that there is even space for transgender topics in comedy, where once transgender people were, and sometimes still are, the subject of ridicule. The solution, once again, is to listen to transgender voices. After critiquing the "transmisogynistic tropes [that] have been a central part of contemporary comedy" (Blaque, 2015, 1:40). Blaque lists ten transgender comedians and one comedy program, redirecting audience desires for transgender comedy to programming that features transgender people making jokes, rather than being treated as jokes.

Riley Dennis, similarly, asserts that "in 2018 we should be able to write fleshed-out, complex, three-dimensional trans characters" (Dennis, 2018, 00:30). Dennis appreciates television programs' efforts to depict transgender characters on screen, but notes that "more often than not those characters aren't handled with very much care" (Dennis, 2018, 00:40). The characters she sees on her screen represent "what cis people think we are rather than what we actually are" (Dennis, 2018, 4:00). Dennis has a clear vision for what she wants to see change in trans representation. Like Blaque, she wants to see transgender characters with "a solid personality and interests outside being trans" (Dennis, 2018, 5:50). Her solution to the problem of inaccurate or harmful representation is simple: "hire trans writers or trans consultants" (Dennis, 2018, 6:20). Dennis argues that cisgender writers "haven't experienced what we have . . . you cannot tell our stories as authentically as we can" (Dennis, 2018, 10:00). The responses of Riley, Dennis, Ross, Ansuini, and others indicate that the absence of transgender voices behind the camera causes a flat singularity of transgender representation on screen. Whether those voices come from transgender comedians, writers, or consultants, it seems that the obvious answer to the problem of representation is inclusion— diverse inclusion.

Blaque's and Dennis's invocation of authenticity calls attention to a larger problem in the entertainment industry, namely exploitations of transgender narratives and disenfranchisements of transgender creators (including comedians, writers, and consultants). YouTube itself offers an alternative entertainment marketplace for transgender creators, though not an ideal one. YouTube has also become a point of contact between retailers and the transgender community through giveaways, sponsorships, and reviews. As such, the site has become a locus of income opportunities for some transgender creators. Chase Ross, Aydian Dowling, Jamie Raines, Stef Sanjtai, and others partner with businesses and private individuals to give away free clothing, prosthetics, and print media to their audiences. Off-market exchanges of goods and promotions occur too. Ash Hardell, for instance, promote a new LGBTQ musician in every video they post, encouraging their subscribers to support emerging artists. Jamie Raines and his wife, and Aydian Dowling and his wife, run their own merchandise companies, often creating events and fundraisers to benefit charities specifically for transgender, LGBTQ, and LGBTQ people of color communities. From product endorsements to book deals, the transgender YouTubers who attract greater audiences can profit in a tangible way from their work.

While YouTube does not provide the exposure or compensation of entertainment industry work, and while it has come under criticism for unabashedly disenfranchising the work of some creators who posts LGBTQ content, transgender creators have turned the site into an alternative industry of representation. Those transgender individuals who publicly share their narratives remind viewers that the lived reality of transition is not a radical leap across the gender binary, as fictional TV characters and public personas would suggest, but rather a kaleidoscope of daily experiences, evolutions, and encounters with the world in which one's social gender is established.

Ultimately, real transgender identities, lives, and stories are much more complex and diverse than their popular media counterparts. The interiority of trans lives and trans subjectivities is much greater than the narrow binary framework of a gender identity routed in medical transition. Transgender people experience transition in a multiplicity of formats: socially, spiritually, intellectually, and yes, also medically. It is reductive to portray transgender narratives as a series of biomedical procedures and accompanying social adjustments. There is hope, however, for the popular public spectrum of trans representation. Progress occurs as YouTubers expand the economic, social, and entertainment influence of their platform; publicized public figures such as Sam Smith embrace nonbinary identity; and others, such as Eddie Izzard, staunchly assert transgender identity despite not matching up with "sense making" grand narratives. Streaming television, already markedly more eager to include transgender characters than its broadcast and cable counterparts, offers programming such as Amazon's *Transparent*, which firmly situates trans life in diverse conversations of identity and lived sociality, rather than in a lockstep of medical steps. As more transgender individuals reclaim authorship of their own narratives and project their voices into public spaces, using platforms like YouTube, hopefully the mainstream media representations of transgender narratives will evolve away from a grand narrative of pathology and strict binarism and toward the exquisite intricacies, grey areas, changing perspectives, and lived realities of all forms of transgender life.

## REFERENCES

ANF Jace. (n.d.). *About Me* [YouTube channel]. Retrieved October 22, 2017, from https://www.youtube.com/user/ANFjace/about.

As/Is. (2015, June 15). *Transgender People React to Caitlyn Jenner's Coming out* [Video]. YouTube. https://www.youtube.com/watch?v=PBVy0xtDoRo.

Blaque, K. (2015, July 28). *Unfunny Transmysogynistic Tropes + Trans Comedy* [Video]. YouTube. https://www.youtube.com/watch?v=hZuC9fRgS54.

Blaque, K. (2015, September 23). *Should Cis Actors Play Trans Characters?* [Video]. YouTube. https://www.youtube.com/watch?v=uaGhMyJ4eqU.

Blaque, K. (2015, October 8). *How Do You Write Transgender Characters?* [Video]. YouTube. https://www.youtube.com/watch?v=D3fbvOX8Zh4.

Day, C., Howeton, G., McElhenney, R. (Executive Producers). (2005–Present). *It's Always Sunny in Philadelphia* [TV series]. FX.

Dennis, R. (2018, August 9). *How to Write a Trans Character* [Video]. YouTube. https://www.youtube.com/watch?v=TDPFZkzN1pA.

DominoAyeJae. (n.d.). *About Me* [YouTube channel]. Retrieved September 20, 2017, from https://www.youtube.com/user/DominoAyeJae.

Falchuk, B. (Writer), and McCrane, P. (Director). (2015, January 16). Jagged Little Tapestry (Season 6, Episode 3) [TV series episode]. In R. Murphy, B. Falchuk, D. Di Loreto, I. Brennan, R. Friend, G. Lerner, and B. Buecker (Executive Producers), *GLEE*. 20th Century Fox Television; 20th Television.

FTMTranstastic. (2016, March 26). *Trans Representation in the Media- Kai & Aiden.* [Video]. YouTube. https://www.youtube.com/watch?v=9mnazQRE-VQ.

GLAAD. (2017). *Where We Are on TV Report—2017*. https://glaad.org/files/WWAT/WWAT_GLAAD_2017-2018.pdf.

Grazer, B., Howard, R., Nevins, D. (Executive Producers). (2003–2019). *Arrested Development* [TV series]. Netflix.

Halberstam, J. (2005). *In a Queer Time and Place: Transgender Bodies, Subcultural Lives*. New York University Press.

Heyes, C., and Latham, J. (2018). Trans Surgeries and Cosmetic Surgeries. *TSQ: Transgender Studies Quarterly, 5*(2), 174–89.

Hodgson, M. (Writer), and Di Loreto, D. (Director). (2015, February 13). Transitioning (Season 6, Episode 7) [TV series episode]. In R. Murphy, B. Falchuk, D. Di Loreto, I. Brennan, R. Friend, G. Lerner, and B. Buecker (Executive Producers), *GLEE*. 20th Century Fox Television; 20th Television.

Kergil, S. (2016, January 8). *FTM Transgender Singer Ryan Cassata Interview* [Video]. YouTube. https://www.youtube.com/watch?v=LKBq0HJmUqw.

Kohan, J. (Executive Producer). (2005–2012). *Weeds* [TV series]. Showtime.

Raun, T. (2015). Video Blogging as a Vehicle of Transformation: Exploring the Intersection Between Trans Identity and Information Technology. *International Journal of Cultural Studies, 18*(3), 365–78.

Ross, C. [FTMTranstastic]. (2016, May 4). *Chase. "Positive" Trans Representation* [Video]. YouTube. https://www.youtube.com/watch?v=nppSz6yXdpU.

Ross, C. [uppercaseCHASE1]. (2017, July 19). *Fantastic Trans Representation on Tv! (interview w/ Amy Fox of The Switch)* [Video]. YouTube. https://www.youtube.com/watch?v=7NN0Y8ZeP70.

Ross, C. [You're So Brave]. (2017, September 11). *Episode #75—Being Out in the Media (Jazz Jennings)* [Video]. YouTube. https://www.youtube.com/watch?v=VMmuKPRxtzY.

Steinmetz, K. (2015, December 9). *Caitlyn Jenner on Privilege, Reality TV and Deciding to Come Out.* TIME. https://time.com/4142000/time-person-of-the-year-runner-up-caitlyn-jenner-interview.

Stryker, S. (2008). *Transgender History*. Seal Press.

Wells, J. (Executive Producer). (2011–present). *Shameless* [TV series]. Showtime.

*Chapter 3*

# Schrödinger's Dick

## *The Transgender Reveal Trope in* Boy Meets Girl

### Finn Lefevre

Dim fluorescent lights pool on Hilary Swank's flesh, as we watch her—playing Brandon Teena—reveal her breasts to a bathroom mirror. A car partially obscures Felicity Huffman as we catch a fleeting glimpse of her (prosthetic) penis. Michelle Hendley emerges from a moonlit lake, exposing her penis to us and her potential suitor.

The *Reveal Scene*: a scene in which a trans character *reveals* themselves to be trans, not by some poignant coming out confession (though these often coexist), but by exposing some part of their anatomy to the audience. This trope, common as it is in films (and plays/books/etc.) with transgender characters, has not yet been documented or theorized, and yet its ubiquity betrays a significant question in trans media. What does this trope actually *reveal* about a trans character? Various viewpoints on the locus of transness, the trans body, and the lines between gender and sex are all condensed and made visible by this reveal scene. This trope has popped up across an overwhelming number of pieces with trans characters, but it is even more potent and telling in those pieces that are intended to portray trans characters as nuanced, complex human beings rather than the butt of the joke, the villain, or the victim (all trans media tropes in their own right). These pieces—*TransAmerica* (Felicity Huffman), *Boys Don't Cry* (Hilary Swank), *The Crying Game* (Jaye Davidson), and the list goes on—glimpse the humanity of a trans character (and most often, a trans woman) only if they first *reveal* their naked body.

The reveal scene trope is most often used to expose some sort of "truth" and express the contradictions of body and self. In exploring this trope, I will contest and complicate both the truthfulness and perceived contradictions in these scenes. This chapter argues that while little is *revealed* by the reveal trope, its use exposes a great deal about the ways trans bodies—and in particular, trans women's bodies—complicate and obfuscate the hegemonic masculine gaze of film. As the list of examples above suggests, this trope appears often in trans narratives, but its use in *Boy Meets Girl* (2014) is especially significant as unlike the previously listed examples, the trans character in this film is played by Michelle Hendley, a transgender actress. The duality of the reveal of a trans character and of a trans person simultaneously offers space to analyze the impact of this trope on actual trans bodies.

I perform this analysis as an audience member, analyzing not the experience of being in the naked trans body, rather witnessing that body and also witnessing the way I am asked to witness it. However, I come to this work both as a performance theorist and as a real-life trans person. As such, my vision is doubled. I am reading these theories both through the lens of their object of analysis, and as a participant in these theoretical debates. I admit I view this film from a place firmly rooted in my transness, but also exterior to the experience of trans womanhood, a distance nearly as great as the positionality of the cisgender folk watching and reviewing the piece alongside myself. I do not have the organ that becomes the object of much of my analysis—the penis. I do, however, belong to a rich community of trans people, many if not most of whom are women, whose words and experiences and bodies color my viewing. My understanding is bifurcated through the split visions of the transness of my body and the academic theories through which my body hesitantly, clumsily, observes. To accomplish this dual reality, this chapter moves between the phenomenological, influenced by the sensuous, visceral encounter with film articulated by queer theorist Katharina Lindner, and the theoretical lenses of trans and performance theories. As I analyze, I switch between these modes, offering both my lived experience and my critical analysis as equal forms of knowledge.

## THE GAZE IN *BOY MEETS GIRL*

*Boy Meets Girl* was written, produced, and directed by Eric Schaeffer, a cisgender straight man. The film premiered at the Frameline Film Festival in San Francisco, CA, in June 2014, with little critical response. It opened a few months later in the United States for a brief theater run to mixed and sub-par reviews. One of its best reviews (which gave the film 2 out of 4 stars), written by Stephanie Merry at the *Washington Post* describes it as "earnestly instructive" and "conspicuously educational" highlighting that the film is intended for cisgender audiences and purports to be revealing of deep truths of the trans experience.

Before even seeing the film, I prepare myself for the gaze through which these "truths" will be told. *Gaze*, as defined by Laura Mulvey, is the perspective through which an audience observes, analyzes, and encodes an object with meaning. Drawing on theorist Jonathan Schroeder (1998), Mulvey is employing gaze as more than seeing, but a relationship of power—as audiences use that power to transform sight into object, and interpret that object through the interpretive lenses of the dominant discourses. This process is seen most readily through the camera lens, as the lens itself is theorized as following the "eyes" of the gaze (we see what the camera sees). Mulvey explains that the male gaze occurs when the audience is put into the perspective of a heterosexual man, denying women in the film subjecthood and relegating them to the status of objects. The theory suggests that women audience members can only view themselves through a secondary perspective (man's perspective). Because this is the dominant and arguably the only gaze through which a female performer can be viewed within Mulvey's theory, rather than "male gaze," she refers to this theory simply as "gaze." Mulvey offers few options for an "outside" to this gaze, and therefore offers a pessimistic outlook on the potential for women to create an alternative gaze through which to view themselves and each other. In *Boy Meets Girl*, it is through Schaeffer's eyes (and camera) that we will see the trans character, and his perspective will color what the audience is allowed to see and asked to believe. Even from the title it is clear that we will be meeting the titular Girl only as the object of Boy's interest, extending Schaeffer's gaze to the Boy. Schaeffer has claimed he chose an intentionally cliché title that "won't be threatening to anyone," which emphasizes that cisgender people are his target audience.

## THE GIRL AND HER SECRETS

In the first moments of the film, we see a preteen girl, Ricky, sitting on a bed, holding up notecards to a webcam a la the YouTube trend. The shot frames both the girl and her own camera, already showing us how Ricky's gender is performed for (and later misinterpreted by) an audience. Her first card: "I HAVE SECRETS." My jaw clenches as I try to keep a painfully, naively open mind. We later learn that her "secrets" are not *just* that she is transgender, but that she believes this to be why her mother left her father, that she has considered suicide, and that her love for family and friends keeps her going. By later, I mean as the credits roll. For now, we are given the impression that this young girl—shown moments later as her adult self, played by trans actor Michelle Hendley—is going to tell us her secrets through this film.

Since Ricky is completely isolated in her transness—no other trans person is ever seen or even mentioned, and she does not report to know of any other trans people (something totally unheard of in all my years of trans rural liv-ing)—we are given her story (or our gaze upon that story) as the only truth. The supposed "rarity" of trans identities exhibited by this film exacerbates the idea that Ricky's narrative is representative of the "trans experience," which is not nearly as monolithic as it is presented.

The assumption of a true trans experience permeates much of the film, offering a strange foil to another of the film's major themes, secrets. The two themes go hand in hand, creating the primary dramatic tension of the film: can there be truth without revealing secrets?

Within trans theory, the truth/secret dichotomy is a fraught discussion. The trans body itself is the site for much of this debate, with theorists argu-ing whether the trans body itself is a truth, and if hiding or altering that body belies or enhances that truth. While Sue-Ellen Case describes a nude trans body as revealing of deep truths, as one that reveals secrets, Susan Stryker offers that hormone replacement therapies are actually excretions of an inter-nal truth expressed on the skin (Stryker, 1999). Whatever her truth is, Ricky has established that she has hidden it, that it is not readily apparent, and despite already knowing that she is transgender, somehow that knowledge is not the full truth. I can assume then that her secret is not her identity, but her body.

In interviews and after the fact, Schaeffer claims Ricky's biggest secret is actually that she is *just like you and me* (again, the assumption is that you and I are cisgender), and yet, the film progresses with ninety-nine minutes of con-fessions, outings, and reveals about her trans identity and bodily experience, presented as her "secrets," a reification of the belief that undisclosed trans status is akin to a secret. The film's structure also suggests that all trans sta-tus is "undisclosed" if not exposed through the reveal of flesh, as she doesn't complete the "secrets" monologue until after her nude scene.

## THE GIRL AND HER PENIS

Soon after this YouTube moment, Schaeffer introduces the crux of the film: a lifelong friendship (with cis guy pal Robby) that may be more, a new love interest (cis lady stranger, Francesca), and the conflicts with both revolving around one thing: a penis. In her first interaction with both characters, Ricky jokes that the thing guys want most is the thing they are most afraid of—a penis. In so joking, she references her own anatomy, confusing Francesca, and providing a moment for the audience to recognize that this is the thing that stands between her and true heterosexual happiness with Robby. Her penis. The joke sends both suiters on separate film-long paths of confusion and self-discovery, and leaves Ricky waiting to see who will receive her.

This is four minutes into the film.

Ricky's joke speaks to the idea of disclosure and its relationship to the "truth" of nude trans bodies. The performance of this truth carries material consequences for trans people—and particularly for trans women, who are much more frequently victims of violent crimes due to their transgender status. While Ricky does not encounter direct violence as a result of her disclosure, throughout the film her reticence to disclose is due, in part, to past negative reactions and a fear of violence. Ricky jokes about her own body scaring people away, but her jokes carry an underlying thread of fear for her personal safety. This fear reflects a dominant discourse around trans disclosure—that trans people who do not disclose are "tricking" people and are therefore deserving of whatever negative reaction they receive.

This fear-based reaction to discovering someone's trans status is often called "Trans Panic." Legal scholars Cynthia Lee and Peter Kwan provide an excellent genealogy of Trans Panic laws, through which I examine these themes. Trans Panic laws are borne from the Provocation Defense, a set of laws that allow perpetrators of violent crime to claim that the victim provoked them. These laws justify the crime if "(1) the defendant was actually provoked into a heat of passion, (2) the reasonable person in the defendant's shoes would have been provoked, (3) the defendant did not have time to cool off, and (4) the reasonable person would not have cooled" (Lee and Kwan 98). This basis has two important elements for consideration in Trans Panic defenses: First that somehow the trans person, by being trans and not properly disclosing the said trans status at the exact right moment (though how they are required to disclose is very unclear), has provoked violence. Second, that any "reasonable person" would feel provoked into violence. Trans Panic defense, then, is described as a legal defense in which a perpetrator can claim provocation if they did not know that a sexual partner (would-be, present, or past) is trans. The language of the law allows for the universality of provocation should a heterosexual man (the language focuses on heterosexual men having sex with a trans women) discover his partner is not a "real" woman, where the "reality" of her womanness is negated by her transness (and especially the presence of a penis) (p. 105).

Lee and Kwan note that this language is eerily close to the now mostly discouraged Gay Panic defense, in which (mostly heterosexual male) perpetrators can be excused for attacking a male attempted suitor. That the Trans Panic law echoes the Gay Panic defense shows still how in the law, as arguably in the dominant discourse, genitalia signify sex. This defense also shows significantly how genitalia are assumed to be used, and that the presence of these genitalia (here a scenario with two people with penises) can only be homosexual—a point that the film affirms later in a conversation between Ricky and Robby.

Opponents of the trans panic defense provide two different strains of recourse: first, that the perpetrator must have known the victim was transgender. Second, that the perpetrator's fear of being seen as gay or participating in a "gay" sex act is not an adequate excuse for violence. (p. 108) The latter point I will not argue. To the former point, I ask: Why? How? Do they believe all trans people are recognizable as such? Given Francesca's confusion at Ricky's joke, it is clear that she does not recognize Ricky as trans, despite her (joking) disclosure.

Proponents of the law argue that a lack of disclosure is both deceit and fraud. To disclose would mean that there is something to disclose, something that is not readily available or intelligible. If, say, a transgender woman is being read as a woman, is she not intelligible as a trans woman? She is both trans and a woman; therefore, she is exactly what a trans woman looks like, and yet we must assume that these scholars mean being read as a cis man or woman. The conflict comes, inevitably, when her clothing is removed. The topography of her nude body is recognized as belonging to a different sex than the gender she is read as, and she is called deceitful. Had she claimed possession of a vagina the case may have been more logical, but had she not claimed the said vagina, was it not his assumption rather than deceit that led them here? If she does have a vagina, must she specify its depth, origins, and smell? The laws seem to suggest so. If to disclose then means to tell the w(hole) truth and nothing but the truth, is not disclosing trans status a lie of omission? Lee and Kwan further question who is asked to disclose:

> One might question whether a transgender woman who does not disclose her biological sex is being deceitful. . . . An individual with an ugly birth defect in a private place might not disclose this to a potential sexual partner, hoping that the relationship develops to a more serious level before revealing such information. (p. 114)

It is significant that nuanced writers as these still make comparisons between the penis of a trans woman and "ugly birth defects" or other deformations/ grotesquery. Besides that choice, this also brings up the question of timing. Must disclosure occur before the clothes come off? Is taking one's clothes off *not* a disclosure? The authors suggest that users of this defense claim that the body was truthful and the person not. Can only the body disclose the "truth" of itself? If the victim claims terms and histories for her body, are they less truthful than the imagined truths as interpreted by the observer? Because this law is founded on the principle that it must be a belief any reasonable, average person could hold, it must be assumed that in order for this to be legal, the majority of people view themselves as better interpreters of trans identity than trans people, and that this truth comes from the body—and particularly the genitals—more than anywhere else.

That the following analysis focuses significantly on Ricky's penis is not accidental, nor a microcosm of theory within a broader story. Her genitalia are literally discussed in nearly every scene and is the crux of every debate/relationship snafu/conflict in the film. It is also important to note that the word "penis" never appears in the film, and yet the organ is ever-present. Queer theorists Edelman and Zimman write that the fact that genitals serve as the first (and often the only) cue used to assign sex at birth leads to a process of *hyper-embodiment*, "wherein only one portion of the body becomes the focal point of personhood," and therefore societal interpretation of gender is reflexively tied to this focal point (p. 675). Just as the laws regarding trans people often boil down to genitalia, so do social constructions of gender. The penis becomes the locus of masculinity in media, humor, sexuality, and more. The idea that Ricky, a woman, can have a penis destabilizes the organ's supposed value as a symbol of masculinity. And yet, this film refuses to acknowledge that instability, instead offering time and again that the penis is troublesome and temporary.

The gaze through which we view Ricky is easily labeled as a male gaze—our director and writer is male, and so is the way his lens hungrily scans the topography of her form. And yet, that gaze is complicated by the trans subject. Mulvey's articulation of the gaze that consumes and creates the female body may not be able to include a trans woman's body, if the trans woman has a penis. Mulvey writes that the gaze depends on phallocentrism, and phallocentrism "depends on the image of the castrated woman to give order and meaning to its world" (p. 833). This is a model in which the woman is portrayed as the lack, and her nude body presented as absence, void, and passive (Mulvey, Case). Must the trans woman's body be castrated to be subjected to this gaze? This question begs another question of what makes a body *female*. Though I would argue that a trans woman's body, since it belongs to a female, is therefore a female's body (and by transitive property, a *female* body) the discourse on trans women's bodies rarely follows this line of thinking. While clothed, Ricky's body is objectified by the gaze just as Francesca's, but we are asked to prepare ourselves through constant reminders that Francesca (and we, through her eyes) will be surprised by what is underneath her clothing.

## THE GIRL AND DISCLOSURE

I thought the story might build dramatic irony between who does and does not know Ricky's trans status, but less than five minutes later (at the ten-minute mark), Robby scolds Ricky for not telling Francesca "the truth," despite having met her only once for two minutes. The risks for outing herself are high, but the film offers no acknowledgment, instead admonishing this "secret" as a betrayal. Ricky's penis jokes and not-so-subtle innuendos are arguable a toe in the water for Ricky, a way for her to test if this potential new friend will react negatively to her trans status. And yet, because Francesca does not understand the underlying message, Robby claims the responsibility is on Ricky to fully disclose, whatever that means. Ricky relents, disclosing her trans status over text to Francesca, seated only a few inches away. Her disclosure leads to an awkwardly typical (to my life at least) conversation in which Francesca moves through the following stages:

1. **Disbelief** (because trans people *look* trans, right?). Again, the assumption is that trans=monstrous/different/recognizable. Francesca's very first reaction is a skeptical glance at Ricky's crotch.
2. **Interrogation.** If this phase continues long enough, it usually leads to a request for some degree of nudity. Demands like "prove it" and "show me" abound. Francesca's responses include "where did you get it?" (unclear what "it" is), "do you like it?" (being trans), and "do you keep it a secret?"
3. **Fetishization/Fascination.** Ricky tries to avoid this one, saying it won't be an issue unless Francesca falls in love with her—to which Francesca says the same is true of Ricky. Here again the gaze is clear, as we watch Francesca observe and decode Ricky through a similar patriarchal scrutiny that has been applied to Francesca's own body.

Performance theorist John Berger offers that the lens through which Francesca views Ricky's body is an effect of gaze—there is no outside to this gaze within a patriarchal society, and as such Francesca's own internalized misogyny plays out on Ricky's body:

> Men look at women. Women watch themselves being looked at. This determines not only most relations between men and women but also the relation of women to themselves. The surveyor of woman in herself is male: the surveyed female. Thus she turns herself into an object. (p. 47)

Francesca quizzes Ricky because she herself has been subjected to this scrutiny. And yet, it is clear that the scrutiny that trans women undergo in "proving" their identity is multiplied by the need to conform to both the performance of the gender and the intelligibility of the sexed body.

Ricky explains, again, that she has a penis, but this time she is quick to add that she will someday get "the full surgery," so it will no longer be an issue.

The ephemerality of her penis is offered as a balm. I assumed this to be in reference to vaginoplasty, or the inversion of a penis into a pre-existing but expanded cavity. Note that vaginoplasties do not involve the removal of the penis, nor the creation of a cavity. The "full surgery" Ricky references does not actually castrate, as is the common assumption, but this reference implies the opposite. While Ricky (as do many, but not all trans women) does desire this kind of gender affirmation surgery, the placement of this line alongside the camera's lingering gaze on what is clearly her well-tucked penis, serves to enforce the castration required in Mulvey's gaze theory.

References to surgery as a solution to the "problem" of her being trans is rhetoric that actual trans woman I know have used to describe their experience, and yet the scene made me cringe. In the two scenes so far in which Ricky has spoken, both times she mentioned her penis. I am not offended by her penis, nor am I offended by her talking about it. Further, I am not offended by her hating/joking about/being offended by her own penis. I am, however, concerned that I do not currently know anything else about her. I am concerned that she has only described her penis thus far in relation to how other people might see it/fear it/dislike it. I am concerned that she is pushed into this admission by her cis friend who says she must tell the "truth" or he will—an outing that could be potentially dangerous for her. She clearly harbors enough fear/resistance to being outed that she does not tell people until provoked, and only then over text, despite sitting 6 inches from the recipient of said texts. Though she claims it is important to keep it "all out in the open," she is resistant to outing herself to Francesca until Robby literally yells "tell her" repeatedly at the pair from several yards away. The scene diminishes the very real consequences trans women face for disclosing their status and suggests that disclosure must include some discussion of genitalia, as if genitalia are the core of truth. Schaeffer presents us with a woman who is constantly having to modify that word—she can never just be a *woman*, she has to be a *trans* woman or a woman *with a penis*, because those cannot be synonymous here.

When Ricky outs herself to Francesca, Francesca eyes Ricky's swimsuit-clad body as proof that Ricky must be lying. Ricky has all the trademark signifiers (breasts, no visible penis) and she is barely wearing any clothing, how could she possibly elude the trans radar? We follow Francesca's gaze on Ricky's body through the mediator of the camera. That the camera traces Francesca's gaze reinforces that this gaze is that of the male gaze consuming the objectified woman, internalized even through another woman. As Francesca's eyes, and alongside them the camera, search Ricky's body, we are asked to look for clues ourselves. The gaze is complicated though, as Francesca's gaze eases into a queer lens, as they continue to flirt. Ricky is reified as a woman, but her body is no longer subject to the same demands as Francesca's here. Francesca then confesses she does not know any trans people (and therefore does not know what one looks like) so we, the audience, are affirmed again knowing that once you have seen a trans person, *then* you will know what they look like.

The conflict in this scene arguably arises from Schaeffer's rejection of "passing." Passing, as I use it, is being seen as/read as a desired gender and/ or sex. Many trans people refer to passing both as their identified gender/ sex and as other genders/sexes. For example, a trans woman may "pass" as a cisgender man at some point in her life, and at other times may also "pass" as a woman. In the former scenario, her "passing" as a man destabilizes the connection between gender and sex, in that someone who has been assigned male at birth has to perform maleness in order to be read as male. Both sex and gender become discursive formations. In the latter scenario, as she "passes" as a woman, she is essentially performing self while also performing intelligible womanness. In either use of the term, her "passing," or success is determined not by the topography of her body, but in how both the body and performance of gender are interpreted by others. That both are performative and interpreted from the outside is also complicated by the fact that one can be reflexively performed (in the Butlerian sense) while the other may be a more practiced performance. I won't specify as to which is which—since different trans people experience the internalization of their gendered performances differently, and may disagree as to which is reflexive and which is conscious. This conscious–unconscious dichotomy is then also destabilized, making the reading of trans bodies ever the more complex, and reinforcing the postmodernist questions of "truth" and what trans theorist Gayle Salamon calls the "necessary fiction" of authentic selves in gender.

In this scene, Schaeffer offers us a trans woman who is passing as a cisgender woman—meeting every expectation of Francesca's (and our) gaze. Ricky's ability to pass is admonished as a secret, that it is somehow her fault that observers have decoded her body in a way that does not match her trans status. The camera provides ample time for our eyes to scan her form, while the dialogue simultaneously undermines our visions: she is woman enough to look at, but only now, only clothed, and only if you know what is underneath. The scene skirts dangerously around the material consequences of passing, ignoring the very real risks to Ricky's life (both from external factors and her own dysphoria), saying instead that passing is akin to lying. The structure of the scene suggests Ricky is the one doing the passing, but my own understanding of passing is the opposite—a trans person exists in the world and an observer either does or does not decode their body in a way that matches their identity. The observer applies their own meanings to the trans body and decides if that body passes inspection. If Francesca has interpreted Ricky's body incorrectly, that is an effect of her own cis-normativity.

This moment, a mere ten minutes into the film, is not the first time we have been asked to think of Ricky's penis as a *trick*. A few moments prior, in a flashback of a Halloween past, we see an older man flash child-Ricky, saying "trick or treat." The costumed princess turns to the flasher, lifts her tulle skirt, and retorts "trick." This is our first instance of the reveal scene trope. Though her body is not exposed to the audience, the scene sets up the pattern we should expect: Ricky's body is objectified, she exposes her penis to correct the objectification. At no point does the scene structure propose that maybe the perpetrator should not sexualize any young girls, just not young trans girls. The immediate disgust she receives implies a dangerous assumption that a young trans girl is less at risk for sexual objectification and abuse if she has a penis. The scene also establishes Ricky's own discourse about her penis as a "trick," which is akin to the language of "trap" used to refer to the trans women victims in Trans Panic defenses, as well as being a common (offensive) term to describe trans people in general.

Within my community, I've known trans people who unironically refer to pieces of their bodies as "tricks," but these are tricks against themselves, some sort of cosmic mix-up. This moment appropriated that rhetoric to present Ricky as a trick to others, saying that you may think you know what she is, but the penis will give away the trick. Watching this moment, I am simultaneously enraged by this rhetoric and yet overjoyed to watch a young trans kid distort and upend the expectations of a pedophile. I catch myself—is he upended by seeing a penis? How engrained must our expectations of gender be that a simple penis can destroy them?

I am stuck in the loop of these questions, oscillating between my position as trans person, and my position as performance theorist analyzing the gaze through which this film objectifies Ricky. From the former position, I recognize the internalized transphobia and specifically transmisogyny that makes us believe she is "tricking" someone. The "trick" can only exist within a discourse of dimorphic sexes that leads to binary genders. While all bodies are analyzed for their gender performativity (a la Butler), trans bodies are given the unfair added labor of being analyzed and critiqued for their abilities to destabilize the "fantasy of stable sex" (Coogan, 26). Trans bodies are made to do the labor of destabilizing gender and sex for the observer even if the trans person performs gender within hegemonic norms, while cisgender bodies—even the most gender non-conforming—are not seen as performing instability.

As a performance theorist, I see the scene as a tool to reinforce a biological determinist standpoint in which Ricky is temporally locked: she is a trans woman for now, but soon she will right the mistakes and no longer trick anyone. She must confess her trick to us, both love interests and audience members, in order for us to correct our gaze on her body. My joy at young

Ricky thwarting the gaze of the pedophile is built on my own desire for sex itself to be destabilized, for its "truth" to be revealed as social construction. This labor is not hers to take on, however. Postmodernist theorists label the trans body as a revolution, as a contestation, as an affront, and while I want to say these things about my own body, the trans body itself has performed no such labor. The trans body itself, and Ricky's young trans body in this scene, is only an affront because the gaze upon it refuses to see it as its own truth. A penis is not a revolution. And yet, as there is no outside to the gaze on trans bodies, maybe it is.

Beyond calling her penis a trick, a feared object, and something she will medically correct, later in the film we hear her penis referred to as a "birth defect," something grotesque, something incapable of achieving its designated purpose, and something inherently male. It is these last two points on which I would like to ruminate. That it does not achieve its intended purpose is expressed to us through an otherwise touching scene in which Ricky pauses Francesca before they have sex for the first time to have "the talk." They each name previous sexual encounters and negotiate the boundaries of this encounter. Francesca asks about protection, and Ricky responds that she is not capable of getting anyone pregnant, that "nothing comes out anymore." It is rare for trans women to entirely stop producing semen, even with androgen suppressors and estrogen. As a trans audience member, this inaccurate claim makes me mistrust Schaeffer, and question if he had any trans people involved in the research/writing process. As a performance theorist, I see this as another castration tactic. As Mulvey articulated castration as key to creating the "object" of woman, in order for the gaze on Hendley's body to properly function, it must filter her through a character, Ricky, who is castrated. Schaeffer has told us time and again that Ricky has a penis, but he must also find ways to negate the expected functionality of the penis in order for her to be objectifiable as a woman. As Mulvey tells us, gaze is predicated on the object of that gaze being a woman, and that womanhood is necessarily shown as the lack. Could Schaeffer objectify Ricky as a woman without negating the functionality (and permanence) of her penis? In reifying an objectifying male gaze on her body, is Schaeffer also cementing her as a woman for us, despite the many modifiers to the label?

The slippage of this gaze is deepened as we encounter another descriptor for Ricky's penis—something inherently male. Granted, it is not Ricky that makes the claim, rather it is her friend Robby when he describes Ricky and Francesca's sexual encounter as "heterosexual" and any encounter between two penises as "homosexual." Ricky asks him to explain his stance, but does not discount it. In direct conflict with this assertion, both allow that fingers penetrating a man are only gay if the fingers belong to a man. Neither name whether the person is deemed male by anatomy or gender. If she had penetrated Francesca (or vice versa) without her penis, would their sex be considered lesbian by this logic? Or does the mere existence of her penis preclude the possibility of lesbian sex? According to their logic, Ricky's use of her penis makes it straight, negating both the sexualities and the genders of those involved. Her penis becomes something she, a woman who had lesbian sex, can*not* have. To Robby, through whom we see Ricky, the two simply cannot coexist.

## THE REVEAL SCENE

These collected contradictions produce and complicate a final impossible moment near the end of the film: the reveal scene. Given the number of times Ricky has outed herself and disclosed her trans status, it is significant that I chose to refer only to the scenes in which she exposes her nude body as "reveal scenes." In this final reveal scene, Ricky is nude, but Hendley is also naked, making the analysis of this scene far more complex than the other films I listed. The actors in those films (Huffman, Swank, Davidson) are cisgender, and their bodies are not subjected to the same kind of scrutiny as Hendley's.

The distinction between nudity and nakedness is also crucial here. Performance theorist John Berger separates the nakedness in life from nudity in performance, arguing the former as exposing of deep truths, and the latter as decoded from the outside. He argues nudity in performance is created through a process of consumption or observation: "To be naked is to be oneself. To be nude is to be seen naked by others and yet not recognized for oneself. A naked body has to be seen as an object in order to become a nude. . . . To be naked is to be without disguise. To be on display is to have the surface of one's own skin, the hairs of one's own body, turned into a disguise which, in that situation, can never be discarded" (Berger, p. 54).

By making this distinction between nakedness and nudity, Berger is claiming that the observer decodes a naked body, creating a socially constructed interpretation of the subject, thereby transforming the skin (hair, nails, etc.) into a costume just like clothes. In order to make this argument, he establishes first that nakedness is pre-observation and interpretation, and somehow pre-discursive. By his own logic, a person looking at their own nakedness would still see the construct (and therefore all of Ricky's descriptions of her body are already filtered through this gaze). This coded nudity is picked up by feminist theorist Elizabeth Grosz, who refers to the *nude body* as a "page . . . ready to receive, bear, and transmit meanings, messages, or signs" (p. 117). Where does this pre-discursive nakedness exist, then? Is there a body beyond or outside of this gaze? Berger suggests that nakedness still holds some kind of truth, describing it as "disclosure," echoing back to the idea that only nakedness can properly disclose trans status (p. 59).

The naked/nude trans body is even more complex. A naked trans body becomes a battle ground for observers' (here, assumed cisgender) debates about gender and sex. A naked trans body without surgical intervention (as Ricky's body is) may be incapable of passing as cisgender—does this make it incapable of passing at all? The conflation of sex and gender throughout this film places Ricky's body in a liminal space: she passes as cisgender and as a woman while clothed, but only as a woman while naked. The observation of her body shifts toward its ability to meet physical, rather than social, standards of sex and gender. As Coogan notes, the material effects and fleshy experiences of the trans body are disappeared/invisibilized by this observation and interpretation. This disappearing is not uncommon for the subject of gaze, in which Case notes that the flesh and tangible body as object is ephemeral, more figurative. I argue that these disappearances are both reflection and exacerbation of the material stakes of the existence of trans bodies. While Ricky (and Hendley) is on screen for most of the film, rarely if ever are we shown her gaze upon her own body. Her relationship to her body is subsumed by others' desires to alter, label, and consume it.

Given my simultaneous desire to remain open-minded and the jaded realism of someone who has shrugged through more than my fair share of reveal scenes, I am both always and never prepared for the moment where I am confronted with the naked body of one of my community and asked to accept this as representative of the individual/their gender/their sex/all trans people/some hidden secret/the TRUTH. I watch this scene hyper aware of not only the ways the gaze is asking me to decode Ricky's body, but also the ways in which that gaze affects Hendley's body in turn. Case argues that the trans body destabilizes our gaze upon it: "More than naked, this body displays itself as a construction at the deepest base of physiological and hormonal structures. Moreover, its very technological intervention is the site of the construction of sexual difference" (p. 195). If, as Case and Rubin have argued, the trans body is expected to perform the labor of making visible our gender constructions, the naked trans body is expected to do so for sex as well. Coogan writes, "transsexuals, through sex-change surgery, are seen as merely refiguring one version of their body's dress code, that of the skin" and are able, through "bodily surface manipulations" to re-encode and re-gender the body (Coogan, p. 30). She theorizes the process of altering the body through medical transitions as a search for truth, as well as a destruction of the stability of sex. The medical interventions (hormones, surgery, etc.) which have often (though not always) reshaped the naked trans body expose the skin itself as a costume that can be altered, refashioned, and made to hold different meanings. In this moment, Hendley's body is asked to perform as a costume for her character, and her own hormonal and surgical interventions (or lack thereof) made to serve as markers of Ricky's journey.

Just prior to this scene, Robby and Ricky have an explosive fight in which Robby confesses that he believes Ricky is not a "real" woman, but also not a real man or a "real anything." His confession drives Ricky out of the house, and as Robby is deciding if he should go after her, Ricky's little brother shows him the YouTube clip from her as a preteen (from the start of the film). Robby watches just long enough to see that Ricky was suicidal (and takes it to mean she is currently suicidal) and goes chasing after her. Once again the structure of the scene provides no agency for Ricky, as Robby is the one who confesses and chooses to go after her. Ricky only receives and responds to the actions put forth by the man, and we are along for the ride watching through a camera lens near Robby's ear. We see what he sees and interpret her as he does, reinforcing his gaze and his/our power over her (Mulvey, 1999).

Robby arrives at the lake where they spent the scene in which Ricky was first outed (to Francesca) to find Ricky, already naked, treading water in the middle of the lake. The moonlight glows off her skin and she looks like a goddess. The camera zooms out to Robby's vantage point and she now looks small, weak, and like she might sink and disappear into the giant pool of dark water. They lock eyes. Moments before, they had an emotionally charged argument in which Robby invalidated Ricky's identity and proved that even he believes all the horrible things that everyone else believes about her (Ricky's words). Robby tells her he saw her video and that he thought his invalidation of her might destroy her. We were asked to believe this as well. And yet we find her at peace, and happy to see him. I hope that she is at peace because she knows she can do better than this guy. I hope Schaeffer is providing us with an out—a way of saying his words does not matter, she will keep on keeping on.

Instead, still floating with water up to her clavicle, Ricky says Robby now knows "all her secrets," and begins walking out of the water, exposing her flesh in the somehow-too-harsh moonlight. As her flesh is revealed, it is almost laughably anti-climactic. There is a musical swell, and the camera sweeps around her body, as if she is not simply a human woman emerging from a pond, but something truly impossible. She walks toward him and we see her from a wide angle, a back angle, and a front angle—we obviously need to see every inch of her body in its entirety from every possible angle—before resuming its position alongside Robby's vision. An ache grows in my chest. I feel the potential power of seeing a naked trans person before me, the potential power of the normalizing of this body, of recognizing this body as beautiful, the potential power of seeing a body like my own presented as something that is real, sexual, and human. I feel this potential so much I could choke on all its deflated energy when Ricky steps out from this water and stands naked and wet, exposed and vulnerable, before Robby and asks "you still think I'm beautiful?"

She does not ask if he thinks she is a woman, if he thinks she is real. She does not say she believes herself to be real and a woman. She does not present herself without modifier or judgment or need of validation. She asks for confirmation that if this body is beautiful in his—and our—eyes. She asks our eyes to confirm that the gaze on her body is working. That we see her, yes, but that we see her the way she is intended: as the object of woman, not the person. I see her *and* I see that in order for her to be, she must be approved. I see her *and* I see the normalization of the self-effacing questions of approval I know I have also asked. I see her *and* I don't, because I see only what Robby and Schaeffer and the gaze on her body allow me to see. Robby kisses her. She says he can "ignore it if [he] want[s]" (not if *she* wants it to be ignored), and we know the "it" in question is her unspeakable penis. He says he won't ignore it, and throws her down on the ground. We accept that she is beautiful, and they have sex right then and there on the grass beside the pond. I can only assume it was gay sex, since they already told us two penises=gay sex.

I feel manipulated and disturbed. Ricky has given up on being recognized as herself just to have someone agree she is sexually appealing. She is recreating and reflecting the gaze on her body. She is seeing herself through the same eyes we see her. And in this moment, I am reminded of another gaze—that of the pornographic lens. Trans women have been made sexual objects in the porn industry in so many ways, and for many men, this is the first and only place they might see a nude trans body. That Ricky is naked for us in a moment specifically designed to titillate and lead to a sexual encounter reinforces this objectification. That she is the only naked body, or even partially naked body, in the entire film isolates and makes her the focal point—just as the penis is the focal point of biological determinist arguments.

Standing naked before us, she is made "woman" by the gaze on her body, the eyes and lens through which we decode her (Berger, 1979; Mulvey, 1999), but the "truth" of her penis tells us otherwise. Robby himself has said she is not a real woman because of it, and though Ricky believes herself to be a woman she also believes her penis to be a trick, a defect, a male object. She is simultaneously presented to us as a woman and not. The gaze is disrupted, and gender as well. But why? As a trans person watching, nothing is disrupted. She is a woman, and her penis does not change this. This moment does not reveal any kind of truth to me. It does not expose her sex, but that her sex is culturally constructed. It does not determine her gender, as her gender has been made clear in her words. It does not betray her beauty, as she is as beautiful now as before her clothes were removed. What purpose, then, does this reveal scene trope serve?

What it *reveals* is that these theories of gaze have not made room for the ways that woman is objectified beyond the "lack" and the "castration." The objectification of her body functions very similarly to the way gaze and the naked female in performance are described (Case, Mulvey, Berger) but it also functions in a way only a trans body can be objectified. Only a trans body can exist and not in this paradox. What it reveals is that writers and directors of trans stories need to gaze upon her body through different eyes, perhaps her own—knowing and showing when that gaze has been mediated by the reflection of the male gaze. It shows that the effects of gaze still permeate trans performance, but that the trans body has to be made intelligible to cis-heteronormative viewers first. It reinforces that we need to see Ricky's feelings about her body beyond its sexual capacity, that we need to see her feelings about her body in relation to the structures that influence those feelings. We need to make room in these portrayals for the complex and multifaceted feelings and experiences of being in a trans body as owners of a "flexible accumulation" of topography, sensations, desires, and capacities (Harvey, 2018). What this trope really *reveals* is that we need to stop being so surprised by women having penises.

## REFERENCES

Berger, John. *Ways of Seeing*. London: British Broadcasting Corp, 1977. Print.

Case, Sue-Ellen. "The Emperor's New Clothes: The Naked Body and Theories of Performance." *SubStance*, 31, no. 2/3, issue 98/99: Special Issues: Theatricality, 2002, pp. 186–200. Internet Resource.

Charles, R. *Lettin' It All Hang Out*. UK: Sphere, 1995.

Coogan, Kelly. "Fleshy Specificity." *Journal of Lesbian Studies* 10 (2006): 17–41. Internet Resource.

Córdova Quero, M. H. "This Body Trans/Forming Me: Indecencies in Transgender/Intersex: Bodies, Body Fascism and the Doctrine of the Incarnation." In M. M. Althaus-Reid and L. Isherwood (eds.), *Controversies in Body Theology*. London: SCM Press, 2008, 80–128. Internet Resource.

del, Mar Pérez-Gil. María. "Undressing the Virgin Mary: Nudity and Gendered Art." *Feminist Theology* 25, no. 2 (2017): 208–21. Print.

Davey, and Gage. "Boy Meets Girl: Another Film That's Not for Us." *Feministing*. Web.

Dolan, Jill. *The Feminist Spectator in Action: Feminist Criticism for the Stage and Screen*. New York: Palgrave Macmillan, 2013.

Edelman, E. A., and L. Zimman. "Boycunts and Bonus Holes: Trans Men's Bodies, Neoliberalism, and the Sexual Productivity of Genitals." *Journal of Homosexuality* 61, no. 5 (2014): 673–90. Internet Resource.

Grosz, Elizabeth. *Volatile Bodies: Toward a Corporeal Feminism*. Bloomington, IN: Indiana University Press, 1994.

Horlacher, Stefan. *Transgender and Intersex: Theoretical, Practical, and Artistic Perspectives*. New York: Palgrave Mcmillan, 2016. Internet resource.

Lee, C., and P. Kwan. "The Trans Panic Defense: Masculinity, Heteronormativity, and the Murder of Transgender Women." *Hastings Law Journal* 66, no. 1 (2014): 77–132. Internet Resource.

Lindner, Katharina. *Questions of Embodied Difference: Film and Queer Phenomenology*. Amsterdam University Press, 2012. Internet resource.

Lizzo. "Like a Girl." *Cuz I Love You.*, Nice Life Recording Company and Atlantic Recording Corporation, 2019, track 2. *Spotify*.

Merry, Stephanie. "A Small-Town Transgender Love Story." *Rev. of Boy Meets Girl. Washington Post* February 12, 2015: n. pag. Web.

Monks, Aoife. *The Actor in Costume*. New York: Palgrave Macmillan, 2010.

Mulvey, Laura. "Visual Pleasure and Narrative Cinema." In Leo Braudy and Marshall Cohen (eds.), *Film Theory and Criticism: Introductory Readings*. New York: Oxford University Press, 1999, 833–44.

Phelan, Peggy. *Unmarked: The Politics of Performance*. London and New York: Routledge, 1993.

Rubin, H. S. "Phenomenology as Method in Trans Studies." *Glq New York* 4, no. 2 (1998): 263–82. Internet Resource.

Salamon, Gayle. *Assuming a Body: Transgender and Rhetorics of Materiality*. New York: Columbia University Press, 2010. Print.

Schaeffer, Eric. "Frameline Interview: Eric Schaeffer On His Trans Rom Com 'Boy Meets Girl.'" Interview by Gary K. Kramer. *IndieWire*, June 25, 2014. Web.

Stryker, Susan. "Christine Jorgensen's Atom Bomb: Transsexuality and the Emergence of Postmodernity." In E. Ann Kaplan and Susan Squier (eds.), *Playing Dolly: Technocultural Formations, Fantasies, and Fictions of Assisted Reproduction*. New Brunswick, NJ and London: Rutgers University Press, 1999, 157–71.

———. "Transsexuality: The Postmodern Body and / as Technology." *Exposure* 30, no. 1/2 (1995): 38–50.

Toepfer, Karl. "Nudity and Texuality in Postmodern Performance." *Performing Arts Journal* 18, no. 3 (September 1996): 76–91.

*Chapter 4*

# The Trans Baby Boom

*Framing Male Pregnancy on Television*

Traci Abbott

The relationship between the transgender and medical communities is complex and fraught with issues of access, power, and choice. Currently in the United States those in the transgender community who seek medical assistance for their transition must rely on regulations called the "Standards of Care" (SOC), set forth by the World Professional Association for Transgender Health (WPATH, 2011). First defined in 1979, the guidelines are in their seventh iteration, last updated in 2011 partly to coordinate anticipated revisions to the diagnostic criteria of "gender dysphoria" in the American Psychiatric Association's *Diagnostic and Statistical Manual of Mental Disorders*, fifth edition (DSM-5) (WPATH, 2011; APA, 2013). Although medical tools such as hormone therapy and surgery have enabled many to transform their physical self to fulfill their gender identity, transgender scholars and activists have disputed this need for "gatekeepers" (Wentling, 2012; Teich, 2012; Glover, 2016). Moreover, the SOC contributes to the presumption that social transition requires medical intervention and that gender identity must correlate to specific bodily changes, particularly genital surgery, often called "transnormativity" (Vipond, 2015; Glover, 2016).

From this perspective, pregnant trans men[1] by definition defy transnormativity since they retain their female genitalia and reproductive organs while living and identifying as male. Yet this chapter raises the contradictory premise that the expertise and authority of medical personnel inherent in medical reality shows affirms this non-normative transgender identity for cisgender (non-transgender) viewers, as seen on *Discovery Health*'s Baby Week, "Transgendered and Pregnant" (Ali and Orstein, 2009), and "Dad's Having a Baby," which is part of the ITV/Channel 4's documentary series *Bodyshock* and airs in the United States on *BBC America* (Keel, 2011). My methodology combines the genre research on medical reality television, feminist media scholarship that quantifies the explicit and implicit bias of such shows, and queer media studies that relate how documentary and reality television produce "affirmational" narratives to bridge identity differences between queer subjects and the mainstream audience. This methodology thus indicates how both episodes rely upon the authority of medical personnel, albeit differently, to demonstrate that pregnant trans men shift gendered notions of pregnancy and even reconfigure the dependence of gender upon anatomical differences. Each episode utilizes the relational element of gender identity to affirm the pregnant man's maleness by others, including family members, but it is more impactful when the medical professionals who supervise his pregnancy and childbirth do not disqualify his maleness, since their gaze, as the program's consistent authority, becomes the audience's "gender mirror" (Straayer, 1997, p. 214). This methodology also integrates trans media research which has exposed the prevalence of transphobic assumptions in visual media, particularly against those who do not conform to the expected trajectory of physical transition. Thus, a third hour-long televised documentary of a pregnant trans man from the ABC news program *20/20* will be integrated into the discussion as a useful contrast, since this example, "Journey of a Pregnant Man" (Goldberg and Paul, 2008), upholds the transphobic perspective of its interviewer/narrator, Barbara Walters, the overall affirmational testimony by medical personnel, family members, or even other transgender parents. As a result, *20/20* frames trans masculine pregnancy as antithetical *to* rather than an extension *of* traditional family structures and anathema to the commonly accepted definition of *pregnancy*.

*Discovery Health*'s "Transgendered and Pregnant" documents Emily and Cai's[2] unexpected pregnancy. Presuming their hormone treatment rendered them infertile, they were unaware of the pregnancy until twenty-eight weeks. Like many pregnancy and birth reality programs, "Transgendered" documents the couple's pregnancy through birth and their return home with their son Dante. *Bodyshock*'s "Dad's" follows a trans masculine couple, Tom and Scott Moore, from the weeks before Scott gives birth to son Miles through their move from a liberal California town to New Mexico and into Scott's second pregnancy. Since *Bodyshock*, airing since 2006, provides "extraordinary and moving real-life stories about the extremes of the human body," the producers offer a more comprehensive overview of this atypical family than *Discovery Health* (2014). Indeed, despite *Bodyshock*'s description, *20/20*, ABC's news magazine, actually utilizes more medical and technological sensationalism in its coverage of Thomas Beatie, who was already a celebrity when *20/20* aired this episode with its premier celebrity interviewer, Barbara Walters. Beatie and his wife Nancy gave Walters unparalleled access to their Oregon home soon after the birth of daughter Susan as well as to their own footage of the pregnancy and birth.

## TRANS BODIES IN VISUAL MEDIA

Trans media studies have demonstrated the challenges of representing trans bodies on visual media. Trans[3] bodies already confront cis-normative expectations of identity, which presume that gender corresponds to the sex assigned at birth, a sex visible anatomically and through one's gender expression (clothes, hair, etc.), based on a "body = sex = gender" equation that preempts the possibility of other combinations or identities (Siebler, 2012, p. 84). Cisgender audiences therefore assign a gender using visual elements over personal proclamations, accepting someone's gender only when they can "*see* the identity on the body in order to believe it" (Booth, 2015, p. 112). A pregnant male body, by definition, visually and conceptually challenges these cis-normative expectations and necessarily forces television documentary producers to affirm transgender identities over the comfort levels of their cisgender audience, an occurrence more often seen in independent films than in mainstream television (Straayer, 1997; Alías, 2010; Sender, 2014; Booth, 2015).

Pregnant male subjects also challenge the most common transgender identities in popular visual media which reify rather than undermine the two gender paradigm. Whether as characters or documentary subjects, producers typically chose identities that replicate one standard of transition, a binary gendered model in which a change in physical sex characteristics accompanies a shift in external gender expression, with masculinity the domain for male-identified persons and femininity for female-identified persons (Siebler, 2012, p. 75). Granted, transgender people often cannot legally change their gender without medical/surgical changes, which has negative repercussions on their ability to work or travel and increases the possibility of harassment and discrimination if they are "outed" as transgender outside of their control (Bender-Baird, 2011; Spade, 2011; Teich, 2012). Yet visual media narratives usually ignore facts to reproduce instead a "born in the wrong body" narrative that arose from journalistic and autobiographical accounts of transsexuals in earlier decades (Catherwood, 2015, pp. 46–47; Stryker, 2008). This stereotypical narrative emphasizes a discomfort or inability to live in one type of body and then celebrates a new sense of self through a thorough physical transformation, perceived to be successful when it follows traditional expectations of their gender identity (Stone, 1991, p. 290). Such narratives therefore heighten the significance of bodily transformation for the transgender subjects as well as their conformity to accepted standards, such as with montages that demonstrate daily acts, like dressing, shaving, or putting on makeup, or that provide visual comparisons before and after permanent medical procedures, as seen recently in National Geographic's "American Transgender" (Schwerin, 2012) and CNN's "Lady Valor: The Kristin Beck Story" (Herzog and Orabona, 2014) (Hladsky, 2013; Serano, 2013; Booth, 2015).

This visual evidence of the body before and after medical transition forces the audience to recognize both the subjects' gender identity and sex they were assigned at birth (Boucher, 2011). Even though the conceptual distance between gendered bodies in this timeline may be illusory (Halberstam, 2005; Hayward, 2008), this juxtaposition still maintains a cis-normative perspective of the gender binary as the subject moves from one gender to the other. In contrast, a pregnant trans masculine body displays the subject's gender history *simultaneously* in a single image and introduces the biological possibility that motherhood and manhood are not mutually exclusive (Norwood, 2013). *Trans masculine pregnancy* by definition thus challenges the dominant, cisgender belief that external markers of gender correlate to bodily markers of sex in the same way for everyone, since the subjects have completed their social transition by living and identifying as men, but their medical transition, by the standard definition, is incomplete[4] (Boucher, 2011). Many trans persons today do not follow the traditional trajectory of the past. Numerous studies (Factor and Rothblum, 2008; Beemyn and Rankin, 2011) conclude that many in the trans community no longer define *gender transition* the same way, particularly the assumption that specific genders require specific genitalia (Cromwell, 1999; Catherwood, 2015). Beatie, Cai, and Scott Moore, in other words, do not rationalize why their pregnant bodies are male but instead explain their pregnant state as part of, not in contrast to, their gendered male selves.

## PREGNANCY AND MEDICAL REALITY TELEVISION

Medical reality television shows, like the reality genre, proliferated in the 1990s and 2000s. Media scholars indicate that even though scripted hospital dramas heightened the fallibility and emotionality of physicians during this period (Pfau, Mullen, and Garrow, 1995; Turow, 2010; Strauman and Goodier, 2011), reality shows continued to offer an uncompromised view of physician competence and authority (Chory-Assad and Tamborini, 2001; Turow, 2010). Critically, one study noted that medical reality programs showcase male physicians (87%) more often than fictional dramas (60%), attributing this finding to the genre's overreliance on plastic surgery as a topic, (Jain and Slater, 2013, pp. 713, 717) yet do not acknowledge that such patients are primarily female, an element of childbirth reality shows, too. Thus, feminist scholars often conclude that pregnancy and birthing reality shows, like *Discovery Health*'s "Baby Week," accentuate the authority of medical personnel, settings, and technologies over the naturalness of the process, culminating in the "crisis" of childbirth which requires constant technological monitoring and medical intervention (Morris and McInerney,

2010; Sears and Goddaris, 2011, Luce et al., 2016). Yet the authority of medical personnel does not necessarily inhibit sympathy for the pregnant subject. One feminist researcher concludes that reality show health practitioners can become role models of empathy for viewers when their voiceovers or interviews specifically connect their professional ethics and expertise to caring for a vulnerable patient during a challenging period (Horeck, 2016). As I further explain, medical personnel on "Dad's Having a Baby" and "Transgendered and Pregnant" utilize both to explicitly affirm these pregnant males' status and their heightened vulnerability during pregnancy and childbirth.

At the same time, the topic of pregnant men may appeal to audiences of medical reality shows through sensationalism, whether by focusing on diagnosing or treating rare conditions, like *Bodyshock*, or on interventions during health emergencies, like *Discovery Health* (Christenson and Ivancin, 2006). In fact, some researchers conclude that this impetus has amplified the authority of obstetrics professionals since the shows highlight the risks of pregnancy and childbirth despite the unlikelihood of these conditions for the average patient (Luce et al., 2016; Morris and McInerney, 2010). Yet the birth process is a common, not rare, condition, so it promotes empathy in viewers who relate to the couple's anxieties and agonies even though they may also watch to revel in the novelty of different individual circumstances (Horeck, 2016).

These producers, though, certainly recognize the "novelty" of pregnant men, which is evident in the extensive media coverage on the topic despite being neither a new nor an isolated phenomenon. In 2000, *The Village Voice* published Patrick Califia's account of partner Matt Rice's pregnancy, who was also profiled in Jules Rosskam's 2005 documentary, *Transparent*, along with nineteen other trans masculine parents, although the majority transitioned post-pregnancy. Yet attention to Beatie's pregnancy in 2008 was unparalleled because he appeared in multiple media outlets, including *People* and *Oprah*, and claimed to be the first male to give birth.[5] While some non-mainstream news outlets have published sympathetic profiles of trans masculine parents (Parker, 2015; Kellaway, 2015), mainstream media in the United States and United Kingdom continue to treat trans masculine pregnancy, like Britain's "first" pregnant men, Hayden Cross and Scott Parker, and Trystan Reese in Oregon, as revelatory and controversial (see, for example, Kelly, 2017; Hassan and Andone, 2017). On one hand, coverage which details these men's routes to conception and current and future medical procedures may encourage more trans masculine pregnancy. While statistical evidence is scarce, recent obstetrics research (Light, Oben-Maliver, Sevelius, and Kerns, 2014; Obedin-Maliver and Makadon, 2016) and a panel at the 2012 Trans-Health Conference suggest, "we're on the cusp of a trans baby boom" (Pérez, 2012). Since some studies have concluded that "the majority of transsexual men desire to have children" (Wierckx et al., 2012, p. 486), many medical professionals encourage transgender patients to consider future reproduction (De Sutter, 2009; Murphy, 2012), and the American College of Obstetricians and Gynecologists (2011) has called for more sensitivity and options for trans patients. On the other hand, mainstream coverage often capitalizes on the topic's controversy by providing photos of the subject's bare stomach or torso. The sight of a man's pregnant belly with his facial hair and a bound or breast-less chest is sensationalist because it intends to shock viewers with the combination of gender markers (Salamon, 2010; Catherwood, 2015). All three of these episodes include some version of the male transbody as spectacle, but an underlying narrative on gender dysphoria can counter the image's startling impact.

## PREGNANT TRANS MEN DOCUMENTARIES AS AFFIRMATION NARRATIVES

Queer media scholar Christopher Pullen has defined the elements required to designate reality documentaries "affirmation narratives," regarding their use of confessional storytelling to establish a group identity that is both worthy of recognition as a valid identity and compatible within traditional frames of reference, like family and community (2007, pp. 145, 163). This component, "intimate storytelling," refers to those moments of emotive display and vulnerability which engage the audience with the subject's experience (Pullen, 2009, p. 118). For these episodes, a couple anticipating the arrival of their child is a touchpoint that fits within the "family" genre, whose popularity has been able to expand the traditionally heterosexual and gendered family to include gay men and lesbians, even to market them as modern pioneers updating conventional paradigms using familiar elements (Pullen, 2007).

It is therefore useful to recall that reality television, such as news programming and other genres that purport to depict "reality," often utilizes the ideology of the viewing majority since ideology itself is, as Burke argues, "a system of political of social ideas, framed and propounded for an ulterior purpose" (Burke, 1969, p. 88; Gitlin, 1980; Holmes and Jermyn, 2004). This connection to the family genre is what moves these episodes away from the medical exposition found in other transsexual documentaries, but then hinges on the framing of pregnant trans men and their spouses as a "family," with references to their parental roles in sometimes traditionally gendered terms (Booth, 2015, p. 116). Both *Discovery Health* and *Bodyshock* immediately affirm the trans men's male identity, though the former is more invested in heteronormativity. This episode opens with a low angle shot of Emily, highlighting her shoulder-length blond hair and pink t-shirt, standing with her arm around Cai, whose belly pushes against his black shirt. They smile as she addresses the camera: "I'm Emily and I got my husband pregnant." Emily later mentions the two were married at a local church, so even though the producers do not include either her or Cai's description of their sexual orientation, they implicitly validate their heterosexuality. Granted, since the producers acknowledge in a caption that "neither Cai nor Emily had completed gender reassignment when they conceived," it is possible for the audience to misgender Cai and Emily while seeing them as heterosexual. Yet since Cai and Emily's repeated declarations as husband and wife are neither implicitly nor explicitly questioned nor connected to their legal status, their stated identities are not undermined by knowledge of their anatomical sex differences, also demonstrated by a traditional "before and after" montage. Cai states early in "Transgendered" that he is still physically transitioning but does not find it incongruent with his current status: "eventually I'll probably have a hysterectomy done, and have top surgery and a reduction done. I'm very much a man, and that's how I'd like society to see me." He later states, "I've always wanted to be a father. I feel blessed," again indicating that the pregnancy does not shift his perspective on either his gender identity or his relationship with his son. *Discovery Health*'s presentation of Emily's and Cai's heterosexual status thus fits the ideological heteronormativity of the pregnancy reality genre, as defined by feminist scholars, while simultaneously reformulating traditionally gendered parental roles (Maher, 2004; Morris and McInerney, 2010; Sears and Goddaris, 2011).

"Dad's," in contrast, presents the Moores' story from the start as two gay men, so that the opening repeats the promotional description on the website: "like most married couples, Scott and Tom still wanted to try for a baby. Unlike most male gay couples, they had the means to do so, as Scott still has working female reproductive organs." The Moores are also referenced as "gay dads" even though they do not explain if Tom is able to adopt Miles after Scott gives birth to him.[6] Both are shown in "before and after" photo montages, but early in the program, Scott connects the pregnancy to his body materiality: "I was very lucky to be able carry Miles. For such a long time my body and being transgendered was such a negative thing for me. . . . And even though the process of being pregnant and giving birth isn't the most comfortable thing, it made me . . . appreciate what I have more and realize that even though it's not the ideal of what I want to be, it's still beautiful." Moreover, even though "Dad's" shows Scott's pregnant torso, it is Tom who provides a rationale for his mastectomy. During an extended shot showering, Tom narrates his dysphoric relationship with his breasts: "I just didn't want to see them. To see them would make me cry. The process of binding [my breasts][7] . . . caused gangrene so when I finally did have to have my breasts removed, . . . I lost my nipples. . . . But in the same instant, it saved my life." *Bodyshock* thus links breast removal to achieving personal autonomy and

health, not a masculine ideal. Gendered body parts and experiences are therefore explained as related to but also not dependent upon gendered identities.
The producers of "Dad's" and "Transgendered" do not question whether the
Moores or Cai are husbands or fathers. They presume that they are, so the
viewers do, too.

In contrast, *20/20* rejects Beatie's gender identification almost immediately. The tone is set in the opening moments, when Walters asks, "Do you
see yourself as a traditional family?" to which Beatie replies, "We do. We
are man, woman, and child . . . a family. Just the same as everyone else." She
then adds in a voiceover, "They are but they are not," seguing into a montage
of press coverage that includes a newscaster's announcement, "this story is
very disturbing." Walters references a photo of Beatie's naked pregnant torso
from the *Advocate* first by calling it a "disturbing picture" and later asking
Beatie why he would send such a "provocative image" to the press, causing
an "uproar" and making him "fodder for the taboids." Walters also relies on
legal definitions to dispute Beatie's gender, despite his male legal status, by
explaining the legal requirement that he be listed as "mother," and by reiter-
ating biological facts: "But it wasn't your sperm. It was your *eggs*. Eggs are
associated with the mother, sperm with the father."

Legal and biological facts are presented differently in "Dad's." The
*Bodyshock* narrator explains that the Moores were able to marry in California
(prior to equal marriage legalization in 2013) because Scott's legal status was
female and Tom's male, but producers immediately follow this admission
with interviews with their two older sons explaining their family as having
"two dads." The narrator similarly contextualizes their decision to go public
not as a publicity stunt, like Walters implies, but because they felt safe in their
tight-knit community and were proud of their growing family, reiterated by
shots of a well-attended baby shower. Thus, when Scott's shirtless photo is
shown, it is normalized as a common, expectant parent phenomenon.

Walter thus uses medical and legal "evidence" to give her own cissexist
perspective on legitimacy. Since Walters is narrator *and* interviewer, her professional credibility underscores her reaction as fitting or informed about *any*
trans masculine pregnancy. She confers further authority on cissexist social
norms with statements such as, "you make a great many people very uneasy,"
and "you know that there are people who say just because you've taken testosterone, cut short your hair, removed your breasts, that doesn't make you a
man." In this way, *20/20* demonstrates how documentary producers present
both sides of an issue to appear objective but then utilize other elements to
directly or indirectly resolve those opposing viewpoints (Pullen, 2007). As
noted, *20/20* starts with a montage of the reactions of the mainstream press,
which Walters then summarizes as "some people called you a freak," and
later adds additional transphobic examples like jokes from late-night talk

show monologues. In contrast, transphobic statements listed onscreen to show what the Moores experienced after the birth of their son, Miles, are framed in *Bodyshock* for what they are, transphobia, and the narrators rightly emphasize that Moores' safety in light of this discourse rather than downplaying them as "some people."

*20/20* includes two transgender parents, trans man Andy New and trans feminine author Jennifer Finney Boylan, to dispute Beatie's self-identification as a responsible trans parent rather than to confirm his legitimacy. Walters explains how "Angie" delayed her transition to becoming "Andy," "in order to get pregnant," without mentioning potential psychological distress. Rosskam's *Transparent* (2005), for example, shows a range of reactions by trans masculine parents who followed a similar route, some of whom found the situation unbearable, "like a constant slap in the face, that here I am, stuck in this female body." Then Boylan's explicit validation of the Beaties, "two people who have done the greatest thing two people can do, which is to have a child," is undercut by her admission that "the concept of a man having a baby . . . freaked me out a little bit at first," a statement that is given additional weight when the producers repeat it in the introduction. Ironically, then, even other trans parents were used to maintain a cis-normative view of Beatie as selfish or freakish.

*Bodyshock* similarly includes dissenting viewpoints that discount the Moores' identities and denigrate their reproductive rights but to underscore their struggle when they are forced to leave California due to a home fire for Las Cruces, described as, "Bible Belt New Mexico." The producers sought out interviews with local townspeople who reject the Moores in religious language, such as a teenager who declares, "God is not mad at the people that are. He's mad at the fact of homosexuality," and a woman who replies, when told about Miles's birth, "God created women to be women and men to be men." The narrator immediately invalidates this viewpoint by stating, "like most transsexuals, Tom and Scott would argue that their transition from one to the other was unavoidable." Tom's sarcastic response also judges the cissexist perspective: "Yes, I choose to be harassed, I choose to be called names, I choose to be different. No, you don't make a choice. It's simply who you are. And it's not an easy life. I've stopped trying to figure out what people think." Moreover, the producers include accepting family members, like Scott's police officer father, who explains to the camera, "Scott thinks of himself as a man and wants to live as a man. . . . He's still got all the organs and functioning parts of a female, so that he lives as a man but is biologically a female. That's the way I see him." Yet rather than counter this remark like *20/20*, the producers instead contrast it to Tom's description of his own father to Scott: "your dad loves you whether you're gay or straight or trans or a pregnant man. He doesn't care. It's like, 'you're my kid and I love you and I'll do what I can help you however I can.' And my dad doesn't even recognize that I exist anymore."

*Discovery Health* producers similarly offer testimony from family members who are accepting of both Cai and Emily's situation and their gender identities as mother and father. Emily's mother exclaims prior to their son's birth, "I've gotten over the difficulty of talking about my transgendered daughter, and so now I'm talking about my pregnant son-in-law. I'm really looking forward to my grandchild." Yet what makes this episode particularly crucial in countering transphobic statements is that the most dissenting view in this episode is by Cai and Emily's physician. In his only scene, their endocrinologist first asks Emily, "how are you preparing for fatherhood?" When she replies, "more like motherhood," he seemingly agrees with her by answering, "Well, both of you to some extent will be mothers, right?" He then disagrees with Cai, however, when he replies, "Not really," by telling him, "Well, you are carrying the baby at this point." Yet when Cai replies, "At this point, in terms of the physical and the genetics, yes. In terms of the social role that we want to play, not so much," the producers affirm his statement by not disrupting the narrative with a rejoinder or a reaction shot of the doctor. Instead, the scene moves on to a discussion of whether increasing Emily's hormones will allow her to breastfeed, another means to privilege their gender identities as biologically compatible with traditional gendered parenting. In contrast, *20/20* seems to justify Beatie's rejection by nine different doctors for assistance in artificial insemination as valid, never mentioning the commonality of his experience for atypical families (Mamo, 2007; Solinger, 2013) nor his later, presumably positive experiences with childbirth personnel.

The most affirming health practitioners included in each episode are midwives. Although most media and health communication scholars focus on only physicians in reality television (Pfau, Mullen, and Garrow, 1995; Chory-Assad and Tamborini, 2001; Cho, Wilson and Choi, 2011; Jain and Slater, 2013), others note that that midwives are rarely shown assisting pregnancy and childbirth, which they characterize as unfairly prioritizing a medicalized model of hospital childbirth over alternative birthing centers or home births (Morris and McInerney, 2010; Sears and Goddaris, 2011). Yet the American College of Nurse-Midwives (2016) reports that certified midwives assisted in 8.2 percent of U.S. births, 94.3 percent of which were in a hospital. Therefore, the dichotomous relationship set up by these scholars may be overstated. In *Discovery Health*, the nurse-midwife appears consistently throughout the episode and is shown assisting the birth along with other hospital personnel. Since the birth of Scott's son and Beatie's daughter were recorded on home video, no hospital personnel appear, yet each program still utilizes midwives with differing effects.

*20/20* includes midwife Stephanie Brill as an expert on trans masculine pregnancy, not because she assisted Thomas Beatie or, like Scott, because he wished to become pregnant again.[8] She testifies to the commonality of Beatie's experience, having assisted around thirty-five to forty trans men in her practice; but Walters first seems to encourage her to criticize Beatie's publicity and then asks, "Beatie says that he is legally a man, but he kept his reproductive organs to have a baby. Isn't he trying to have it both ways?" Brill replies, "I think he is trying to have it *his* way. He had the capacity to have a baby. That didn't invalidate him being a man." Walters immediately counters her statement with a voiceover, "Of course, not everybody would agree to that," again reasserting the cissexist view as "logical" and dismissing Brill's perspective, despite her professional expertise.

In contrast, Cai's nurse-midwife explicitly states that she sees Cai's gender identity as compatible with her medical mission: "Our [practice's] motto is, listen to the pregnant woman. In this case, the pregnant woman is a man, for all intensive purposes. He considers himself a man, although he's pregnant." Other hospital personnel who assist in the delivery also treat the couple with sensitivity and respect, including a lactation specialist who sets up a supplementary nursing system for Emily. Therefore, the culminating effect of the medical personnel who assist Cai thus forces the cisgender audience to acknowledge the fact that if obstetrics professionals can de-gender pregnancy from femaleness, than they can as well. As the midwife succinctly explains, "What I see is a loving couple. They love each other, and they're going to love this baby. They didn't realize that they could get pregnant, but now that they are pregnant, they're very happy." *Bodyshock*'s midwife bridges these examples, as she is supportive to Scott as he contemplates a second pregnancy and is noted by the narrator as having a specialization in trans masculine pregnancies, such as how to conceive using artificial insemination. Yet "Dad's" is even more explicit in its affirmation of a flexible identity system, modeling for practitioners—and by extension, the audience—how to address the gendered language of pregnancy. The midwife explains that a pregnant man should not "have to endure . . . somebody referring to him with female pronouns and female body parts as though he wasn't a man at all. . . . I put the pronouns in front of them, you know, like 'your man ovaries' or 'manhole,' or 'down here.'. . . I actually get a lot of referrals based on the idea of sensitivity. I'm really not doing anything for them that I don't do for anyone else except my language." This comment is thus significant. By being sensitive to the way pregnancy is traditionally gendered through language, the midwife exemplifies for the audience how to decouple gender from any experience, a shift that requires nothing but an open attitude.

## CONCLUSION

This chapter asserts that medical reality television can affirm transgender identities and a de-gendered view of pregnancy which further encourage acceptance of non-normative families and those in the transgender community who no longer follow a "one size fits all" medical and social transition or gender identity. Granted, the paucity of transgender identities in mainstream media outside of the transnormative model is already a challenge for media scholars (Siebler, 2012; Capuzza and Spencer, 2017). Yet future research on such representations has the potential to shape trans media studies as well as other fields, particularly feminist theory, as Noble (2012) explains: "critical *trans* perspectives should be making it harder to make truth claims about the universalizability of 'women'—experientially or otherwise—without at least using it with much more precision to identify a relation to 'woman' no longer reducible to the female body or the nefarious 'women's experiences'" (p. 50). In my view, the producers' decision to utilize the affirming authority of medical personnel as part of their promotion of trans masculine pregnancy within mainstream values of family and childbirth is what makes them a powerful tool for shifting cis-normative perspectives. Even though an affirmative narrative or sympathetic affect for the media subject is "highly contentious" and subjective, media scholars have demonstrated that the trans community seeks and deserves a place within the familial ideological frameworks provided by television that do not devalue their differences, one that "positions them as unique—defined by a difference that warrants recognition and affirmation, and fully average—defined by everyday concerns and mundane experiences" (Pullen, 2009, p. 145; Cavalcante, 2018, p. 177). Indeed, other trans men have stated their appreciation for these attempts to show the cisgender public how to uncouple pregnancy from femininity. Activist Matt Kailey asserts on his blog, "Beatie is doing us a favor. He's showing the world that . . . that being a man can mean nurturing children and even giving birth to them," a sentiment another trans man echoed: "the greatest legacy [Andy] Inkster and Beatie may leave is the challenge they represent to our ideas of manhood" (Cascio, 2014). Another trans masculine blogger also credits Beatie with such power by writing about his conversation with a "middle class mother-of-two," who commented, unaware she was speaking to a trans man, "If a couple wants to have children, then I'm all for it," forcing him to conclude that, "people who are uneducated about us, who are never exposed to us, . . . [will] come around to accepting us if trans people like Thomas Beatie pop up right in front of them and say, 'Hey, I am here and I'm a good person and I'm not that different from you and I only want the same things that you want'" (Anderson, 2015). Two forums with substantial comments about *Discovery Health*'s "Transgendered" episode do demonstrate the positive impact on the cisgender audience: the Facebook (2009) page advertising the episode and a BabyCenter Community thread entitled, "Transgendered and Pregnant . . . WTF?!?" (2009) Although both comment threads start out with transphobic statements, predictably by people who refuse to watch the show, a more progressive and sympathetic ethos eventually asserts itself. These initial reactions get called out as "haters," and Cai's ability to have a child unexpectedly is a "miracle." Given the more balanced tone in recent mainstream publications, like *Time* magazine's "My Brother's Pregnancy and the Making of a New American Family," or *Cosmopolitan*'s, "This Transgender Couple Got Pregnant in a Groundbreaking Way," perhaps male pregnancy will become more routine and less sensational in the twenty-first century (Hempel, 2016; Moore, 2015). This could enhance all of us, since "the more scripts for pregnancy expand to include men, the less gendered pregnancy will become, and the more flexibility for gendered bodies and selves there will be" (Shapiro, 2010, p. 186).

## NOTES

1. I use the term "trans men" to refer to those whose gender identity is male but were assigned a female sex at birth due to their female genetic and physiological traits, also referred to as "female-to-male" or FTMs. My use of "trans masculine" or "trans men," however, is not meant to invalidate their gender as "male" or "men," nor to suggest that it is inauthentic compared to cisgender (non-transgender) males or men.

2. Neither Cai nor his wife Emily's last name is given in the documentary or subsequent press.

3. I use the term "trans" here as an adjective to denote more broadly those who experience an incongruence between their sex as assigned at birth and their gender, including those who identify outside of the gender binary. I acknowledge both "trans" and "transgender" are debated terms whose use continues to evolve (Serano, 2013).

4. Surgical procedures for trans men that would preclude reproduction include sex organ removal (vaginectomy, hysterectomy, and oophorectomy) and new genital construction (phalloplasty or metioplasty).

5. States vary on their requirements for a legal change of gender and whether they issue a new or amended birth certificate. Since Beatie was born in Hawaii, he was able to change his gender to male because his mastectomy qualified as a "sex change operation."

6. The episode also does not indicate if Scott legally adopted Tom's sons Logan and Gregg, but does mention that Tom adopted them after his relationship with their mother ended and she committed suicide.

7. Binding is a common practice among some butch females and trans men intended to hide or flatten the breasts, especially because it is relatively inexpensive since it can be easily achieved by layering clothing or using drugstore bandages, although a chest binders are becoming more easily accessible through the Internet.

8. In fact, Beatie announced his second pregnancy during his interview with Walters, who notably seems shocked and does not offer her congratulations. Beatie gave birth to a son in June, 2009 and another son in July, 2010.

## REFERENCES

Ali, S. (Writer and Director). (2009). Transgendered and pregnant [Television series episode]. In A. Orstein (Executive producer), *Discovery Health.* Silver Spring, MD: Discovery Communications.

Alías, M. E. (2010). Shattering gender taboos in Gabriel Baur's *Venus Boyz. Journal of Gender Studies, 19*(2), 167–79. doi: 10.1080/09589231003695880.

American College of Obstetricians and Gynecologists. (2011, December). Health care for transgender individuals. Retrieved from http://www.acog.org/Resources-And-Publications/Committee-Opinions/Committee-on-Health-Care-for-Underserved-Women/Health-Care-for-Transgender-Individuals.

American College of Nurse-Midwives. (2016). CNM/CM-attended birth statistics in the United States. Retrieved from http://www.midwife.org/CNM/CM-attended-Birth-Statistics.

American Psychiatric Association. (2013). *Diagnostic and statistical manual of mental disorders.* 5th ed. Washington: American Psychiatric Association.

Anderson. (2014, May 16). Why I thank Thomas Beatie [Blog post]. Retrieved from https://americantrans man.com/2010/04/25/why-i-thank-thomas-beatie/.

*Babycenter Community.* (2009, December 1). Transgendered and pregnant . . . WTF?. Retrieved fromhttp://community.babycenter.com/post/a19300605/transgendered_and_pregnant...wtf?cpg=4&csi=2088320776&pd=-1.

Beemyn, G. and Rankin, S. (2011). *The lives of transgender people.* New York, NY: Columbia University Press.

Bender-Baird, K. (2011). *Transgender employment experiences: Gendered perceptions and the law.* Albany: State University of New York Press.

*Bodyshock.* (2014). Channel 4 (UK). Retrieved from http://www.channel4.com/programmes/bodyshock.

Booth, E. T. (2015). The provisional acknowledgement of identity claims in televised documentary. In L. G. Spencer and J. C. Capuzza (Eds.), *Transgender communication studies: Histories, trends and trajectories* (pp. 111–26). Lanham, MA: Lexington Books.

Boucher, M. J. (2011). 'Do you have what it takes to be a real man?': Female-to-male transgender embodiment and the politics of the 'real' in *A Boy named Sue* and *Body Alchemy.* In E. Watson and M. E. Shaw (Eds.), *Performing American masculinities: The 21st-century man in popular culture* (pp. 192–231). Bloomington: Indiana University Press.

Burke, K. (1969). *A rhetoric of motives.* Berkeley: University of California Press.

Califia, P. (2000, June 20). Family values. *The Village Voice,* pp. 45–48. Retrieved from http://www.villagevoice.com.

Capuzza, J. C., and Spencer, L. G. (2017). Regressing, progressing, or transgressing on the small screen? Transgender characters on US scripted television series. *Communication Quarterly, 65*(2), 214–30. doi: 10.1080/01463373.2016.1221438.

Cascio, J. (2014, February 21). The reproductive rights of trans men [Blog post]. Retrieved from https://goodmenproject.com/featured-content/reproductive-rights-trans-men.

Catherwood, R. (2015). Coming in? The evolution of the transsexual memoir in the twenty-first century. *Genre, 48*(1), 35–71.

Cavalcante, Andre. (2018). *Struggling for ordinary: Media and transgender belonging in everyday life.* New York, NY: New York University Press.

Christenson, P. and Ivancin, M. (2006). The "reality" of health: Reality television and the public health. The Henry J. Kaiser Family Foundation. Retrieved from https://kaiserfamilyfoundation.files.wordpress.com/2013/01/7567.pdf.

Cho, H., Wilson, K., and Choi, J. (2011). Perceived realism of television medical dramas and perceptions about physicians. *Journal of Media Psychology, 23*(3), 141–48. doi: 10.1027/1864-1105/a000047.

Chory-Assad, R. M., and Tamborini, R. (2001). Television doctors: An analysis of physicians in fictional and non-fictional television programs. *Journal of Broadcasting & Electronic Media, 45*(3), 499–521.

Cromwell, J. (1999). *Trans men and FTMs: Identities, bodies, genders, and sexualities.* Champaign: University of Illinois Press.

De Sutter, P. (2009). Reproductive options for transpeople: Recommendations for revision of the WPATH's Standards of Care. *International Journal of Transgenderism, 11*(3), 183–85. doi: 10.1080/15532730903383765.

Discovery Life Channel. (2009, December 1). Transgendered and pregnant [Facebook post]. Retrieved from https://www.facebook.com/DiscoveryLifeChannel/videos/188053234581/.

Factor, R. and Rothblum, E. (2008). Exploring gender identity and community among three groups of transgender individuals in the United States: MTFs, FTMs, and genderqueers. *Health Sociology Review, 17*(3), 235–53. doi:10.5172/hesr.451.17.3.235.

Gitlin, T. (1980). *The whole world is watching: Mass media in the making and unmaking of the new left.* Berkley, CA: University of California Press.

Glover, J. K. (2016). Redefining realness?: On Janet Mock, Laverne Cox, TS Madison, and the representation of transgender women of color in media. *Souls, 18*(2–4), 338–57. doi: 10.1080/10999949.2016.1230824.

Goldberg, A. (Writer) and Paul, G. (Director). (2008). Journey of a pregnant man [Television series episode]. In D. Sloan (Executive producer), *20/20.* New York, NY: ABC News.

Halberstam, J. (2005). *In a queer time and place: Transgender bodies, subcultural lives.* New York: New York University Press.

Hassan, C. and Andone, D. (2017, June 8). My body is awesome: Trans man expecting his first child. *CNN.* Retrieved from http://www.cnn.com/2017/06/08/health/trans-man-pregnant-trnd/index.html.

Hayward, E. (2008). More lessons from a starfish: Prefixial flesh and transpeciated selves. *Women's Studies Quarterly*, *36*(3–4), 64–85.

Hempel, J. (2016, September 16). My brother's pregnancy and the making of a new American family. *Time*. Retrieved from http://time.com/4475634/trans-man-pregnancy-evan.

Herzog, M. and Orabona, S. (Directors). (2014, 4 September). *Lady Valor: The Kristin Beck Story* [Television series episode]. In M. Herzog and C. G. Cowen (Executive producers), *CNN Presents*. New York, NY: CNN.

Hladky, K. N. (2013). The construction of queer and the conferring of voice: Empowering and disempowering portrayals of transgenderism in *TransGeneration*. In J. Campbell and T. Carilli (Eds.), *Queer media images: LGBT perspectives* (pp. 101–10). Lanham, MD: Lexington Books.

Holmes, S. and Jermyn, D. (2004). Introduction: understanding reality TV. In S. Holmes and D. Jermyn (Eds.), *Understanding reality television* (pp. 1–23). London, UK: Routledge.

Horeck, T. (2016). The affective labour of *One born every minute* in its UK and US formats. *Critical Studies in Television*, *11*(2), 164–76. doi: 10.1177/1749602016642917.

Jain, P., and Slater, M. D. (2013). Provider portrayals and patient–provider communication in drama and reality medical entertainment television shows. *Journal of Health Communication*, *18*(6), 703–22. doi: 10.1080/10810730.2012.757388.

Kailey, M. (2009, June 10). Thomas Beatie's second baby. *Matt Kailey's Tranifesto*. Retrieved from https://mattkailey.wordpress.com/2009/06/10/thomas-beatie-second-baby.

Keel, A. (Writer and Director). (2011, April 7). Dad's having a baby. (Television series episode). In J. Wilkins (Executive producer), *Bodyshock*. London: Channel 4.

Kellaway, M. (2015, June 21). 9 trans dads share what they love about fatherhood. *The Advocate*. Retrieved from https://www.advocate.com/families/2015/06/21/9-trans-dads-share-what-they-love-about-fatherhood.

Kelly, T. (2017, July 9). Tale of two VERY modern dads. *The Daily Mail* (UK). Retrieved from http://www.dailymail.co.uk/news/article-4680190/The-tale-two-modern-dads.html.

Light, A. D., Oben-Maliver, J., Sevelius, J. M.., and Kerns, J. L. (2014). Transgender men who experienced pregnancy after female-to-male gender transitioning. *Obstetrics & Gynecology*, *124*(6), 1120–7. doi: 10.1097/AOG.0000000000000540.

Luce, A, et al. (2016). "Is it realistic?" The portrayal of pregnancy and childbirth in the media. *BMC Pregnancy and Childbirth*, *16*(1), 40–50. doi: 10.1186/s12884-016-0827-x.

Maher, J. (2014). Something else besides a father: Reproductive technology in recent Hollywood film. *Feminist Media Studies*, *14*(5), 853–67. doi:10.1080/14680777.2013.831369.

Mamo, L. (2007). *Queering reproduction: Achieving pregnancy in the age of technoscience*. Durham, NC: Duke University Press.

Moore, L. (2015, December 28). This transgender couple got pregnant in a groundbreaking way. *Cosmopolitan*. Retrieved from cosmopolitan.com/sex-love/news/a51353/transgender-couple-groundbreaking-pregnancy.

Morris, T., and McInerney, K. (2010). Media representations of pregnancy and child-birth: An analysis of reality television programs in the United States. *Birth, 37*(2), 134–40.

Murphy, T. F. (2012). The ethics of fertility preservation in transgender body modifications. *Journal of Bioethical Inquiry, 9*(3), 311–16. doi: 10.1007/s11673-01209378-7.

Noble, B. (2012). Trans. Panic. Some thoughts toward a theory of feminist fundamentalism. In A. Enke (Ed.), *Transfeminist perspectives: In and beyond transgender and gender studies* (pp. 45–59). Philadelphia, PA: Temple University Press.

Norwood, K. (2013). A pregnant pause, a transgender look: Thomas Beatie in the maternity pose. In J. Campbell and T. Carilli (Eds.), *Queer media images: LGBT perspectives* (pp. 65–75). Lanham, MD: Lexington Books.

Obedin-Maliver, J., and Makadon, H. J. (2016). Transgender men and pregnancy. *Obstetric Medicine, 9*(1), 4–8. Retrieved from http://journals.sagepub.com/doi/full/10.1177/1753495x15612658.

Parker, S. (2015, June 21). 11 transgender parents share their paths to parenthood. *Buzzfeed*. Retrieved from https://www.buzzfeed.com/sydneyparker/fathers-day-tk1mvmm?utm_term=.hwXZEbxxz4#.ogxgz3KKQD.

Pérez, M. (2012, June 18). Preparing for the trans baby boom. *Rewire*. Retrieved from https://rewire.news/article/2012/06/18/preparing-trans-baby-boom.

Pfau, M., Mullen, L. J., and Garrow, K. (1995). The influence of television viewing on public perceptions of physicians. *Journal of Broadcasting & Electronic Media, 39*(4), 441–58.

Pullen, C. (2007). *Documenting gay men: Identity and performance in reality television and documentary film*. Jefferson, NC: McFarland & Company.

Pullen, C. (2009). *Gay identity, new storytelling and the media*. New York, NY: Palgrave Macmillan.

Rosskam, J. (Producer and Director). (2005). *Transparent* [Motion Picture]. United States: MamSir Productions.

Salamon, G. (2010). *Assuming a body: Transgender and rhetorics of materiality*. New York, NY: Columbia University Press.

Schwerin, L. (Writer and Director). (2012, 1 May). *American Transgender* [Television documentary]. *National Geographic Television*. Washington, DC: National Geographic.

Sears, C. A., and Godderis, R. (2011). Roar like a tiger on TV? Constructions of women and childbirth in reality TV. *Feminist Media Studies, 11*(2), 181–95. doi: 10.1080/14680777.2010.521626.

Sender, K. (2014). Transgender, transmedia, and transnationality: Chaz Bono in documentary and *Dancing with the Stars*. In C. Carter, L. Steiner, and L. McLaughlin (Eds.), *The Routledge companion to media and gender* (pp. 300–310). New York, NY: Routledge.

Serano, J. (2013). *Excluded: Making feminist and queer movements more inclusive*. Berkeley, CA: Seal.

Shapiro, E. (2010). *Gender circuits: Bodies and identities in a technological age*. New York, NY: Routledge.

Siebler, K. (2012). Transgender transitions: Sex/Gender binaries in the digital age. *Journal of Gay & Lesbian Mental Health, 16*(1), 74–99. doi: 10.1080/19359705.2012.632751.

Solinger, R. (2013). *Reproductive politics: What everyone needs to know.* New York: Oxford University Press.

Spade, D. (2011). *Normal: Administrative violence, critical trans politics, and the limits of the law.* Brooklyn, NY: South End Press.

Stone, S. (1991). The empire strikes back: A posttranssexual manifesto. In J. Epstein and K. Straub (Eds.), *Body guards: The cultural politics of gender ambiguity* (pp. 280–304). New York, NY: Routledge.

Straayer, C. (1997). Transgender mirrors: Queering sexual difference. In C. Holmlund and C. Fuchs (Eds.), *Between the sheets, in the streets: Queer, lesbian, and gay documentary* (pp. 207–23). Minneapolis: University of Minnesota Press.

Strauman, E. C., and Goodier, B. C. (2011). The doctor(s) in house: An analysis of the evolution of the television doctor-hero. *Journal of Medical Humanities, 32*(1), 31–46. doi: 10.1007/s10912-010-9124-2.

Stryker, S. (2008). *Transgender history.* Berkeley, CA: Seal Press.

Teich, N. (2012). *Transgender 101: A simple guide to a complex issue.* New York, NY: Columbia University Press.

Turow, J. (2010). *Playing doctor: Television, storytelling and medical power.* Ann Arbor: University of Michigan Press.

Vipond, E. (2015). Resisting transnormativity: Challenging the medicalization and regulation of trans bodies. *Theory in Action, 8*(2), 21–44. doi: 10.3798/tia.1937-0237.15008.

Wentling, T. (2012). Am I obsessed: Gender identity disorder, stress, and obsession. In A. Ferber, K. Holcomb, and T. Wentling (Eds.), *Gender, sex and sexuality: The new basics,* 2nd ed. (pp. 208–18). New York, NY: Oxford.

Wierckx, K, et al. (2012). Reproductive wish in transsexual men. *Human Reproduction, 27*(2), 483–87. Retrieved from https://academic.oup.com/humrep/article/27/2/483/2919320.

The World Professional Association for Transgender Health (2011). *Standards of care for the health of transsexual, transgender, and gender nonconforming people.* Retrieved from http://wpath.org/site_page.cfm?pk_association_webpage_menu=1351.

*Chapter 5*

# Where's the "T"? *RuPaul's Drag Race* and Transgender In/Exclusion

Peter Piatkowski

In a March 2018 interview with *The Guardian*, self-proclaimed Supermodel of the World and drag legend RuPaul (born RuPaul Andre Charles) proudly asserted that drag is "a big f-you to male-dominated culture." This quote exemplifies the narrative RuPaul pushes when doing press for his successful reality TV/competition show *RuPaul's Drag Race*. Despite the show's popularity among non-queer audiences, its growing viewership, and its multiple awards, including thirteen Emmy wins (The Academy of Television Arts & Sciences), RuPaul still works hard to maintain the subversive nature of drag. This dogged grip on the inherently rebellious tone in drag is a marked way of combating calls that the show has spoiled the art of drag as the show's super-sized success has pulled the art from into the mainstream; *Drag Race* alumna Jasmine Masters colorfully declared in her YouTube video that the show has "fucked up drag," by encouraging the contestants to hew to a seemingly monotonous style of drag, insisting that the drag scene had gone "downhill" in response to the oversized influence the show has on the scene (2016) . The need to remain an outsider looking askance at mainstream (read: straight, white, cis) places the show—and by extension—RuPaul and his career into the narrative that includes such revolutionaries as Marsha P. Johnson, Sylvia Rivera, Stormé DeLarverie, and other heroes of the Stonewall Rebellion. Much of RuPaul's ethos as an entertainer is about being outside the main-stream, and therefore, the show carefully maintains the narrative that it is a destabilizing work that disputes gender roles and mores. Many times through-out the show's run, RuPaul has affirmed the show's outsider status, publicly bristling at the notion that the show has made drag respectable, maintaining that "Drag is naughty. Drag is not politically correct . . . I don't really want it to be acceptable. Drag is dangerous" (Kegu, 2019).

*The Guardian* interview—conducted by Decca Aitkenhead (2018)—for the most part is a fawning puff piece that makes the case for *RuPaul's Drag Race* as "the most radical show on TV." During the exchange between Aitkenhead and RuPaul, the subject of the trans community comes up. The journalist admits that she does not understand how a trans woman could participate in the competition, and contestant Peppermint comes up. Peppermint, a runner-up on the ninth season of the show, is the first transwoman who came out as trans prior to the show's airing (Hawkins, 2017), though other contestants have come out during their seasons or after their seasons have aired.

When Explaining Peppermint's "special" circumstance to Aitkenhead, RuPaul says, "Peppermint didn't get breast implants until after she left our show; she was identifying as a woman, but she hadn't really transitioned." When asked if a transgender woman who has transitioned would be considered as a contestant, RuPaul went on to say,

> Probably not. You can identify as a woman and say you're transitioning, but it changes once you start changing your body. It takes on a different thing; it changes the whole concept of what we're doing. We've had some girls who've had some injections in the face and maybe a little bit in the butt here and there, but they haven't transitioned. (2018)

Soon after, RuPaul went on Twitter and tweeted "You can take performance enhancing drugs and still be an athlete, just not in the Olympics" (RuPaul, 2018a). As expected in a social media–saturated pop culture, his comments were quickly criticized by members of queer communities, including former contestants of *RuPaul's Drag Race*, such as Courtney Act, Sasha Velour, Willam, and Gia Gunn, among others. And the story reached its predicted conclusion with the celebrity apology—again, disseminated via Twitter:

> Each morning I pray to set aside everything I THINK I know, so I may have an open mind and a new experience. I understand and regret the hurt I have caused. The trans community are heroes of our shared LGBTQ movement. You are my teachers. (RuPaul, 2018b)

After the *mea culpa* was released, the controversy settled, and despite the brush of bad publicity, RuPaul and his show moved on steadily, winning more awards and earning even higher ratings. Though this was the most notable controversy for the show when it comes to trans issues (there are problems with race and class as well), it has gotten criticized for its representation of trans communities. In particular, there was a recurring segment on the show called She-Mail, a play on both email and She-male, the latter being an oft-derogatory and exploitative slur against transgender women. After complaints from viewers, the show dropped the offensive segment starting from its seventh season in 2015, though RuPaul disagreed with the decision, insisting, "I would not have changed it, but that's (the network's) choice" (Nicholson, 2015).

To criticize *RuPaul's Drag Race* for bias against trans identities and trans communities might appear contradictory to the show's impact and its message. But it's clear that though the show has been an invaluable representation of queer people (in particular, queer people of color), there are blind spots when addressing trans identities; these blind spots mirror general ignorance and prejudice within the larger queer community, where cisgender queer folks will stumble or fail when addressing trans identities.

## *RUPAUL'S DRAG RACE*: A BRIEF HISTORY

*RuPaul's Drag Race* premiered on February 2, 2009, on Logo TV. Initially, the show could have been grouped with other reality competitions, which dominated television in the 2000s. *American Idol* created a template of sorts: a panel of celebrity "expert" judges that critiques contestants weekly, eliminating one person each episode until a winner is declared. One of the features of these kinds of shows—such as *American Idol, America's Next Top Model, The Starlet, The Next*—is the use of celebrities who have experienced success in their careers but who have also recently seen their careers and professional fortunes dim. By 2009, RuPaul was in just that position, after an initial burst of fame and popularity in 1993 with his hit song "Supermodel (You Better Work)" as well as a series of well-received appearances on TV talk shows and sitcoms. He was able to ride a relatively hospitable time in queer pop history in the early 1990s, which he attributed to the optimism of Bill Clinton's election and a general leftward shift in politics and society (Hall, 1993).

The show's parent channel, Logo TV was a niche channel that was originally aimed at a queer audience. Launched in 2005, it was a platform for a variety of programming, including reality TV, newsmagazines, comedies and dramas, as well as syndicate programs, all with either queer content or skewed toward queer audiences. The show's initial aesthetic was defined by its low budget that added to its camp value. As the show went through its seasons, it grew steadily into a mainstream hit, its success solidified by its move from Logo to the more accessible channel VH1, and that move brought the show to a much wider audience (Logo is still available on a few cable subscription packages).

*RuPaul's Drag Race* was celebrated as a source of exposure and representation of various queer identities as well as intersectionality with race, class, nationality, age, HIV status, and trans identities. The show also made celebrities of its contestants and branched out into merchandising and television franchising, spinning off CDs, books, television programs, web series, films, fashion lines, and cosmetic lines. RuPaul even hosts a series of fan conventions that feature past contestants who have developed followings of their own through various channels of social media. Like the most successful of television shows, *RuPaul's Drag Race* has established a series of franchises, including *RuPaul's Drag U* (one of the few *Drag Race*-adjacent projects that flopped); *RuPaul's Drag Race All Stars*, a reunion show that gives past favorites the chance to redeem themselves; a recent spin-off that has celebrity contestants compete for charity; as well as international *Drag Race* series in the United Kingdom, Australia, Thailand, Canada, and Chile. The show has also branched out into various live programs, holiday specials, drag and comedy tours, and variety shows.

For the most part, the show was rightly praised for its cast of contestants; however, it has a problematic relationship with trans identities—either by erasure or by ridicule. Slurs like "tranny" and the aforementioned pun, she-mail was used throughout the show's early history. Tranny is a word that has caused a good deal of controversy among RuPaul's fanbase. It's a word that has spawned debates on language, tone policing, and the questions of who has the right to use certain words. Because RuPaul is a cis man, his use of the word has been found as problematic because we have to ask whether he has the right to use the word. When asked about the controversy over the word, RuPaul dismissed the debate, enthusing that "I love the word 'tranny.'" He later makes the dubious claim that "no one has ever said the word 'tranny' in a derogatory sense" (Signorile, 2012). When comedian Marc Maron (2014) suggested that trans folks find the word offensive, RuPaul dismissed the claim, insisting that "No, it is not the transsexual community. These are fringe people who are looking for story lines to strengthen their identity as victims." He tells Maron, "It's not the trans community because most people who are trans have been through hell and high water and they know, they've looked behind the curtain at Oz and went, 'Oh, this is all a fucking joke.'"

But RuPaul's enthusiasm and self-proclaimed love for the word isn't without some dispute. To appreciate the problematic relationship that RuPaul has with the word, one needs to briefly look at how he understands trans identity. E. Alex Jung sums up Ru's attitude toward trans people as being "essentialists, whereas drag queens are not" (2018). Essentially, RuPaul's attitude toward drag is that it exposes how "gender is inherently performative." And RuPaul has pointed out that tranny has been used to describe drag queens and his many years of performing, activism, and advocacy have given him the right to use the word (Maron, 2014). He not only used the word in the past, but has folded it into his work, including recording two songs that used the word: "Tranny Chaser" which appears on his 2009 album *Champions*;

and "Responsitrannity," a tortured portmanteau of responsibility and tranny which is included on his 2010 album *Glamazon*. His use of the word in his pop culture work is just a small part of a larger trope of using the word in queer/pop culture. Outside of pornographic films, b-films that embrace schlock have used the word in their titles: self-referential projects such as *Trannysnatchers!* (2012), *Killer Tranny* (2011), and *Ticked-Off Trannies with Knives* (2010) are a few of the titles that play with the word tranny, alluding to the exploitative titles found in porn. The use of the word in these titles—as well as in Ru's music—is a tongue-in-cheek appropriation of the word to elicit a reaction from its audiences that are reared in schlocky camp. It's an embrace of an irreverence that speaks to RuPaul's characterization of the word's opponents as humorless and overly sensitive. Also, the queens who did well did so by adopting very heteronormative ideals of femininity (albeit highly exaggerated). Queens who defied the feminine aesthetic prized on the program were often chastised for being "too boy" and often queens were reminded that this was a "drag competition" when they ventured on the runway wearing clothing that was a departure from the cartoonish glamor, like, for example in season 6, when Milk decided to strut down the runway in RuPaul-out-of-drag drag in the runway challenge of "Night of a 1000 Ru's Runway" in which the queens adopted some of Ru's most iconic looks; another example had season 5 frontrunner Alaska Thunderfuck getting criticism for choosing to do a Pee-wee Herman-esque male character in a maxi-challenge. The only time it seems that the queens are allowed to dress in boy drag without criticism is when they essay male celebrities in the Snatch Game. There is also the complicated use of tragic queer spectacle to engage with audiences' sympathy. The show was not above editing the queens' histories to create narratives of tragedy and pain to create compelling story lines. These backstories of trauma included ostracization from family and friends, homelessness, teen parenthood, homophobia, violence, and HIV status. Contestants are encouraged to replay and share these moments of tragedy for the cameras, all in aid of positioning RuPaul as a parental figure, tending to broken, damaged figures. These moments of candor are either played out on the runway or in the workroom. Often these instances of confession take place on the runway, late in the season, in which the queens are instructed to give inspirational advice to pictures of their five-year-old selves. Audiences will see the queens tearfully promise their younger selves that though their queerness others them as children, it will become the key to their success as adults. The runway is often also a site for catharsis when queens share deep and personal traumas (usually after doing badly in a challenge and getting heavy criticism). And because the workroom is also a safe place for the queens to be honest (even though they're being filmed), audiences are also privy to heart-to-hearts, as the queens busily beat their faces. In these moments we learn harrowing histories such as the death of Trinity Taylor's mother to AIDS; Charlie Hides surviving the AIDS crisis, but seeing many of his friends die; BenDeLaCreme's trauma from being bullied as a child for being overweight and gay and losing his mother at a young age; or Latrice Royal's struggles after being incarcerated.

The revelation of trans identities are braided into these moments, as well, presented as cathartic moments of truth-telling, when queens tearfully share these memories, which are often answered by pop psychology bromides by RuPaul, who insists that the show is their family (he is even referred at times as Mama Ru by some of the contestants). The show leans heavily into the concept of queer families—most of which are made up of friends because queer folks are often ostracized by their birth families. In season 6, after Roxxxy Andrews lands in the bottom two, she tearfully recounts a tragic story of being abandoned by her mother. As she dissolves into sobs, leading the other queens to dab their eyes, Ru puts on a parental persona, saying

> We love you. And you are so welcome here. You know, we as gay people, we get to choose our family. You know, we get to choose the people that we're around. You know what I'm saying? I am your family. We are a family here. I love you.

## RUPAUL'S DRAG RACE AND ITS PLACE IN HERSTORY

*RuPaul's Drag Race* was neither the first program to feature drag queens nor queer people. Drag has been a popular art form in the entertainment industry, not just in queer circles, but in mainstream entertainment. For many entertainers, drag was used as comedy. Flip Wilson, Milton Berle, John Inman, Paul O'Grady, Barry Humphries, and Martin Lawrence have all used drag—or cross-dressing—as a comedic element in their work. And during his first height of fame in the 1990s, RuPaul was also a popular media figure, appearing on television chat shows and sitcoms, cameoing in drag as a spectacle.

But the drag that is represented by *RuPaul's Drag Race* is distinct from the drag-as-a-punchline, even in the case of comedy queens who use drag as an essential part of a comedic persona (i.e., Bianca Del Rio, Bob The Drag Queen, Miz Cracker). For the comedy queens, drag is not the punchline, but the vehicle in which the delivery comes. The drag from the show has its roots in Black ball culture and heritage (underground competitions in which queens would engage in pageant-like contests for prizes and trophies—a precursor to *RuPaul's Drag Race*). It relies heavily on razor-sharp wit, an eye for style, and an ingenuity for being able to produce hot drag with limited resources—a major part of the show's many themes is how impoverished some of the queens' backgrounds are—we see queens like Chi Chi DeVayne or Heidi N Closet share stories of their financial insecurity as well as their struggles to create drag on par with queens who have more resources. *RuPaul's Drag Race* is unique in the sum of its parts, but it relies heavily on the legacy of Jennie Livingstone's seminal documentary *Paris Is Burning* (1990), which is a groundbreaking work that chronicles the lives of Black and Latinx trans women and gay men who compete in the drag balls in New York City. *RuPaul's Drag Race* has appropriated many elements of drag ball culture as well as elements of Livingston's film; the show works both as a derivative work as well as a tribute to the queens portrayed in the documentary. Like *Paris Is Burning*, *RuPaul's Drag Race* gives viewers a backstage look at how a drag show is put together—from when the queens design and blueprint their conceptual looks, to the eventual unveiling of the finished product—and the viewers get to see the queens interact with each other and share their stories of how they found drag. RuPaul is a veteran of the drag ball scene, and so is Visage, a former voguer who was mentored by her drag father, legendary dancer and Alvin Ailey member, Cesar Valentino.

Interestingly enough, RuPaul's statements in his interview with *The Guardian* run counter to what the ball culture in *Paris Is Burning* shows; trans women in various degrees of transitioning are featured heavily in the film. Some of the film's most memorable and oft-quoted subjects—Octavia St. Laurent and Venus Xtravaganza—were transgender women who found great success and cult legendary status as drag performers. One of the most popular and iconic episodes in the film is when Venus reads someone:

> Now you wanna talk about reading? Let's talk about reading. What is wrong with you, Pedro, are you going through it? You're going through some kind of psychological change in your life? You went back to being a man? Touch this skin, darling, touch this skin honey, touch all of this skin! Okay? You just can't take it! You're just an overgrown orangutan! (Livingston, 1989)

Venus's read has become a catchphrase among drag queens and has been referenced throughout the show's history and RuPaul himself has name-checked the popular line "Touch this skin, darling, touch all of this skin" in his minor hit song "Looking Good, Feeling Gorgeous" (2004). Reading is an important part of drag culture and *Paris Is Burning*, and to a larger extent, *RuPaul's Drag Race* has made reading a popular sport among mainstream audiences, too. The patois developed among the Black and Latinx queens in the drag scene has also been popularized through the show—and much of the lingo the contestants use is found in Livingston's film, too. "No tea, no shade," "throwing shade," and "slaying" have found their way into contemporary, mainstream slang in much the same way Yiddish words and phrases had worked their way into speech.

## REALNESS: PERFORMING FEMININITY AND ESTABLISHING BEAUTY HIERARCHIES

Arguably, the most important part of an episode of *RuPaul's Drag Race* is the judging segments. Queens create outfits with some kind of themed challenge that culminate in a runway show in which the queens strut down a catwalk in front of a panel of judges (RuPaul, Visage, and a celebrity judge or two) As the series progresses, it's clear that a certain kind of drag is favored by others—namely a hyper-feminine drag that is pretty and that heightens and stylizes traditional ideas of femininity and standards of beauty, which was largely cis-presenting and white, for much of the show's run. Though among the show's twelve winners we have queens like Sharon Needles or Yvie Oddly who represent a shift away from pageant glamor, for the most part, for a queen to succeed, she does best when conforming to the kind of polished look that RuPaul himself sports, which is largely inspired by old Hollywood glamor. Even comedy queens like Bianca Del Rio and Bob the Drag Queen glammed it up, eschewing the kind of alternative drag that won Sharon or Yvie the crown.

Unless there is a certain challenge specifically asking for some nod toward innovation or alternative form of drag—particularly genderfuck—androgyny and "boy" drag is frowned upon. A popular criticism from the judges is "I see too much boy." Success on the show is predicated on being able to create an illusion of femininity through a variety of cosmetic ways, including imaginative padding, tucking (the act of hiding one's genitalia between the legs), breast plates, and corsets. At times, when queens fail to or choose not to engage in these practices, they are often scolded or not chosen to win—in one example, the popular and talented Adore Delano was criticized for abstaining from wearing a corset to give her body a waist (as it fits into her rougher drag aesthetic), and is rewarded by the judges (especially Michelle) when she finally dons a corset, gifted to her by an increasingly maternal Bianca.

While few of these "rules for winning" are explicitly anti-trans, they do contribute to an unwritten rule that there is a certain aesthetic that is sought out by the judges, and cis "fishiness" (as well as white female beauty) is prized. When queens strut on the runway in beautiful gowns and extravagant makeup with mountains of hair they are rewarded with plaudits from the judges as opposed to the queens who either cannot or will not perform these attempts at lacquered beauty. As a result, the tension can be quite traumatic for the queens who do not conform to more conventional pageant, as evident in the difficulty season 6 queen Milk had when confronted on the runway for opting out of wearing a gown and choosing instead to emulate RuPaul's workroom look of a natty suit and a bald cap in response to a challenge in which the queens were instructed to copy looks from Ru's career. Judge Santino Rice pans Milk's look, wanting for something more glamorous, pointing out that the judges haven't seen anything glamorous from her up to that point. In her defense, Milk said

I could go more glam, but it wouldn't be staying true to my aesthetic. . . . Honestly, sometimes, I do feel that, if I were to put on a beautiful dress like these girls and beautiful hair like them, I would stand out for the wrong reasons, and people would just laugh at me, and I wouldn't be able to laugh at myself. (Murray, 2014)

Instead of accepting her stance on her self-defined aesthetic—which has been marked by a more avant-garde, club kid look—RuPaul and the judges urge Milk to adopt a more feminine, traditional look, opting to define and characterize Milk's commitment to maintaining her aesthetic as refusing to be open or vulnerable to the judges and audiences. Milk is being read because the judges are contextualizing her challenging drag as false—a cover operating to hide the "real" Milk.

## TRANS PRESENCE IN *RUPAUL'S DRAG RACE*

Though most of the contestants in *RuPaul's Drag Race* were cis queer men, but some have come out as trans or gender non-conforming: Gia Gunn, Jinkx Monsoon, Kenya Michaels, Stacy Layne Matthews, Carmen Carrera, Sonique, Peppermint, Jiggly Caliente, Monica Beverly Hillz, Fernanda Brown, Courtney Act, and Meannie Minaj.

During the show—few of the contestants actually came out during the show's airing—none of the queens came out as transitioning while filming it. A number of the queens came out in various stages of transitioning after their time on the show—this fact allows for the show to claim representation of trans women without countering RuPaul's discomfort and angst about allowing for trans women who have had surgery.

As mentioned earlier, the show's editing and packaging uses and exploits trans narratives as plot arcs. These stories are often shared during the workroom scenes while the queens are constructing their looks. They turn to each other and share their experiences with adversity, while facing the mirror (the mirrors act like two-way mirrors for the audience). These instances are often used to create plot license to create empathy with audiences (as well as to further the social justice mission of the show to promote progressive, liberal attitudes toward sexual minorities).

Though RuPaul has admitted discomfort with the concept of trans identities, he seems to be fine with trans bodies as long as they serve some kind of purpose—meaning as long as they can contribute to the success of the show. Whether right or wrong, RuPaul's main focus on the show is its success. As season 7 contestant Pearl shared, when she gushed like a fan upon meeting RuPaul, her enthusiastic entreaties were answered by a curt "Nothing you say matters unless that camera is rolling" by a business-as-usual RuPaul.

The presence of trans women in *RuPaul's Drag Race*'s alumni network contributes to the debate of the role of trans women in drag. The question remains, "Why is there a need for a debate when historical evidence proves that trans women have been part of drag and ball culture since its inception?" RuPaul repeatedly stated that drag is a way to subvert patriarchy, gender norms, and male-dominated culture. How do trans women fit into that narrative of subversion and protest? If RuPaul's flawed logic is followed, then transitioning trans women affirm rather than challenge gender norms and are therefore acting as an ameliorate to the subversive nature of drag itself. Does RuPaul see transgender identities as aligning themselves with gender roles? If that is the case, then that guess could explain his hesitation in allowing for post-op trans women to compete (this does not even begin to discuss why cis women are excluded from being part of the *Drag Race* story).

And what about the backlash? Though brief, the controversy surrounding RuPaul's statements was sustained and large enough that he responded quickly with an apology. Testimonies given by various drag queens and celebrities via social media—and in Peppermint's case, through an open letter in *Billboard* magazine (Peppermint, 2018)—celebrated and spotlighted the history of trans women in drag as well as the contribution that trans women make to drag culture.

## CONCLUSION

*RuPaul's Drag Race* is one of the most prominent products of queer culture on television today, with an unprecedented reach due to its popularity and the popularity of its hosts and a number of the contestants (many of whom did not make it very far into the competition, but made a mark due to their charisma, comedic talent, or gregarious personality). The show has been credited with expanding the definition of *queerness* and exposing audiences to aspects of queer culture that are normally hidden. Instead of the palpable and easy-to-relate culture of *Will & Grace*, *RuPaul's Drag Race* pulls its viewers into a world that is alien to many. The show has exposed its viewers to queer history, providing historical context for the queens' art. Difficult issues such as AIDS/HIV, homelessness, family estrangement, hate crimes, and anti-gay legislation are discussed on the show, and most importantly, these discussions are conducted by queer people. Throughout the show's twelve seasons, viewers are privy to a representation of queer life and queer culture that are almost exclusively created and curated by queer artists.

While all of these accomplishments are laudatory and important, the show still seems to struggle—as does the larger queer community as well as mainstream culture—to integrate all kinds of trans identities, as well (trans identities that defy easy definitions are marked by surgery and presentation). Language is still developing and sensibilities are still evolving around these questions and despite her groundbreaking work as an activist and an artist, RuPaul is not immune to these blind spots, either. What does it mean when the most important representative of queer culture cannot seem to be fully invested in trans identities without certain conditions? If a large part of the audience for *RuPaul's Drag Race* is non-queer/cis, does it allow for there to be equivocation in the acceptance of trans people? And does this tension in the show reflect a larger tension among the queer community (particularly the cis members of the queer community)? *RuPaul's Drag Race* is a show that offers an unprecedented platform for queer voices—particularly queer voices of color. Before the show's existence, queer voices were often presented through a straight filter. But excluding an important part of the queer community from benefiting from this platform seems antithetical to the thesis of the show. Trans women in all stages of transition make up an important part of drag, but are otherized on the program, leading many viewers to take RuPaul's lead and discount the importance and contribution of trans women to the art of drag.

Part of RuPaul's persona—one that she shares proudly when interviewed—is one of the wise elder who is tired of political correctness. She dismisses political correctness and does not seem particularly concerned about offending anyone. She proudly dismisses the notion of political correctness and has little patience for what she sees as self-indulgent behavior. She bridles at the concept of "participation trophies," diagnosing younger generations as ill-equipped to handle adversity because parents "just decided they were going to right the wrongs of the world by putting their child . . . in a position where they don't have to feel the slings and arrows of an unkind world" (RuPaul and Visage, 2015). In RuPaul's mind, this failure in our culture is boiled down to the beginning of what he calls "the politically correct movement."

As of June 2020, the debate around trans representation still lingers. Despite Ru's apology and public pronouncement of his support of the trans community, trans activists, *Drag Race* alumni, fans, and supporters still feel the show hasn't done enough to rectify its past. Drag artist and trans activist Mistress Sara Andrews has been one of the most vocal proponents of trans inclusion in *Drag Race*, using her platform to highlight the inequities that cis queer folks in power, like RuPaul, perpetuate. Season 5 *Drag Race* queen and *All Stars* runner-up, Detox urged the show to "start putting your money where your mouth is" (Detox, 2020a) and slammed the show for excluding "an integral part of the drag community" (Detox, 2020b). Former *Drag Race* contestant Carmen Carrera, who identifies as trans, went further, opining in a since-deleted Tweet that RuPaul is "the Hitler, false prophet, anti-Christ of the LGBTQ community" (Keating, 2020).

The spring and summer of 2020 have been particularly significant for the trans community and the seismic shifts in the national conversation has brought up *Drag Race*'s continued erasure into focus. U.S. President Trump's administration has rolled back a slate of civil rights that his predecessor Barack Obama instituted, though on June 15, 2020, the Supreme Court announced in a decisive ruling that federal civil rights laws protect LGBTQ+ workers. Public demonstrations and civil unrest have spread throughout cities in the United States as well as in some cities in Europe in response to the murder of George Floyd. A renewed wave of anti-racist protests inspired by the Black Lives Matter movement took place and the summer of 2020 also saw the Black Trans Lives Matter movement, spurred on by the disproportionately high number of Black trans people who are murdered, including the May 27, 2020, shooting of Tony McDade; the June 2020 murders of two trans women—Dominique Fells and Riah Milton—who were killed within 24 hours of each other; and the disturbing video of Iyanna Dior being beaten by a mob after a reported fender bender.

In light of these impactful episodes, *Drag Race* and RuPaul are starting to look increasingly out of touch with the evolution of the queer movement and its acknowledgment of identities. Though, one can dismiss this controversy as simply a TV show—especially in light of Black activists being beaten by the police—as mentioned earlier, *RuPaul's Drag Race* isn't simply a television show, but a platform for queer people to attain access to financial security and career advancement. It's the drag version of the NLF draft, and the show's large influence has changed the industry and its economy, (Nolfi, 2020) making it almost necessary to appear on the show to become competitive and bankable. If trans drag queens are systematically excluded from the show, they also become excluded from this dominant avenue of opportunity. The resultant is that trans drag queens become even more marginalized, professionally, that they have been before.

## REFERENCES

Aitkenhead, D. (2018, March 3). *RuPaul: 'Drag is a big f-you to male-dominated culture.' The Guardian.* https://www.theguardian.com/tv-and-radio/2018/mar/03/rupaul-drag-race-big-f-you-to-male-dominated-culture.

Detox. [@TheOnlyDetox]. (2020a, January 23). *And to @RuPaulsDragRace: Enough with the feigned inclusivity. Time to start putting your money where your mouth is.#AllDragIsValid.* Twitter. https://twitter.com/TheOnlyDetox/status/1220442901198536704Detox. [@TheOnlyDetox]. (2020b, January 24). *It's not* *about political correctness\*, it's about the conscious exclusion of an integral part of the drag community . . .* Twitter. https://twitter.com/TheOnlyDetox/status/12206 21207193538561.

Hall, A. (Presenter). (1993, May 28). Episode 156 [Television Program]. In Arsenio Hall (Executive Producer), *The Arsenio Hall Show.* Los Angeles: Paramount Domestic Television.

Hawkins, K. (2017, May 25). *The 'RuPaul's Drag Race' season 9 cast is filled with some of the most talented queens the show has ever seen.* Bustle. https://www.bus tle.com/p/the-rupauls-drag-race-season-9-cast-is-filled-with-some-of-the-most-ta lented-queens-the-show-has-ever-seen-46587.

Jung, E. A. (2018, March 6). *Why RuPaul's reversal on trans issues is so surprising.* Vulture. https://www.vulture.com/2018/03/rupaul-on-drag-and-trans-identity.html.

Kegu, J. (2019, May 8). *Why RuPaul isn't trying to make drag "acceptable."* CBS News. https://www.cbsnews.com/news/rupaul-on-drag-race-being-an-outsider-and -why-the-met-gala-was-a-fancy-bar-mitzvah/.

Livingston, J. (Director). (1990). *Paris Is Burning* [Film]. Off White Productions.

Maron, M. (Host). (2014, May 19). RuPaul Charles—Episode 498 [Audio Podcast Episode]. In *WTF with Marc Maron.* PRX. http://www.wtfpod.com/podcast/episo des/episode_498_-_rupaul_charles.

Masters, J. [Jasmine Masters]. (2016, January 28). *Jasmine Masters RuPaul Dragrace fucked up drag.* [Video]. YouTube. https://www.youtube.com/watch?v =gf25Xzhpz_k.

Murray, N. (Director). (2014, March 24). Snatch Game (Season 6, Episode 5) [TV series episode]. In F. Bailey, R. Barbato, S. Corfe, RuPaul, and M. Salangsang (Executive Producers), *RuPaul's Drag Race.* World of Wonder.

Nicholson, R. (2015, June 3). *RuPaul: 'Drag is dangerous. We are making fun of everything.'* The Guardian. https://www.theguardian.com/tv-and-radio/2015/jun/ 03/rupaul-drag-is-dangerous-we-are-making-fun-of-everything#_=_.

Nolfi, J. (2020, June 12). *How* RuPaul's Drag Race *changed the global drag economy. Entertainment Weekly.* https://ew.com/tv/rupauls-drag-race-legitimized-bus iness-drag/.

Peppermint. (2018, March 6). *Peppermint responds to RuPaul's apology over controversial interview: Exclusive.* Billboard. https://www.billboard.com/articles/news/ pride/8233000/peppermint-rupaul-apology.

RuPaul. [@RuPaul]. (2018a, March 5). *You can take performance enhancing drugs and still be an athlete, just not in the Olympics.* Twitter. https://twitter.com/RuPau l/status/970709820364881920.

RuPaul. [@RuPaul]. (2018b, March 5). *Each morning I pray to set aside everything . . .* Twitter. https://twitter.com/RuPaul/status/970810665685299201.

RuPaul, and Visage, Michelle (Hosts). (2015, 25 February). Anti-Porn unicorn with Colleen Ballinger and Miranda Sings—Episode 24 [Audio Podcast Episode]. In *RuPaul: What's the Tee with Michelle Visage.* The Paragon Collective. https://op en.spotify.com/episode/1Am3ye2YwBifUB3lZ5uaPG.

Signorile, M. (2012, January 14). *RuPaul sounds off on new season of 'RuPaul's Drag Race,' Obama, The Word 'Tranny,' and more. Huffington Post.* https://ww w.huffingtonpost.co.uk/entry/rupaul-on-rupauls-drag-race-obama-tranny_n_120 5203?ri18n=true.

## Chapter 6

# How to Define *Fair*?

## *Examining Transgender on the "Level Playing Field"*

### John C. Lamothe

During prime-time coverage of the 2016 Rio Olympics, Nike launched a new ad campaign entitled "Unlimited Courage," with a thirty-second commercial on NBC featuring Chris Mosier, the first known openly transgender athlete to earn a spot on the U.S. men's national team. The commercial begins as Mosier, a competitor in the duathlon, jogs down a stereotypical New York street early in the morning, upbeat music playing in the background, when an omnipresent narrator introduces the athlete and cheerfully says, "Morning, Chris" (IncomeIT, 2016). Mosier responds to the disembodied voice, "Morning," as he continues his run. During a training montage throughout the city, the narrator explains Mosier's distinctive success and then starts to question him. "How did you know you would be fast enough to compete against men," to which Mosier responds, "I didn't." Volleying back and forth throughout the commercial, the narrator asks how Mosier knew he would be accepted, allowed to play, and so on, and each time Mosier responds "I didn't." In the final ten seconds, as Mosier runs a race, the volleying concludes:

"That must have been tough. Didn't you ever just
    want to give up?" asks the narrator.
"Yeah, but I didn't," responds Mosier.
The words "Unlimited Courage" and "Just Do It" then flash on the screen.

This ad is what first sparked my interest in transgender issues. I have not been a gender scholar in the past; my background is in rhetorical theory and sports rhetoric, but the idea of breaking down gender categories, especially the sports arena where so much emphasis is placed on splitting participants into categories such as male/female or professional/amateur for competition's sake, intrigued me.

Mosier's breakthrough success at securing a position on the U.S. men's national team and the subsequent Nike commercial and notoriety it brought him could be considered nothing but a huge win for the LGBTQIA+ community, and in particular the trans community. Mosier's breakthroughs continued as he successfully petitioned the International Olympic Committee (IOC), which is the governing body for Olympic (and subsequently most international) rules, to allow him to compete once he made the U.S. national team. Under the previous rules, he would have had to undergo genital reassignment surgery before being allowed to compete, but after a short legal battle, the IOC changed the rules so that any female-to-male transgender athlete would be eligible for competition immediately without surgery or any other kind of gender-affirming procedures.

Also in 2016, Mosier participated in *ESPN The Magazine*'s annual "Body Issue," which spotlights the spectrum of athletic bodies by featuring them nude or semi-nude and primarily in poses that showcase characteristics idealized in sports—strength, poise, balance, physical fitness, etc. Mosier was the first transgender athlete to appear in the magazine, and in an interview about the issue he says, "I think the reason I felt so inspired to do it is that I'm finally at a place where I feel very comfortable with my body. And as a trans person, being in a body that didn't really fit me for 29 years, now I feel very comfortable in my own skin" (qtd. in Kahrl, 2016).

On the surface, it may seem surprising that Mosier found success as a transgender athlete as quickly as he did. In a relatively short span, he was accepted on a men's national team despite being assigned female at birth, got a major international governing agency to review and change its policies, and was praised in the media, earning himself a national television commercial and magazine spread. And his accomplishments *are* amazing. Some might argue that his efforts were aided by the fact that the sporting community—at least at the higher levels of policymaking and media coverage—has for years been considered more progressive than other areas of society when it comes to transgender. Caitlyn Jenner, who obviously can speak from experience about both transgender and sports issues, said in an interview with Tucker Carlson that, "The Olympic committee is way ahead of the rest of the world when it comes to dealing with/identifying transgender issues in competing," going on to explain that since at least the 1970s when Jenner competed that the IOC has conducted gender tests on athletes and ever since then has researched non-conforming gender and its impact on competition, especially extensive research on hormone levels (Fox News, 2017).

Another example of sports supporting the trans community can be seen in the National Collegiate Athletic Association's (NCAA) response to the North

Carolina bathroom bill. In 2016, then-governor Pat McCrory signed into law the Public Facilities Privacy and Security Act, better known as House Bill 2, which mandated that individuals using restrooms in government buildings (including public schools, parks, etc.) must use the facilities that correspond with the gender assigned on their birth certificate. The bill garnered criticism from groups nationwide as it specifically targeted transgender individuals, and the NCAA opposed the bill and banned all championship events from occurring in the state. Not only would the ban have a financial impact on the state, but it also struck home with many sports fans in North Carolina, a state that is fanatical for collegiate sports such as basketball and football. The NCAA's move was a significant factor in the bill getting repealed the following year.

Despite these recent victories for the trans movement, to say that the sports community has accepted all transgender athletes would only tell a very small part of the story. When it comes to female-to-male transgender athletes, like Mosier, the sports community has been fairly accepting, but when someone assigned male at birth transitions to female and enters competition, the situation is much murkier. Controversy swirls around questions of whether these athletes have an unfair advantage, whether policies enacted to balance competition are actually "gender policing," whether trans athletes are taking the spots and awards that should go to "real" females, and whether *fairness* refers to competition or inclusion. As numerous case studies over the past ten years bear out, these questions occur at every level of sport, and to answer these questions, we must determine what it is we want sports to be.

Take, for example, the situation that Mack Beggs, a transgender male high school wrestler in Texas, found himself in during his 2017–2018 high school season. Despite being in the process of transitioning to male and taking steroids and hormones as part of that process, the University Interscholastic League (UIL), the governing body for all Texas high school athletics, forced Beggs to wrestle against females because of a rule that requires all athletes to compete as the gender assigned on their birth certificates (Domonoske, 2017). Beggs won the 2017 state championship easily with a 57–0 record, and he went on to repeat as champion in 2018, both years defeating the same athlete, Chelsea Sanchez, in the final. Beggs has stated that he would have preferred to wrestle against boys, but his only option to compete was against females because of the Texas rule. "It's not like I'm just doing this because I want to like call myself a boy and just dominate all these girls. What do I get out of that? I don't get anything out of that" (qtd. in *Guardian sport*, 2017).

As one might expect, his championships generated controversy. Much of the media criticism was aimed at the UIL birth certificate rule, which was universally ridiculed by both those who supported Beggs and those who felt he should be banned from wrestling. And if judging the situation strictly by major media coverage, it painted a picture that most were in support of Beggs. Quotes from his family, teammates, and those in his local community dominated the coverage. However, when you listen to video from the actual 2017 championship match, you hear almost as many "boos" from the audience as you do cheers, and that is not at all common for a sporting event at this level (Robinson and Muaddi, 2017).

After Beggs's victory, one would think that the UIL would consider repealing its birth certificate rule, if for no other reason than to ensure that students compete against athletes who are perceived as having the same physical and hormonal abilities. Instead, the Texas state legislature introduced a bill that would have banned Beggs and athletes in similar situations from competing at all. During the wrestling season, several female athletes withdrew from competition against Beggs because they feared for their safety in competing against someone with so much more strength, which was believed to stem from his hormone replacement therapy (HRT). The state legislature grasped onto that fact and introduced a bill that would force transitioning athletes to submit their medical records to the UIL. The governing body could then declare the student ineligible if the league "determines that the safety of competing students or the fairness of a particular competition has been or will be substantially affected by the student's steroid use" (SB 2095, 2017). The bill did not mention transgender; instead, it was marketed as a measure against teenage steroid use. However, a 2015 report about the UIL's statewide steroid testing program found only two cases of steroid use out of over 2,600 athletes screened (Allen, 2017). The timing of the bill, immediately after Beggs's victory, seems more than a little questionable. The bill passed the State Senate, but after sharp criticism in the media, it withered in a House committee and was never signed into law.

On the one hand, we could say that the very fact Beggs was allowed to compete is a far cry from the conversation we would be having if this had taken place ten years ago—if we would have any kind of conversation at all. However, clearly the IOC's guidelines have not filtered down to the high school level where each state decides its own rules and regulations when it comes to transgender athletes. Texas is not the only state to have a birth certificate rule, and several states require genital reassignment or documentation of hormone therapy before transitioning athletes can compete.

But even on the international scale, where the IOC's guidelines prevail, female transgender athletes are far from being embraced, especially by fellow athletes and fans. In March 2017, Laurel Hubbard, a New Zealand weightlifter made history as the first transgender female to win an international weightlifting competition, beating the second-place competitor by roughly 42 pounds, a significant amount. Hubbard became eligible for competition after submitting a year's worth of blood tests that showed her testosterone levels within the female range, an IOC requirement for female transgender athletes. However, competitors were vocal about what they saw as an unfair advantage. Two-time weightlifting Olympian Deborah Acason said, "If I was in [Hubbard's weight] category I wouldn't feel like I was in an equal situation. I just feel that if it's not even, why are we doing the sport?" (qtd. in Payne, 2017)

Tracy Lambrechs, Hubbard's teammate on the New Zealand team, said, "I'm more than happy that she has become a female, I have no problem with that as everybody needs to do what they need to do to be happy with life. Personally I think they should be able to compete, but they shouldn't be able to take spots from other female athletes" (qtd. in Payne, 2017). The obvious contradiction here is that if Lambrechs truly is happy that Hubbard has become female and believes she should be able to compete, why does she then argue that Hubbard should not be able to take spots from other females. In what category does she think Hubbard should compete?

The runner-up to Hubbard, Somoan weightlifter Luniarra Sipaia, said after the match, "I felt that it was unfair because all in all, Laurel is still a male even though he already had an operation to change his gender. It only changed the physical side but her emotions, her strength and everything is still a male. So I felt that it was unfair because we all know a woman's strength is nowhere near a male's strength no matter how hard we train" (qtd. in Seva'aetasi, 2017).

Fans have echoed these sentiments. The comments sections of the articles published on mainstream news sites are overwhelmingly against Hubbard and transgender people in sports. Along with the vitriol concerning transgender in principle and commentaries that Hubbard is a cheater, many comments claim that transgender women have an unfair advantage.

Determining the extent of Hubbard's advantage (and the advantage of other male-to-female transgender athletes) is far from simple. The IOC's regulations look strictly at testosterone levels, and although testosterone plays a role in strength and performance, it certainly is not the only factor. Commenting on the Hubbard article in *The Washington Post*, a fan noted "The hard cold fact of the matter is, she grew all that upper body muscle when she was still a he. Testosterone levels going down is one thing. But you can clearly see the difference in upper body development. That doesn't go away just because your T levels are down" (qtd. in Payne, 2017). Hubbard started transitioning in her mid-thirties, which meant she had years of weightlifting experience and development before transitioning to female. Although she underwent hormone therapy to reduce testosterone, many would argue that HRT does not remove the years of physical and mental experience she gained previously.

Scientific research into the effects of HRT on athletic performance is still in its infancy. However, a 2019 study titled "Muscle Strength, Size, and Composition, Following 12 Months of Gender-affirming Treatment in Transgender Individuals" (Wikk et al) demonstrates that although transgender men showed a significant increase in muscle mass and strength after the year of testosterone treatment, transgender women showed minimal decrease in muscle volume and nominal strength loss after hormone replacement was completed. This research appears to support arguments that male-to-female athletes, such as Hubbard, may have a strength advantage in some sports even after following the IOC's requirement for a full year of HRT before competition.

The Hubbard case highlights flaws in the IOC's attempt to incorporate transgender into competition. And despite Jenner's belief that the IOC has this all figured out, privileging testosterone levels as the exclusive determinant of who can compete is problematic. Testing testosterone probably is the easiest protocol, but the research behind its effects on athletic performance is mixed. Certainly, research shows that testosterone can translate into more power, but some studies have shown that athletes with higher levels of testosterone do not necessarily perform better than those with lower levels (Karkazis et al., 2012). Furthermore, research published in 2014 in the *Journal of Clinical Endocrinology and Metabolism* found that in female athletics in particular, no clear scientific evidence proves that increased levels of testosterone have a significant impact on performance and success (Fagan, 2015). Even if research did support the common assumption about testosterone's impact on athletics, it is certainly not the only factor, as the Wikk study shows. Osteological and biomechanical differences between those born with XX chromosomes and those with XY (not to mention other chromosome combinations) also have an impact on performance (Sutherland, Wassersug, and Rosenberg, 2017), and there are many other factors that affect performance. Determining *which* factor has *what* effect on any given athletic performance is an impossible task.

Another issue is how sports regulating authorities determine what is an acceptable level of testosterone. The case of Indian sprinter Dutee Chand is a perfect example. At eighteen, Chand was India's 100-meter champion in the eighteen-and-under category, but afterward she was banned from competing against other female athletes on an international level. Chand was born with hyperandrogenism, which means her body produces natural levels of testosterone that are significantly higher than what is considered normal for females. As a result, the International Association of Athletics Federations, the governing body for track, prohibited her from competing unless she lowered her testosterone levels below the male range by either taking hormone-suppressing drugs or having surgery to limit the amount of testosterone her body produces (Macur, 2014). Chand refused to do so, and for several years she fought the ban in court. In July 2015, she won her case and was allowed to return to international competition, but the ruling came late and her training for the 2016 Rio Olympics was limited. Although she did qualify and ran in the women's 100 meters, she did not make it out of the opening heats. However, in 2018, she won two silver medals at the Asian Games, and early in 2020, she was on track to qualify for the Tokyo Olympics before they were postponed due to the global pandemic.

Chand's case is interesting because her condition occurs naturally, yet she has been accused of having an unfair advantage due to her higher-than-normal testosterone levels. And here we see the crux of the transgender in sports debate: how do we define what is "an unfair advantage." Despite having testosterone levels within the female range—and really the lower end of the female range—Hubbard was accused of capitalizing on an unfair advantage by fans and her competitors, and they made reasonable arguments. Chand's testosterone levels were high, but they were naturally occurring, and she was still banned from competing. When Chand steps on the track with other elite athletes, some would argue that the playing field is tilted in her favor; however, the idea of a level playing field becomes problematic when extended beyond physical playing fields and the rules. And yet, more often than not, the level playing field argument is used to imply that all athletes should have the same chance of success as their competitors.

Athletes are not born equal, and sporting events would be much less interesting if they were. Natural, genetic gifts have always been an important element in athletic performance. A 7-foot-tall basketball player has a distinct advantage over an equally talented player who is 6-foot tall. Much has been said about Michael Phelps's body proportions and double jointedness. He has a longer "wing span" than is typical of elite swimmers, and his joints allow for a much wider flexibility range. He has a physical advantage over most swimmers when he steps onto the pool deck, and in a sport where winning and losing are often separated by milliseconds, his physical proportions play a role. Far from being "unfair," this is an essential part of athletic competition.

Clearly, the IOC is attempting to be inclusive. Their own policy states, "it is necessary to ensure insofar as possible that trans athletes are not excluded from the opportunity to participate in sporting competition" (International Olympic Committee 2015, p. 2). But when it comes to weighing the importance of inclusion over fairness, that same policy makes it very clear that fairness trumps inclusion: "the overriding sporting objective is and remains the guarantee of fair competition." Hubbard's experience and physical development as a male certainly gives her an advantage, but how do we determine if that advantage is *unfair*? Saying that all advantages are unfair ignores the full spectrum of human development and possibilities. Sipaia, the runner-up to Hubbard, is Somoan, a people known for their physical strength. A quick Google search will reveal numerous articles on why the Somoans are genetically predisposed to excel at sports like American football, rugby, or mixed martial arts. Is that not an advantage for a weight lifter, especially if we start comparing to other ethnic groups, such as Ethiopians? Does that make her advantage unfair? These types of physiological advantages are not easy to quantify, unlike something such as testosterone levels, which can be determined by a simple blood test. And even if an athlete has a potential advantage, how do we determine how much it would affect the outcome. Saying that Hubbard had an unfair advantage because of her experience as a male completely disregards all the training, development, and determination she has as an athlete, regardless of gender. What if Hubbard simply trained longer and harder than her competitors?

Another complication with the emphasis on testosterone is that the IOC policy could be perceived as discriminatory against women. According to researcher Adam Love, "while the IOC's guidelines may signal a new level of inclusion for transgender athletes in some ways, they still work to reinforce restrictive assumptions about sex, hormones, and athletic performance" (2017). Take, for example, the NCAA's rules about transgender athletes, which got its cue from the IOC policy. In the NCAA, transgender men are eligible to compete immediately on a men's team; no medical history is required, and the athletes do not need to undergo any hormone treatment. Men's teams with transgender players are not effected or penalized in any way. However, if a transgender woman wants to compete on a female team, that team is barred from competing in any championship games. Transgender women must submit a year's worth of medical records documenting their hormone treatments and testosterone levels. Only after one year is that female team allowed to compete in all matches. ESPN sports writer Kate Fagan has rightfully called this "gender policing of women," citing a *New York Times* article from 2012 by two researches that states, "Scientifically, there is no clear or objective way to draw a bright line between male and female" (2015).

Because of the "gender policing" that some see within the IOC and NCAA rules, critics from within the LGBTQIA+ have been quick to praise the kinds of inclusive policies seen in numerous states at the interscholastic (i.e., high school) level. In 2007, the state of Washington, through its Washington Interscholastic Activities Association (WIAA), became the first to adopt a formal policy on transgender athletes (Love, 2017). Specifically, the WIAA policy allows athletes to participate "in a manner that is consistent with their gender identity, irrespective of the gender listed on a student's records" (qtd. in Love, 2017, p. 198). Unlike the IOC, NCAA, and other interscholastic rules such as the one that Beggs faced in Texas, states following the WIAA model do not require surgery, medical evidence, hormone tests, birth certificate changes, etc., in order for transgender high school students to compete within the gender category that they identify. Mosier, who founded

TransAthlete, a resource for athletes within the LGBTQIA+ community that explains different policies, bills, and laws related to transgender athletes nationwide, has long supported the kinds of inclusive policies seen within the WIAA (Allen, 2017). Helen Carroll, who co-authored the NCAA's 2011 guidelines for transgender athletes, also praises the simplicity and inclusivity of interscholastic policies. "Your transgender boys play on boys' teams, your transgender girls play on girls' teams, and everybody's happy," she said while commenting on the Beggs situation (qtd. in Allen, 2017). In a 2010 report she co-authored for high schools and colleges, Carroll argues that fears about any unfair competitive advantage are exaggerated:

> [T]ransgender girls who do not access hormone blockers or cross-gender hormones display a great deal of physical variation, just as there is a great deal of natural variation in physical size and ability among non-transgender girls and boys. Many people may have a stereotype that all transgender girls and women are unusually tall and have large bones and muscles. But that is not true. A male-to-female transgender girl may be small and slight, even if she is not on hormone blockers or taking estrogen. It is important not to over generalize. (Griffin and Carroll, 2010, p. 15)

However, assertions like Carroll's that inclusive rules have a minimal effect on "fair competition" have recently come under greater scrutiny. Some are now calling such inclusion policies an infringement on a female's rights under Title IX, a 1979 law that bars discrimination on the basis of sex within educational programs that receive federal funds. In early 2020, a federal lawsuit challenged the Connecticut Interscholastic Athletic Conference's (CIAC) transgender inclusion rule (similar to the WIAA's) allowing athletes to compete in accordance with their gender identity. Although Connecticut is one of eighteen states with similar rules allowing transgender athletes to compete without undergoing HRT or other gender-confirming measures, the "Constitution State" has been under the microscope because of two transgender female high school students, Andraya Yearwood and Terry Miller, who dominated women's indoor and outdoor track and field in the state from 2018 to 2020.

Title IX applies to a range of issues on educational campuses including things such as admittance of females into institutions of higher education and how colleges and universities must report and investigate accusations of sexual abuse or misconduct. It also applies to athletics, with Title IX being the key legal requirement for colleges and universities to keep a balance between male and female athletic programs and scholarships. The law was intended to promote inclusion, but now some are arguing that in order to preserve female rights under Title IX, transgender athletes must be excluded.

The Alliance Defending Freedom (ADF), the organization that filed the lawsuit, argues that its clients, three female track runners who competed against—and generally lost to—Yearwood and Miller were harmed by Connecticut's inclusive policy. "We're looking for a return to a level playing field," said Christiana Holcomb, the attorney for the ADF. "It's our position that what's happening with the [CIAC's] policy is that by allowing males into the female category [. . .] they're denying female athletes opportunities and failing to accommodate physical differences between the sexes" (qtd. in Barnes, 2020). Throughout the legal filing, the ADF had continued to refer to the transgender girls, Yearwood and Miller, as males (Barnes, 2020).

Around the same time as the ADF's lawsuit, the Idaho state legislature began debating House Bill 500, called the Fairness in Women's Sports Act, which stipulates that at all levels of state competition (interscholastic through collegiate), teams designated as female "shall not be open to members of the male sex," which would include transgender females (qtd. in Barnes, 2020). Representative Barbara Ehardt, who is sponsoring the bill, says that, "I am not trying to exclude trans people from living a full, healthy life. This is about competing in the biological sex which you were born" (qtd. in Barnes, 2020). Of course, Ehardt is saying that a trans person's full and healthy life cannot include organized athletic competition, which seems hypocritical coming from a former women's basketball coach who should understand the crucial role that athletics play in many people's full, happy lives.

As female athletics appear poised as the next major battleground for trans rights in America, the central debate will revolve around what we want sports to be. Are they simply an empirical measure of athletic skill, or are they meant to impart something more, something loftier but less tangible? Unfortunately, the answer may not be a one-size-fits-all. At the professional level, and possibly even the collegiate level (which with the billions of dollars invested every year could be characterized as "semi-pro"), one could argue that the primary goal is to determine winners and losers. If that is the case, the concept of "fairness" really does equate to an evaluation of "advantage," an idea that is as impossible to quantify as it is to ignore. Perhaps that is not what sports should be, even at the professional level. The IOC's own *Olympic Charter* boldly claims that "The practice of sport is a human right. Every individual must have the possibility of practising sport, without discrimination of any kind and in the Olympic spirit, which requires mutual understanding with a spirit of friendship, solidarity and fair play" (International Olympic Committee 2019, p. 11). Despite the IOC's noble claim, it would take a monumental cultural shift to move us away from the perspective that the primary goal of professional sports is to determine who is "better" during athletic competition.

However, at lower-level competitions, from youth sports through high school, many educators and policy makers would argue that the primary goal of sports is not simply to crown a winner. In her report to the NCAA about including transgender athletes, Carroll argues that, "the benefits of school athletic participation include many positive effects on physical, social, and emotional well-being. Playing sports can provide student athletes with important lessons about self-discipline, teamwork, success and failure—as well as the joy and shared excitement that being a member of a sports team can bring" (Griffin and Carroll, 2010, p. 6). The CIAC made similar claims when responding to the ADF lawsuit. "The purpose of our organization is about giving kids an opportunity to develop social, emotional, cognitive, physical, and mental health and well-being," said CIAC executive director Glenn Lungarini. "We believe our inclusive policy . . . gives the best opportunity for all kids to benefit from those aspects of participation in sports" (qtd. in Barnes, 2020). In this regard, "fairness" could take on a different meaning. At this level, is it more "fair" to allow all to compete and reap the likely benefits of athletic competition, or is it more "fair" to exclude some in the name of creating a level playing field for determining athletic achievement?

## REFERENCES

Allen, S. (2017, May). The Texas Law That Could Disqualify Trans Athletes from Competing. *Daily Beast*. https://www.thedailybeast.com/the-texas-law-which-could-disqualify-trans-athletes-from-competing.

Barnes, K. (2020, June). The Battle of Title IX and Who Gets to Be a Woman in Sports: Inside the Raging National Debate. *ESPN*. https://www.espn.com/espnw/story/_/id/29347507/the-battle-title-ix-gets-woman-sports-raging-national-debate.

Domonoske, C. (2017, February 27). 17-Year-Old Transgender Boy Wins Texas Girls' Wrestling Championship. *NPR*. https://www.npr.org/sections/thetwo-way/2017/02/27/517491492/17-year-old-transgender-boy-wins-texas-girls-wrestling-championship.

Fagan, K. (2015, July). It's Time We Got Away from Determining Who Is "Female Enough" to Compete. *ESPN*. https://www.espn.com/espnw/news-commentary/story/_/id/13343132/got-away-determining-female-enough-compete.

Fox News (2017, April). *Caitlyn Jenner: Easier to Come Out as Trans than Republican* [Video] YouTube. https://www.youtube.com/watch?v=f4RJTEVKObM.

Griffin, P. and Carroll, H. J. (2010, October). *On the Team: Equal Opportunity for Transgender Student Athletes*. NCAA. https://www.ncaa.org/sites/default/files/NCLR_TransStudentAthlete%2B(2).pdf.

Guardian sport. (2017, March 2). Mack Beggs, Transgender Wrestler Who Won Texas Girls' Title: "Boo All You Want." *The Guardian*. https://www.theguardian

.com/sport/2017/mar/02/mack-beggs-transgender-wrestler-state-title-winner-texas
-law.

IncomeIT. (2016, December 4). *Nike—Unlimited Courage* [Video]. YouTube. https:/
/www.youtube.com/watch?v=xtl3oMVV4aU.

International Olympic Committee. (2015). *IOC Consensus Meeting on Sex
Reassignment and Hyperandrogenism*. International Olympic Committee. https
://stillmed.olympic.org/Documents/Commissions_PDFfiles/Medical_commission
/2015-11_ioc_consensus_meeting_on_sex_reassignment_and_hyperandrogenism-
en.pdf.

International Olympic Committee. (2019). *Olympic Charter*. International Olympic
Committee. https://stillmed.olympic.org/media/Document%20Library/Olympi
cOrg/General/EN-Olympic-Charter.pdf.

Kahrl, C. (2016, June). Chris Mosier Becomes First Known Transgender Athlete in
World Duathlon Championship. *ESPN*. https://www.espn.com/sports/endurance/
story/_/id/15976460/chris-mosier-becomes-first-known-transgender-athlete-comp
ete-world-duathlon-championship.

Karkazis, K., Jordan-Young, R., Davis, G., and Camporesi, S. (2012). Out of Bounds?
A Critique of New Policies on Hyperandrogenism in Elite Female Athletes. *The
American Journal of Bioethics*. https://www.tandfonline.com/doi/full/10.1080/
15265161.2012.680533.

Love, A. (2017). The Tenuous Inclusion of Transgender Athletes in Sports. In E.
Anderson and A. Travers (Eds.), *Transgender Athletes in Competitive Sport* (pp.
194–205). Routledge.

Maccur, J. (2014, October). Fighting for the Body She Was Born With. *The New
York Times*. https://www.nytimes.com/2014/10/07/sports/sprinter-dutee-chand-fi
ghts-ban-over-her-testosterone-level.html.

Payne, M. (2017, March). Transgender Woman Wins International Weightlifting Title
Amid Controversy over Fairness. *The Washington Post*. https://www.washingt
onpost.com/news/early-lead/wp/2017/03/22/transgender-woman-wins-internation
al-weightlifting-title-amid-controversy-over-fairness/?utm_term=.73589658b586.

Robinson, F. H. and Muaddi, N. (2017, February 27). Transgender Boy Wins Girls'
Wrestling Championship in Texas. *CNN*. https://www.cnn.com/2017/02/27/us/t
exas-transgender-wrestler-trnd-hold/index.html.

SB 2095. (2017). *Bill Analysis*. https://capitol.texas.gov/tlodocs/85R/analysis/html/
SB02095I.htm.

Seva'aetasi, S. F. (2017, March). Woman Lifter Beaten by Transgender Speaks Up.
*Somoa Observer*. https://www.samoaobserver.ws/category/samoa/8993.

Sutherland, M. A. B., Wassersug, R. J., and Rosenberg, K. R. (2017). From
Transsexuals to Transhumans in Elite Athletics: The Implications of Osteology
(and other issues) in Levelling the Playing Field. In E. Anderson and A. Travers
(Eds.), *Transgender Athletes in Competitive Sport* (pp. 173–93). Routledge.

Wiik, A., Lundberg, T. R., Rullman, E., Andersson, D. P., Holmberg, M., Mandic,
M., Brismar, T. B., Leinhard, O. D., Chanpen, S., Flanagan, J. N., Arver, S., and
Oustafsson, T. (2020, March). Muscle Strength, Size, and Composition Following
12 Months of Gender-affirming Treatment in Transgender Individuals. *The Journal
of Clinical Endocrinology & Metabolism*. https://academic.oup.com/jcem/article
/105/3/e805/5651219.

*Chapter 7*

# Gender Identity in Transgender Comics

Jacob Muriel

Within the past ten years, the comics industry has seen an upsurge in trans-centric storylines and characters. Of course, trans characters have featured in comics from around the world before. The trans woman Wanda from Neil Gaiman's *Sandman* series and Rumiko Takahashi's *Ranma ½*, in which the titular character supernaturally transitions continually between male and female, serve as popular examples of twentieth-century fictional transgender comics characters. Avid comics readers can find plenty of other contemporary examples, particularly within Japanese *manga*, as well as recent American superhero comics—one example being Alysia Yeoh, Batgirl's transgender friend introduced by comics author Gail Simone in the 2011 *Batgirl* #1 comic (although the character did not come out as transgender until *Batgirl* #13). Recently, however, the comics medium has seen an increase of transgender graphic memoirs. As comics scholar Hillary Chute writes, "LGBTQ comics may be the fastest-growing area of comics right now," an area she broadly defines as "comics that feature in some way the lives, whether real or imagined, of LGBTQ . . . characters" (2017, p. 349). These are (auto)biographical comics that depict the real-world experiences of contemporary trans individuals, as well as additional realist fiction comics inspired by the transgender cartoonist's own experience.

Consistent with the rise of "literary graphic novels" and graphic memoirs during the late twentieth and early twenty-first centuries, then, there has been an increase in transgender graphic narratives rooted in and depicting the contemporary, lived experience of trans-identifying people. Unlike the past transgender representations in comics, more comics are being created by those identifying as transgender about their own and other's experiences in identifying as trans in contemporary Western society. Some notable examples include Dylan Edwards' *Transposes* (2012), a collection of six graphic short stories about transgender men, and Julia Kaye's *Super Late Bloomer* (2018), a comic diary recording the author's first months in transition. Biographically based fictional comics include the ongoing web comic *TransLucid* as well as the German comic *Nenn mich Kai* (English: *Call Me Kai*) by Sarah Barczyk (2016). These comics range from fictional to (auto)biographical; yet, all are inspired by the lives of trans people, whether the author or others, and all aim to depict the real-world experience of trans people across modern Western culture.

Comics provide an interesting opportunity for depicting the lived experience of trans people. Comics' hybrid text-image format may perhaps be understood as mirroring a similar key juxtaposition constituting the transgender individual's own life: that between a felt gender identity and a socially assigned gender status. Judith Butler argues in her seminal book *Gender Trouble* that gender does not exist outside of a social environment, and within Butler's philosophy, the social world is constructed by and through language. Thus, for Butler, each individual's gender identity becomes established through the performance of various linguistic and social customs a host culture assigns to respective genders. Gender becomes something imposed on the individual from sociolinguistic surroundings rather than arising from within (Butler, 2007, pp. 33, 45). The National Center for Transgender Equality (NCTE) speaks of transgender people experiencing a dissonance—officially termed *gender dysphoria*—at odds with Butler's theory however. The NCTE describes this dissonance for trans people as "the difference between the gender they are thought to be at birth and the gender they know themselves to be" (2016). The first part of this description—one's assigned gender identity—is that which Butler theorizes, a gender attributed to an individual through a sociolinguistic code. The second half of the NCTE's description—that gender one knows themselves to be—defies Butler's gender theory in suggesting there does exist a gender identity outside the linguistic realm. These two halves of the gender dissonance experienced by many trans-identifying people would seem to generally align with comics' text-image binary—text linguistically assigning gender identity while the image depicts a more immediate and visceral gender experienced by the author and/or character.

The comics image, however, is not necessarily free from society's linguistically enforced gender system. Alison Bechdel, author of the famous graphic memoir *Fun Home* (2006), writes in a Foreword to the comics collection *Transposes*, "Comics also solves an interesting problem inherent to the trans experience. Language can be confusing when discussing someone's pre-transition past. But that problem recedes when the storytelling is primarily visual . . . there's no need to encumber them with pronouns" (Edwards, 2012, n.p.). This language difficulty is a familiar and personal topic for many trans people, and Bechdel's remark seems to offer an easy solution; when stumbling between referring to the pre-transition individual as either he or she, drawing a picture ostensibly elides the problem altogether. The problem with Bechdel's claim, however, is that images and pictures are employed every day in order to code gender, from the international insignia for men and women to the association of certain colors with specific genders. One commonplace and culturally relevant example appears near the end of the fictional German comic *Nenn mich Kai*, in which the eponymous male-to-female character Kai attempts to enter a gym locker room. The comic panel portrays Kai standing in front of two doors, both identically marked *Umkleide* (English: *locker room*), differentiated only through familiar and divergent stick figure signifiers, one signifying a woman, the other, a man. Kai pauses and thinks, "Oh, I never even thought of that" (translation my own), before eventually entering the men's room untroubled (Barczyk, 2016, p. 71). This everyday occurrence exemplifies the use of images to code and signify gender outside of language.

Images code and signify gender in many other ways. Pictures, drawn or photographed, operate through resemblance and representation. Comics critic Harry Morgan explains how, for economic and practical reasons, comics characters during the twentieth century came to rely on graphic caricature, a custom that has carried through today (2009). While Morgan never notes how this caricature plays into gender representation within comics, one can see it most overtly in many comic book serials—characters such as Wonder Woman, Barbarella, and Lucy van Pelt are coded as women through gender-specific visual motifs, for example, long hair, full lips, eyelashes, or dresses, characteristics typically lacking in their male counterparts. Such minor graphic details are employed to differentiate male from female characters and code characters as female. With just these examples, it becomes clear that "graphic representation is a socialized act involving many codes and constraints," particularly as regards gender (Baetans, 2001, p. 152). While Bechdel perceives comics as offering a visual freedom in depicting gender, the graphic economy described by scholars such as Baetans and Morgan suggest comics may not be as liberating as Bechdel believes. If comics rely on a culturally determined system of visual codes, then the visual depiction of gender in comics is likewise affected, and even determined, by the various signs associated with respective genders throughout a comic's host culture.

This method of signifying gender through iconography connects with the emphasis on appearance in many (auto)biographically based transgender comics. In these comics, transgender characters universally, and seemingly unintentionally, equate *being* a specific gender with *appearing* as that gender. For example, in *Super Late Bloomer*, Julia Kaye documents the first months of her male-to-female transition and her incumbent psychological and material struggles. One key personal issue throughout is whether she can viably appear as feminine. While transitioning, she experiences a nerve-racking self-consciousness over whether others perceive her as a woman, that is, how feminine she looks, (2018, p. 39) so that whenever others compliment her appearance, her cartoon representation blushes with enlarged doe eyes surrounded by stars (2018, p. 32). Reading her daily cartoon entries, the reader is often left with the impression that Julia's day is determined either as good or bad based on whether or not others recognize her as a woman—she even admits to succumbing to this external validation (2018, p. 41). Likewise, Kaye is often discouraged by thoughts that she looks more like a man than a woman, (2018, pp. 38, 65) moments that contrast with a disparate self-admiration over her own increasingly feminine appearance (2018, p. 25). The underlying logic seems to be that, in order for her to attain a full femininity, at least in the eyes of others, Kaye must appear fully feminine.

Kaye thereby highlights the importance of perception and self-image to her own trans experience—although self-perception is a universally human concern as well. She writes in one strip dated June 26, 2016, "On bad days, I see a man playing dress-up in the mirror. On good days, I actually see myself, I recognize myself" (2018, p. 38). In strips like this—similar strips can be found throughout Kaye's book—Julia Kaye demonstrates her own tendency to code her body as masculine rather than feminine based on appearance while wrestling with the appearance-related aspects of her transition. The problem is thus not only how others visually code her gender, but also Kaye's tendency to do so as well. A subsequent strip dated July 1, 2016 documents a similar moment. Kaye writes, "I've gone through a dress phase recently. A symbol of femininity, it was an armor I could wear to remind myself and others I'm a girl" (2018, p. 43). The dress functions as a visual signifier of Julia's femininity, "a symbol of femininity" as she calls it. She here speaks to the cultural tendency to visually code gender, much like the traditional bathroom signs Kai encounters. For example, a female restroom stick figure is considered different than a male figure based on the existence of, primarily, a dress, and maybe long hair. The dress, as Kaye points out and the bathroom sign demonstrates, visually codes femininity in Western culture and so serves as a means for Kaye to affirm and establish her gender status as woman, both for others and in her own mind. It thereby demonstrates her use of visual cultural signifiers to solidify her self-identified gender, both socially and psychologically.

Returning to the German comic *Nenn mich Kai*, the female-to-male Kai likewise models his own appearance after traditionally masculine tropes as a way of concretizing his status as a man. In one sequence, while walking down the street, Kai encounters a French fashion poster portraying a model of traditional masculinity—the six-pack-wielding, strong-jawed, and short-haired male model found only in advertisements. Looking into a reflective window disparagingly, Kai immediately enters a barber shop, reappearing shortly thereafter with a short, traditionally male cut. The scene demonstrates the importance of appearance for Kai, being one overt instance in which Kai directly models himself according to Western society's socially regulated image of traditional masculinity. Throughout the comic, Kai seeks other means of manifesting a masculine appearance, whether through purchasing a binder, using makeup to create an artificial five o'clock shadow, or purchasing rubber genitalia. In these ways, much as with Kaye's own experience with her dress and gaff, Kai demonstrates the primacy of appearance in establishing gender identity both psychologically and socially. Throughout *Super Late Bloomer* and *Nenn mich Kai*, the protagonists' status within their self-identified gender is reinforced by appearing in accordance with traditional visual tropes associated with that gender.

Another exemplary instant of visually establishing gender identity in transgender comics can be found in the ongoing web comic *TransLucid*, a fictionalized, yet autobiographically inspired, account of the author's own male-to-female transgender experience. Much like Kaye, the main character Sarah often worries over a felt failure to appear feminine. For example, in one strip dated September 5 2014, Sarah (pre-transition) expresses her worries to her then-romantic partner over the viability of appearing sufficiently feminine post-transition. In response, the romantic partner shaves Sarah's legs and clothes her in a wig and dress, leaving Sarah shocked over how feminine she can actually appear, thereby relieving her transition worries. The strip makes clear that Sarah's fears over her impending transition are not whether she will *be* a woman post-transition in some esoteric metaphysical sense, but whether she will viably *appear* as a woman. In fact, for Sarah, the latter question seems to constitute the first. As Julia Kaye often seems to do in her own comic, so *TransLucid*'s autobiographically based Sarah associates being a woman with appearing as a woman, thereby making the matter of ontologically being a woman actually a matter of visually passing as a woman.

The final example of this association between appearance and gender identity occurs in a June 2018 post by the political satire comics website *The Nib*. The post consists of six, brief comics by transgender cartoonists depicting their transgender experiences. The second panel of a comic by Binglin Hu is most relevant to the present discussion. The panel portrays two versions of the author, one dressed femme and the other masculine, coded red and blue, respectively (a similar gender-specific color-coding technique is utilized in the web comic *TransLucid*). The image is accompanied with text about the author's past, "I'd have what I mentally referred to as 'boy days' and 'girl days.' It was empowering, but scary" (2018). This panel, when taken within the four-panel comic's focus on the author's dress, infers that the author's identification as a boy or girl was associated with how they chose to dress that day, for example, "boy days" signify the days they chose to dress in traditional masculine clothes and identified as male. In this way, the author not only creates an intimate, even synonymous, relationship between appearance and gender identity, but between their own fluctuating gender identity and culturally conditioned visual significations of gender, for example, dresses for girl days and loose-fitting jeans for boy days.

All of this isn't to say one must appear in accordance with traditional Western tropes of masculinity or femininity in order to truly be considered a man or a woman, respectively, or even that this is the right way to approach gender. There obviously exist gender-identified men who do not dress like traditional men, and the same is true of women as well. The purpose is rather to show the frequency of non-linguistic visual codes for gender and their effect on transgender individuals in contemporary Western culture. This counters Alison Bechdel's earlier quotation on the freedom found in representing transgender individuals unencumbered by the gender-classifying force of language via comics' reliance on visual representation. The narratives here considered reveal the propensity for even images to define gender status and categories. If Kai wants to be a man, both in his own mind and in the eyes of society, he must successfully appear as a man, or so he seems to believe. Kai's journey toward becoming a man is equally a journey toward appearing as a physical man. The same applies to both Julia Kaye in *Super Late Bloomer* and Sarah in *TransLucid* in regard to their male-to-female transitions. For all of these transgender characters, real or fictional, the gender transition is largely a material transition; it is about appearing like a (wo)man and evidencing traditional physical features and clothing associated with (wo)manhood.

Importantly, these transgender characters not only fixate on appearing as their identified gender, but on appearing as that gender in accordance with cultural norms. Both Julia Kaye and Sarah, with the aim of being a woman, wear dresses and makeup and grow out their hair. Similarly, Kai receives a short haircut and pursues a traditional masculine build in accordance with culturally enforced images (think of his encounter with the French fashion poster) in order to achieve the social status of a man. In this way, these transgender comics show how images are not entirely free of the gender-enforcing power Bechdel infers them to be. It likewise demonstrates how visual images are employed in the sociolinguistic construction of gender proposed by Judith Butler. Consistent with Butler's theory of gender as produced through social discourse, these comics illustrate how one's status as a given gender occurs through participation within a series of visual rituals and practices. Within these narratives, to be a given gender means to appear as that gender.

But although these comics emphasize the appearance, and so social, nature of gender, their concurrence with Judith Butler's socially constructed notion of gender is only superficial. While these transgender comics characters do focus on appearing as their specified genders, for them, their gender identity is not constructed by participation in a gendered visual culture, but rather, the characters see visual gender signifiers and social practices as the means to manifest a felt internal reality. Gender status may be constructed in social practices and discourse as Butler argues, but not gender identity. These comics represent gender as an internal and ineffable reality that one manifests through social practices. The focus on appearance emerges from a desire to materially manifest one's internal self. In this way, these transgender comics narratives flip Judith Butler's theory of gender. Rather than affirming with Butler that gender identity is constructed through language and social practices, they suggest that such practices actually serve as a culturally coded means to manifest one's personal gender identity.

This understanding of manifesting the psychological through the physical and social permeates the transgender comics considered here. In a strip dated June 2, 2016, Julia Kaye portrays herself looking in the mirror, ostensibly disappointed with what she considers her lack of a sufficiently feminine appearance. In the final panel, her facial features concealed in shadow, she remarks, "It's hard going through life knowing others can't see the real you" (2018, p. 15). A related moment appears several pages later. The first panel of this strip portrays a feminine Julia looking into the mirror as a more bulky and mustachioed (i.e., masculine) version stares back with the text, "On bad days, I see a man playing dress-up in the mirror" (2018, p. 38). In the next panel, Julia smiles into the mirror, her equally feminine reflection smiling back, accompanied by the text, "On good days, I actually see myself, I recognize myself" (2018, p. 38). Likewise, in a *TransLucid* strip dated July 20 2013, a pre-transition Sarah looks hopefully into the mirror, thinking of her impending transition, "I'll finally be myself, the REAL me, and she will be looking back at me every morning through this mirror" (2013). In such moments, these transgender comics juxtapose a psychological "real" gender at odds with the character's social or biological gender status, a dissonance between their internal gender identity and the character's ability to adequately manifest that identity socially.

This internal-external juxtaposition smells of a sort of mind-body dualism in its conflict between the transgender individual's internal and external selves. It suggests a latent psychological essentialism, as though one's identification as a specific gender is a matter of internal, psychological identification regardless of the physical body. For example, this thinking would hold pre-transition Julia Kaye to be a psychological female and physical male, her hormone transition working to harmonize her physiological self with her psychological self. The aforementioned comic strip of Kaye gazing into her mirror and seeing a man illustrates this logic. In such strips, Kaye understands her feminine appearance as a way to manifest her real—that is, internal—self. Her masculine body pre-transition prevents others from, in her own words, seeing the real her, the woman she internally knows and feels herself to be. Creating a feminine appearance enables Kaye and others to materially see her real self, for it is then she can, as she writes, recognize herself.

In one interview from a 2019 issue of the journal *Studies in Comics*, Kaye remarks on this use of mirrors throughout *Super Late Bloomer*:

> I'm not super happy with how often mirrors show up in *Super Late Bloomer*. Not out of embarrassment or anything. It's just a stereotyped way to talk about the trans experience. The depressed trans person staring sadly into a mirror, possibly with their arm out, seeing themselves as a completely different person. It definitely was an easy shorthand for communicating a more complex idea. (Murel, 2019, p. 143)

Earlier in this same interview, Kaye notes her belief that language inevitably fails to express her own, and possibly others', lived experience as trans. It is in this regard that the mirror appears to operate as an easy—if cliché in Kaye's opinion—shorthand for expressing Kaye's experience as a trans woman. Yet Kaye's reservations over the mirror image suggest that even this shorthand, despite the incumbent metaphoric power of visual language, cannot fully communicate her own lived experience as trans. While Alison Bechdel interprets comics' visual language as liberating, enabling people to express themselves and others free of society's linguistically enforced gender code, Kaye suggests this visual language may not be altogether liberating. For Kaye, the visual language of comics can serve as a ready shorthand for concepts and experiences that may be otherwise difficult to express in written or spoken language; yet, even comics' pictography fails at a point. In other words, Kaye's internal gender identity—that is, her feeling of being a woman apart from society's declarations—cannot be fully captured in either the textual or imagistic aspects of comics.

Visual language's inability to liberate, and its juxtaposition with an a-linguistic experience of gender, tacitly surfaces in another of Kaye's strips, dated June 7, 2016. Therein, Kaye writes, "I may have been born into a testosterone-producing body, I may look masculine, I may sound masculine, but I am more than the sum of my parts. I'm a woman" (2018, p. 20). The first panel depicts a doctor holding a baby Kaye, a speech bubble containing the male gender symbol extending from the doctor's mouth. In the next panel, a grown (and seemingly mid-transition) Kaye voices a speech bubble containing the female gender symbol. The placement of these insignia alone within speech balloons speaks to the intimate connection between the visual and language as means for coding and assigning gender. In the strip's final panel,

Kaye writes, "I am more than the sum of my parts. I'm a woman," thereby appealing to a conception of gender outside of the body, and even language, altogether (2018, p. 20). That is, however Kaye may appear or sound, she is a woman. For Kaye, her identity as a woman exists beyond the realm of verbal and visual language—her experience and identity as a woman can neither be entirely expressed nor constituted by any linguistic code. She appeals to her internal, felt gender identity as the ultimate determination of her "real" gender over and above language.

A similar juxtaposition between linguistic and a-linguistic conceptualizations of gender occurs in one of the six comic short stories comprising Dylan Edwards' *Transposes*. On the penultimate page of the short story "Henry," the eponymous female-to-male queer character voices his thoughts on his being a "man." He remarks "I'm far too faggy to be a 'real man.' Now I don't even know that I'm so bent on being a 'man.' I do sometimes wish my body were more like a genetic man's, but surgery is expensive and I have other plans for my money" (2012, p. 33). Henry here equates *real man* and *man* with *genetic man*. His terminological progression infers a conflation of these three terms consistent with traditional Western conceptions of gender, that the only real man is a genetic man. Indeed, those who oppose transgender recognition in America often appeal to the material body as the locus of one's gender identity, refusing to accept another as man or woman if the person in question was not biologically born as male or female, respectively. But by placing quotations around *real man* and *man*, Henry questions the validity of these classifications, suggesting they may be nothing more than misguided signifiers for what is only a genetic man, and so inferring there exist other types of non-genetic men, such as the internally male-identifying individual born with a female body.

The traditional Western system, as Henry tacitly points out, defines a "real man" as a genetic man. It is this cultural belief that prompts Henry to consider surgery as a means of obtaining a biologically male body, and thereby socially establish himself as a "real man." In this consideration, Henry risks buying into the belief that his status as a true man is determined by whether or not he possesses the proper, culturally approved physiology. The power of visual gender markers is powerful and alluring. Julia Kaye says in an interview,

[I]t helps to play into certain gender stereotypes physically in order to maintain a sense of our internal gender, our gender real- ity, for others who might not otherwise see it. Symbols can be powerful, especially when you're living in a different mode of being externally for decades of your life. In one sense, the trans person is playing into societal expectations to be seen how they want to be seen, but there's also euphoria involved with certain symbols as gender markers. We hold these ideas to be powerful in our minds until we arrive at a place where we feel comfortable living and expressing ourselves as we normally would without them. (Murel, 2019, p. 141)

His refusal to follow through with surgery, however, amounts to a refusal to participate in this biologically based social concept of gender, instead adhering to the more personal conceptualization favored by Kaye. Henry, like Kaye, bears a gender identity outside the sum of his parts. Henry silently abjures the physiological as an exclusive determinant of gender, instead adhering to a gender identity apart from the biological and linguistic, one that is felt but can still be expressed through these mediums.

Returning to the aforementioned strips of Julia Kaye staring into the mirror, her expressed sentiment of recognizing herself and wanting others to see her real (i.e., felt) self expresses a far more basic and universal sentiment: to be seen as one feels one's self to be. For Kaye, as well as the other transgender comics characters here considered, this can be achieved by matching one's physical appearance with one's psychological experience, thereby bridging the mind-body gender gap and so harmonizing one's internal and external selves. Further, the physical transition serves a practical social function for the transgender individual. As Kaye notes, "The physical hormone transition is all about trying to change the way you are seen in society to abate your gender dysphoria" (Murel, 2019, p. 143). If Kaye appears like a woman, people will approach and regard her as a woman, thereby affirming who she knows herself to be. This should not be taken as inferring one's physical hormone transition is only a matter of external validation. Rather, I suggest the above quote from Julia Kaye means that physical hormone transition serves as a means of bringing both one's physiological (i.e., hormonal) makeup and one's treatment by society into alignment with who that person knows themself to be. Hormone transition is understood as filling the gap characterizing gender dysphoria by physiologically manifesting the reality of one's internal identity.

On a macro level, the transgender character's transition reverses the logic inherent to how Western society visually codes gender according to signs and symbols drawn from physical appearance. Rather than allowing their individual gender identities to be orchestrated and determined by a gender status assigned based on their physiological makeup at birth, these transgender comics characters take control of such customs and appearances in order to manifest their psychological, and more substantive, selves. This approach flips Judith Butler's dominant gender theory. For Butler, gender is performative, meaning it results from dominant societal norms acting upon every individual—gender is constructed through discourse, whether linguistic or visual (Butler, 2007, p. 34). (Auto)Biographical transgender graphic narratives likewise approach gender as performance, but in the more colloquial understanding of the word contra Butler's technical philosophical definition. For transgender characters such as Kai and Kaye, their gender performance aims to manifest a felt reality—Kaye attempts to appear as a woman because she feels herself to be a woman. Despite whatever body with which Kaye was born, she knows herself to be a woman and so molds her appearance and body to match that experiential reality. Gender may be coded through norms and practices, but each individual can take control of such customs in order to manifest his/her own psychological reality.

In these transgender comics, gender is a felt internal reality that one expresses through social rituals and appearance. Consider the aforementioned four-panel comic by Binglin Hu. On days Hu felt themself to be a man, they dressed as a man, whereas when Hu considered themself a woman, Hu dressed as a woman. While Hu was, indeed, participating in societal gender norms by dressing in specific, gender-coded ways, Hu's decision on which gender to code themself as was dictated by whichever gender Hu felt themself to be that day. The same is true of Kai and Kaye. Kai participates in societal norms of visual masculinity because he feels himself to be a man, as Kaye does with femininity. These transgender comics, the product of transgender experiences, suggest, like Butler, that gender is set of societal acts and rituals. But contra Butler, these are the sort of norms with which one can choose to engage and even manipulate. For them, gender is not so much something done to one's self, as Butler understands it, but rather a subjective reality manifested through culturally regulated norms and actions, revealing the potential limits of Butler's theory.

Stephen Whittle writes in a Foreword to *The Transgender Studies Reader*, "Is the basis of gender identity essential and biologically based, or is it socially constructed? Frequently, many non-trans theorists have used trans identities to support constructivist arguments. But increasingly, trans people are questioning whether the deeply held self-understandings they have can be entirely due to nurture and environment" (2006, p. xiii). Contra the claims of post-structuralist thinkers like Judith Butler, biographically based transgender comics narratives suggest an understanding of gender outside of language. This is a theory of gender existing outside nurture and environment, beyond language, visual signs, and social practices—in short, outside of the social altogether. These comics testify to an experiential gender identity, one that arises from within the individual regardless of outside sociolinguistic forces. In these transgender graphic narratives, the transgender individual experiences a gender identity at odds with the physical and linguistic but finds harmony when those conform to his/her/their felt gender. The physical and linguistic do not define the transgender individual's gender, but are instead employed as the mere means of manifesting an internal gender reality.

In the penultimate strip of Julia Kaye's memoir, she writes, "I know I've been told I read as a woman. But makeup still feels like a protective shield. All that's stopping me from being visually misgendered" (2018, p. 157). She can only be misgendered visually or linguistically if she possesses a gender identity existing apart from either of these. Her gender must be independent of them in order for her to be misgendered by them. As she writes in an earlier strip, "I am more than the sum of my parts. I'm a woman" (2018, p. 20). Kaye's identity as a woman exists regardless of her physical body or how others signify her. Appearance and pronouns do not constitute her gender but are the means of manifesting it. In this way, she appeals to an intangible source for her gender identity. Like the pre-modern conception of the soul, this sense of quasi-essentialist identity cannot be located in language, actions, or the body, but exists apart from these altogether while expressing its self through them.

With this approach to gender, biographical transgender comics portray the potential limits of Judith Butler's dominant theoretical model by testifying to the transgender individual's ineffable sense of gender at odds with language and societal norms. While the juxtaposition between academic theory and everyday experience is nothing new, and others such as Stephen Whittle have prior noted its relevance to transgender studies, the dissonance has to date remained unexplored in the realm of transgender comics studies. The gap suggests a possible re-evaluation of the dominant social constructivist approach to gender, one that accounts for the transgender experience as documented in literature, film, and comics. By re-evaluating this social constructivist theory, academics may aid in bridging the age-old gap between academia and popular culture, a sort of societal mind-body gap as it were, and so follow the example of these transgender comics characters.

## REFERENCES

Baetans, Jan. (2001). Revealing Traces: A New Theory of Graphic Enunciation. In Robin Varnum and Christina T. Gibbons (Eds.), *The Language of Comics: Word and Image* (pp. 145–55). Jackson, MS: University Press of Mississippi.

Barczyk, Sarah. (2016). *Nenn mich Kai*. Köln, Germany: Egmont Verlagsgesellschaften.

Butler, Judith. (2007). *Gender Trouble: Feminism and the Subversion of Identity*. New York, NY: Routledge.

Chute, Hillary. (2017). *Why Comics?: From Underground to Everywhere*. New York, NY: HarperCollins.

Edwards, Dylan. (2012). *Transposes*. Seattle, WA: Northwest Press.

Hu, Binglin. (2018, June 22). [Untitled Comic]. *Visibility Has Its Rewards: Six Cartoonists on Gender and Transition*. Retrieved from: https://www.thenib.com/tr ansition-response?id=the-response-x&t=author.

Kaye, Julia. (2018). *Super Late Bloomer: My Early Days in Transition*. Kansas City, MO: Andrews McMeel Publishing.

Morgan, Harry. (2009). Graphic Shorthand: From Caricature to Narratology in Twentieth-Century Bande dessinée and Comics. *European Comic Art*, *2*(1), 21–39.

Murel, Jacob. (2019). An interview with Julia Kaye. *Studies in Comics*, *10*(1), 135–43.

National Center for Transgender Equality. (2016). *Frequently Asked Questions about Transgender People*. Retrieved from: https://www.transequality.org/issues/res ources/frequently-asked-questions-about-transgender-people.

Tresenella. (2013–6). *TransLucid*. Retrieved from: https://www.translucidcomic.com.

Whittle, Stephen. (2006). Foreword. In Susan Stryker and Stephen Whittle (Eds.), *The Transgender Studies Reader* (pp. xi–xvi). New York, NY: Routledge.

## Chapter 8

# Transgender Talk and Conservative Christians

## *Framing a Persuasive Conversation*

### Jim Shoopman

While progressives struggle to heal the suffering and expand the rights of transgender persons, one of the major stakeholders objecting to such expansion are conservative Christian communities. They are a vocal minority and significant voting bloc at election time. This chapter will suggest rhetorical strategies that might be productive in the personal and public discussions that progressives have with the people in these communities. There are pathways to successful dialogue that can, at least sometimes, get past name calling and refusals to discuss the matter any further. Some arguments might even be persuasive.

By "transgender rights" this chapter refers mainly to the right of transgender persons to legally define themselves—on a driver's license for instance, or in a public restroom, by the gender with which they identify. This also refers to the right to obtain gender reassignment surgery as a medically necessary procedure and not as an elective procedure. Transgenders should also have the right to seek redress if they experience violence, harassment, or discrimination, as a protected minority in a culture that overwhelmingly privileges the heterosexual majority. This includes protection from discrimination in hiring and housing, and the right to receive the same business and government services enjoyed by everyone else.

By religious conservatives, this chapter refers primarily (though not exclusively) to two large groups in the United States—evangelicals and conservative Roman Catholics. Neither religious community should be characterized monolithically. Much to the chagrin of European Catholics, Roman Catholicism in the United States is a very complex community that cannot be easily pigeonholed. American Catholics revere their pope and priests but reserve the right to their own opinions on a whole host of social issues, from birth control to the rights of sexual minorities. A 2019 survey by the Public Religion Research Institute reports that 68 percent of responding Roman Catholics were more comfortable in supporting transgender persons than they were five years ago (Greenberg et al., 2019). Despite this range of American Catholic opinion, in June 2019 the Vatican issued an official statement entitled "Male and Female He Created Them: Towards A Path of Dialogue on the Question of Gender Theory in Education." According to one online analysis this official Catholic statement argues that the transgender movement is an instance of placing human desires over an obviously divine mandate (Horgos, 2019). Traditional Catholic argument usually stresses their concept of natural law as an expression of divine intention. Despite these official stances, there exists organized advocacy for sexual minorities within the Roman Catholic church through such associations as Equally Blessed, which describes itself as "a coalition of three Catholic Organizations that have spent more than 120 years working on behalf of LGBT+ people and their families" (Equally Blessed, 2020).

Evangelical Protestants are often lumped together and perceived in popular terms as a religious bloc of predictable social conservatives, but this also is not entirely accurate. Evangelicals themselves cannot even agree on exactly what the term "evangelical" really means. It may be best defined theologically, as the body of Christians who identify the Bible as the primary source of divine revelation, with reason, church tradition, and emotional intuition coming in behind. (While this is a good definition, it is not necessarily always the popular understanding.) It is true, far more so than among Roman Catholics, that a clear majority of these people are social and political conservatives, but not all of them are. Among Baptists for instance, the largest denomination of evangelicals in the United States, there are some who clearly identify as social progressives. In the northern denomination referred to as the American Baptists, there exists an organized minority calling itself the Association of Welcoming and Affirming Baptists, specifically "welcoming and affirming" to LGBTQ people (Association, year). In the southern United States there are two splinter groups from the old Southern Baptist Convention: the mixed and moderate Cooperative Baptist Fellowship (CBF) and the more liberal Alliance of Baptists, who publish and either tolerate or openly promote welcoming and affirming attitudes. The Alliance of Baptists has been "out" on this issue since their 1994 publication "A Clear Voice: Report of the Task Force on Human Sexuality," which sought to welcome and affirm sexual minorities (Alliance, 1994). The CBF is presently divided over hiring policies for sexual minorities. Progressive evangelicals are most certainly a minority, but in private interviews, even with ordinary conservative Southern Baptists, a researcher would likely discover all manner of unlikely individuals who do not necessarily agree with their pastors about sexual identity and orientation issues. All this is to say dialogue is not necessarily fruitless, and these religious groups are not monolithic; many of these people can be reasoned with in private conversations.

For any such dialogue to be fruitful, progressives must move beyond framing religious conservatives within restrictive stereotypes—as people resistant to reason.

It is not uncommon in academia to assume that religious conservatives simply see themselves as guardians of ordinary cultural norms. At one time that might have been true, when large majorities perceived America as a Christian culture, but that has not been the case for quite a long time now, and religious objectors to the LGBTQ social agenda are oftentimes willing to be seen as social outcasts in order to remain consistent with their ideological commitments. Like any other community, they like social approval if they get it, but they do not primarily see themselves as defenders of traditional cultural standards. A recent article in *Christianity Today*, a flagship evangelical periodical, reviewing popular cultural acceptance of transgender rights concludes, with a mixture of pride and sadness, "Evangelical Christians are clearly in the minority on this issue" (Green, 2016). They are sorry for this state of things but not socially embarrassed.

Conservative Christians are also quickly dismissed by academics and progressives, *en-masse*, as bigots toward sexual minorities. Many of them certainly are, but for a great many Christian conservatives, something more complex is at stake. Christian conservatives primarily seek to be biblical and it would be impossible to overstate the importance of this concern. It is their primary intellectual and emotional guidance system. They believe the Bible is a perfect revelation of the creator's nature and God's requirements for human conduct. They will struggle to remain faithful to their best understanding of biblical revelation, even if that religious understanding is out of step with majority culture all around them. They will even romanticize this as a costly rebellion against cultural norms. Whether their immediate local culture affirms or challenges their mores, their understanding of the Bible is what they find most important. Regardless of whether religious conservatives raise a compassion argument, that transgenders and gay or lesbian people are not and cannot be truly happy, or raise a fear argument, that sexual minorities are by nature predators on children and teens (as infamous evangelical celebrity Anita Bryant did in the late 1970s), they are actually struggling against an even greater fear, often unspoken in public debate—that if they affirm social acceptance among sexual minorities, they will be calling the Bible's validity and authority (for most its inerrancy) into question.

For various reasons, both theological and sociological, conservative Christians simply will not do this. An entire body of doctrine, and more basically, an epistemic system for religious knowledge, has developed within all of Christendom, and especially stressed in the evangelical wing, to reinforce the belief that the entire Bible is divinely inspired, meaning it was brought about under God's intentional direction. Regarding the Bible, the Roman Catholic Catechism declares "104: In Sacred Scripture, the Church constantly finds her nourishment and her strength, for she welcomes it not as a human word, 'but as what it really is, the word of God'" (Roman Catholic Catechism, year). On the very first page of a now classic work *Protestant Biblical Interpretation*, evangelical scholar Bernard Ramm declares, "That God has spoken in the scriptures is the very heart of our faith, and without that we would be cast upon the uncertain waters of the relativity of knowledge" (Ramm, 1970, p. 1). The creedal statement that Southern Baptists affirm, the Baptist Faith and Message, declares that the Bible is "inerrant in all that it affirms" (Baptist Faith and Message, 2020). Conservative Christians see the whole body of biblical text hanging together as a meta-narrative which helps them to see the universe as good, just, and ultimately friendly. Like other serious religions that rely on sacred text, Christians perceive the message of the Bible as their path to hope, spiritual forgiveness, and, most of all, *meaning*. Christians believe their religious narratives provide eternal meaning, and this is not something they will easily trade away.

So, in arguments with religious conservatives, progressives who are angry, contemptuous, or dismissive of the Bible, will not get very far in any discussion of any issue. Any persuasive rhetorical strategy will be wiser to treat the sacred text with reasonable respect. Even people who understand the possible value of reasoning about the Bible rather than condemning it, may be reluctant to adopt this strategy, since most progressives know little about biblical literature and academic biblical studies are now a specialty for scholars who spend years on this material. It is no longer a subject of broad general knowledge, and careful scholars are reluctant to deal in literature they really do not know all that well. Argument out of ignorance is certainly slippery ground, but fortunately, to craft a successful argument, a vast body of biblical knowledge is not necessary. The effective arguments in this case, are mostly about *how* the Bible is understood and interpreted, and those concepts can be discussed by any intelligent person.

## THE ARGUMENT FROM CHRISTIAN LOVE—A RHETORICAL DEAD-END

First, progressives sincerely trying to dialogue with religious conservatives require a cautionary note about an argument from biblical content that is often tried but turns out to be ineffective. Doesn't Jesus say in Matthew

22:39, "Love your neighbor as yourself?" Doesn't St. Paul say in Romans 13:8, "Owe no man anything except to love one another?" Wouldn't it be more "loving" to accept the transgender person who wants to join the church, just as he or she is? This ought to work well, but a quick-thinking Christian conservative may immediately remind a progressive academic that "you are not being kind to your student if you tell her that her work is fine when it is in fact riddled with errors." In academia, some educators call a failing grade tough love. Southern Baptist Ethicist Andrew Walker, author of *God and the Transgender Debate*, has written one of the most irenic and gentle conservative salvos into the transgender debate. Walker acknowledges the pain and disorientation of Gender Dysphoria—the agonizing sense that trans people often report that they are, at the core, a different gender than their bodies. Walker is sympathetic and refuses to dismiss or minimize Gender Dysphoria. In the end, however, he insists that "Love does not mean looking someone in the eyes and affirming every desire they experience" (Walker, 2017, p. 98). He suggests that those who suffer from such dysphoria will have a morally better and emotionally more satisfying life if they endure this pain as a sacrifice toward faithful commitment to a Christian conversion. Walker maintains that to be a faithful Christian, some people must accept Gender Dysphoria as the price. As another evangelical argues, regarding engagement with transgenders, "We should seek their wellbeing—but also prepare for strong disagreement on what that entails" (Gilson, 2018).

Walker argues that this sacrifice is necessary because every individual is created with a literally God-given gender and a person has no right to change the divinely ordained nature of one's creation. Alongside the original creation story in which Genesis 1:27 declares *Male and female He created them . . . and it was very good*. The conservative interlocutor will point to biblical passages like Psalm 139:13, *For you created my inmost being; you knit me together in my mother's womb*, and the Book of Jeremiah, where God tells the prophet, "Before I formed you in the womb I knew you, before you were born I set you apart." These Bible verses suggest to the religious conservative that every single individual is a separate and specific creation, made to be exactly the way they are. Even more than the gay marriage rights debate, the transgender rights debate gets into deep territory as an argument about the theology of creation itself. But there are some very significant hidden assumptions behind the argument that people are intended to live "just as they are," coming out of the womb. The most important conservative assumption in this argument is that God *intends* all of human creation to be either purely male or female, and if people insist that their anatomy does not match their true gender, they are telling God that he made a mistake—and that is impossible. The characters cannot tell the author, "I am different than you wrote me to be." As the Apostle Paul argues in Romans 9:20 (regarding a very different issue), *Shall what is formed say to the one who formed it, "Why did you make me like this?"* From the conservative religious perspective, a trans person who does this is living in defiance of God's obviously manifest will, and perhaps like the poor term paper writer in a professor's class, needs to be corrected for her own good. That *is* loving her as you love yourself.

Walker believes he has the right to call for this "correction" of a transgender person because he frames trans person longing for cultural acceptance and a gender reassignment procedure as a "desire," much akin to the strong desire for a particular kind of pleasure or satisfaction. This resembles the line of thought in the 2019 pontifical pronouncement that referred to transgender drives as "nothing more than a confused concept of freedom in the realm of *feelings and wants*" (Vatican, "Male and Female He Created Them" (italics mine), 2019). It is difficult to imagine anyone accepting the onslaught of social rejection and alienation dished out toward lifetime, simply on the basis of an ordinary sense of "desire." Granted, desire is at play, but there is most certainly something much more serious involved than a desire for a particular pleasure or form of satisfaction. The desire to feel authentic to one's public identity and the desire to put an end to Gender Dysphoria are far more serious than wanting to scratch an itch. It is a desire to alleviate a very peculiar and particular kind of pain.

Generally, in twenty-first-century America, when someone is in some form of pain, deprivation, or dysfunction, we address this need with medicine, surgery, or other forms of therapy. In the transgender friendly book *Transforming: The Bible and the Lives of Transgender Christians*, Lutheran theological trans advocate Austen Hartke argues "while we may believe that imperfections in eyesight are related to the fall [from the initial perfection of divine creation], . . . that doesn't mean that getting fitted for glasses is wrong" (Hartke, p. 38). As a matter of compassion, most people today allow and even encourage others to seek relief for their pain—unless their pain arises from their assigned gender identity. An evangelical reviewer of Hartke's book, Rachel Gilson, is critical of the logic behind Hartke's analogy of getting fitted for glasses to correct imperfect vision, referring to it as "a strange metaphor, given that glasses help weak or damaged eyes do what they were designed to do, whereas a movement to affirm a gender identity separate from biological sex impacts a (usually) healthy, fully functioning body. The glasses metaphor misfires" (Gilson, 2018). Hartke's evangelical reviewer imagines that she has scored a clever point against Hartke's argument, but this is only because she refuses to take into account the very real pain of Gender Dysphoria. Transgender persons do not feel "healthy" in the bodies of their birth. On the contrary, they feel a continuous sense of unhealthy disease that can be alleviated through the redefinition of their physical genders.

Religious conservatives assume that if a person is born with healthy and unambiguously male or female genitalia then God created that person to conform to the sex of his or her genitalia. Any desire to be a different gender than the presenting genitals is regarded by conservatives as a mental disorder and it is the mind which is perceived to be out of order, not the genitalia. In 2017, the Trump administration revoked a federal policy on the provision of gender reassignment treatments for transgender military personnel. It is this author's memory that one White House aid was quoted to explain, "I'm not obligated to pay for a surgery just because some crazy guy thinks he's a woman." While this memory cannot be properly documented, it speaks for a common attitude of both religious and secular conservatives.

It is, of course, possible, that some folk who see themselves as transgender are just "crazy guys" who think they are women (or women who imagine they are men), but when people are in pain, it is usually best to trust their own description of the discomfort. Transgenders do not report their pain as a "crazy" sense of being out of control. They do not run around, out of touch with everyday reality, crying out, "I'm a woman, look at my dress! Call me Mary, right now!" Rather they are in a special kind of agony in which they feel like they need to be women (or in the inverse case men) in order to feel whole—fully human and at ease in their own skin. Left unaddressed, they live in grief at a lost life that might have been for as long as they have breath. The problem does not seem to be as simple as something fixable by mental health therapy and at present, mental health professionals do not see psychotherapy, hormone therapy, or genetic therapy as a useful solution, but do suggest that gender reassignment surgery may alleviate some of the internal pain these people feel. In a 2017 Amicus court-brief filing, the Litigation Center of the American Medical Association declared "It is now understood that being transgender implies no impairment in a person's judgment, stability, or general social or vocational capabilities," the brief stated. "Gender dysphoria is a condition characterized by clinically significant distress and impairment of function resulting from the incongruence between one's gender identity and the sex assigned at birth" (Henry, 2019).

Sexuality, for function and identity, is an astonishingly complex blend of physiology and psychology, where ideas, feelings, nerves, muscles, and hormones must interact in very precise ways to arrive at the "standard" sexual identity and function. Despite the many ways this mix can vary, the vast majority of people come out of the womb in what we have come to call the "normal" way—their genitalia match their internal sense of gender identity and they are sexually attracted to the opposite sex, but with so many factors involved, it's easy to understand how, once in a great while, someone might get a different mix.

A different mix, something out of the ordinary, is what seems to have happened when people report either Gender Dysphoria or same-sex attraction. Faced with such anomalies, religious conservatives accuse transgenders of saying "God got my gender wrong, and I wish to correct God's handiwork." But this is not what most transgenders are "saying" when they seek to align their gender with their internal compass. It is also not what most "normal people" are saying when they seek to accommodate other kinds of birth anomalies. Left-handed folk are not saying "God created me incorrectly and I must adjust for his poor handiwork." While sexual birth anomalies are relatively rare, birth anomalies in general happen often, in various ways. Some people seem "born" to superior intelligence, physical strength, or a greater height, that can be wisely accommodated to great advantage. Other people are born with physical handicaps or mental limitations or are born left-handed in a right-handed world, often to great disadvantage. Mozart was composing sonatas at three years old, while the accomplished physicist Stephen Hawking developed Lou Gehrig's disease early in life. If Mozart had been discouraged—"You are too young to be playing a piano," or if Stephen Hawking had been rejected rather than accommodated in dealing with his medical condition, "people who can't walk or talk normally can't work with other theoretical physicists," the world would have been a great deal poorer. In the gospel of John, chapter 9, when Jesus encountered the man born blind, he did not say, "Since this man was born blind, it is clearly God's will that he remain blind." Most modern religious conservatives do not seek to block accommodation or reversal of most birth anomalies (advantageous or disadvantageous) with the exception of matters related to sexual identity and preference.

In matters of sexual identity and attraction, most well-informed religious conservatives, using Walker as one example, no longer deny the existence of gender dysphoria or same-sex attraction, but they seem to suggest that these birth anomalies are functions of a disordered, spiritually fallen world and exist for the same reason as disease in general or tornados and hurricanes—as tragic challenges to be endured or (in the case of sexual anomalies) temptations to be overcome. They hold a theology of creation that assumes each individual is specifically made to order and every birth anomaly is divinely allowed for a reason. It provides the opportunity to build character or lead a person to depend upon God. The anomaly is a part of one's fated journey toward spiritual development.

Such a theology is tremendously insensitive to the enormous pain endured by countless persons born out of step with their culture, out of step with their time, or even out of step with ordinary bodily needs. While in graduate school, I once knew a nurse at Tulane Hospital who worked on the neo-natal ward. One night she was called to hold and rock an infant born without an outer layer of skin, a ball of unrelenting pain that cried itself to death over the course of a few hours, probably *Aplasia Cutis Congenita* (Aplasia, 2020). It is impossible to discern a divine purpose behind such an anomaly. Thankfully, such un-relievable pain is rare, but even one such birth should call the standard monotheistic theologies of creation into serious question. In a world where myriad individuals are born to lifelong pain in countless ways, the standard monotheistic theological belief that each individual birth is carefully overseen and directed from heaven needs to be rethought. This chapter is not the place for that conversation, but in the meantime, as Christians, Jews, and Muslims labor over theologies of birth, at the very least they are obligated to offer compassionate solutions for the pain of those who are not born to the norm. Andrew Walker may think he is sufficiently generous to acknowledge the pain of gender dysphoria, but "tough it out for God," when some amelioration of such pain is available, is not a compassionate response.

Before leaving Walker's argument, it is worth mentioning that he rightly points out transgenders are not entirely freed from psychological problems and anxieties, even after they undergo gender reassignment surgery (Walker, 2017, p. 67). He brings this up as if it were the clincher to his whole argument against a transgender person trying to adopt a different gender than the one provided at birth. It is as if he is saying, "You think you will solve all your gender identity issues by adjusting your sex to your desires, but this does not solve all your problems at all." He is no doubt correct. No person alive ever views all their sexual dilemmas or painful problems through some mythological rearview mirror. The question for the transgender person is, given that you will never escape all of your sexual problems or anxieties, which set of problems would you rather deal with—those of a person struggling with gender dysphoria and nearly impossible longings, or the problems of a person who is transitioned to a better or even perfect fit?

Because of Walker's belief that one's genital-gender is a biblical mandate, he and his allies counsel endurance of gender-disorientation for the whole of one's life. So, how do progressives argue with someone who is certain they have all they need to know from a source in which they have absolute confidence? Progressives could tell them to dismiss the source of their confidence but given the value that religious conservatives attach to sacred text, that will probably just end the discussion. The key to a more successful rhetorical response is to talk about how to see the answers in the book differently. This is often the approach of religious leaders in debate with each other about how to interpret their sacred texts. Think of conservative Christians as a separate subculture, with a key textual-language, who can be reasoned with, if their language and assumptions are at least respected. There are at least three avenues toward more progressive arguments that could successfully engage religious conservatives, using language they can relate to and respect.

## STRESSING SOUND SCIENTIFIC RESEARCH:
## THE ETHOS OF AUTHORITY

One might think an appeal to scientific authority would *not* be a very productive way to go, since religious conservatives often seem to be hostile to good science. "My mind is made up, don't confuse me with the facts." Some of them certainly seem to be resistant to the theory of evolution and the science of climate change, for instance. But looking carefully at how most religious conservatives frame their response to such challenges, you will see that *everyone* in the Western world lives in a post-Galileo universe, including religious persons. A handful of Old Testament Bible passages unambiguously suggest that all the heavenly bodies revolve around the earth. In the early 1600s, Galileo changed the scientific understanding of this matter, eventually forcing the church to a different understanding of those Bible passages. There are still a few flat-earthers out there, but by and large no Bible-believing Christian today interprets the scripture to require belief in an earth-centered universe. In his book, *Myths, Models and Paradigms: A Comparative Study in Science and Religion*, Ian Barbour argues "religious beliefs . . . are highly resistant to falsification, but the cumulative weight of evidence does count decisively for or against them in the long run, in comparison to alternative interpretations" (Barbour, 1974, p. 131). He suggests even a recalcitrant religious community will eventually reinterpret religious beliefs in terms of what is proved to be there by the science. Since the time of Galileo's argument, and in view of its long-term success, it seems clear that all of Western culture, including Christian culture, has struggled to scientifically verify beliefs about the world and how it works. This is why some conservative Christians have created a discipline called "creation science" to challenge evolutionary theory on its own ground. This is why they insist that climate change is not scientifically proven to be a man-made phenomenon and why Walker finds it necessary to belabor the idea that "The best research has offered no conclusive evidence that experiences of gender dysphoria are the result of any particular factor or factors" (Walker, 2017, p. 34). Because all modern religious conservatives are post-Galileo thinkers, if the science is eventually irrefutable, they will eventually be forced to adjust their interpretation of these scriptures.

There are two ways they can go with scientific evidence that internal gender identification is an irreversible condition of birth: they can affirm that God created some people transgender and these people have every right to pursue this to its logical conclusion, or second, they can affirm that anomalous conditions of birth are usually random accidents of nature and these people have every right to adjust for this, in accord with what is useful to alleviate pain and make some level of happiness or fulfilment possible.

These two directions of thought are strictly suggestions, and there may be other ways they could reason their way toward tolerance, but to begin with, they need to be convinced of the science, or at least convinced of the sincerity of people's personal experience with gender. In either case, however, conservative Christians are faced with the need to reinterpret what appears to be "the plain meaning of scripture." So is such significant reinterpretation something they can be successfully encouraged to do.

## STRESSING THOSE IDEAS IN THE BIBLE
## THAT HAVE BEEN REINTERPRETED

The fact is all religions adjust their understandings of sacred texts to new understandings of the world and how it works. A recent Supreme Court decision ruled that the 1964 Civil Rights Act protects the employment of LGBTQ persons. In protesting this decision, Russell Moore, the President of the Southern Baptist Ethics and Religious Liberty Commission said "There's a common assumption in secular America that evangelicals and Roman Catholicism and other forms of religion will morph and change along with it . . . I don't think that's true" (Dias, *New York Times*, 2018). On the contrary, Christians have been "morphing" and changing in reaction to new information and changing ethical perspectives since the beginning of the religion; Galileo's previously mentioned heliocentric discovery is only one example. The most important instance of Christian biblical reinterpretation in American history is related to the problem of slavery. Conservative Christians need to be reminded of such reinterpretations. This is a roundabout appeal to the ethos of "virtu," an appropriate reflection of what the community has come to value.

Today one will not find a single mainstream conservative Christian community which believes it is right for one person to own another. There probably are a very few, very small wing-nut racist sects that would be fine with it, (some of them probably marched in Charlottesville), but practically speaking, Christians around the world have abandoned the idea that slavery is a "biblical" notion. And yet, the Old Testament assumes slavery to be part of the ordinary course of things, and that divinely given Mosaic Law regulates its practice. Granted, the Old Testament calls for humane treatment of slaves in a time when that was unusual, but it never calls for abandoning the practice as unethical (Exodus 21:1–11). Later, the Christian scriptures encourage slaves to gain their freedom if they can (1st Cor. 7:21), and the Apostle Paul even encourages Philemon, a slave owner, to free the slave Onesimus (Philemon vs. 6), but Paul does not encourage Philemon to free all of his slaves; in Ephesians 6:5–8, he calls on Christian slaves to be the best slaves they can be, in order to prove the life-changing nature of the believer's message.

Most Christians are unaware that slave ownership is *not ever forbidden* in any part of the Bible. Before the American Civil War, southern preachers argued from a great many biblical passages that slavery was an institution sanctioned by God and that "abolitionism was "the final antichrist" (Gourley, 2010, p. 2). Church historian Mark Noll says, "With relentless pressure, skillful defenders of slavery insisted that any attack on a literalist construction of Biblical slavery was an attack on the Bible itself. . . . To propose for whatever reason that the Bible did not sanction slavery was to attack not just slavery but the Bible as well" (Noll 51–52). The similarity to the argument among Christians today regarding equality and freedom for LGBTQ people is striking. During the Civil War, a southern woman's diary repeated the "commonplace charge that Yankees had thrown away their Bibles to embrace fanaticism" (Rable, 2010, p. 224).

Despite all this, today, Christians of almost every stripe, everywhere in America have come to hold <u>zero</u> tolerance for slavery of any kind. This is a genuine change from the New Testament's literal teaching on this issue. To arrive at this conclusion, most conservative Christians have eventually embraced the belief that certain biblical laws or customs are limited to the cultural mores of a particular period. Previously mentioned evangelical scholar Bernard Ramm cautions, "We must interpret the Bible with the realization that it is a progressive revelation" (Ramm, 1970, pp. 80, 90). This approach to the Bible saves them from being forced to support Old Testament laws that would be considered immoral or meaningless by today's standard. The Bible's text has not changed, but in the matter of slavery, moved by better information and a sense of compassion, nearly all Christians have come to interpret biblical text in new ways that allow them to perceive "God's perfect will" differently. In modern Christian churches, the passages about slaves and masters are now applied to the relationships between employers and employees. Please note this interpretive change does not involve anything the Bible says but involves reasoning *about* the Bible and how it might reveal religious truth.

This general interpretive principle of seeing much specific biblical law as conditional to its time is now commonly accepted, even by very conservative Christians, if for no other reason than it gets the Bible off the hook for affirming actions that we would regard as criminal today. We do not, for instance, stone rebellious children to death (Deuteronomy 21:18–21). The more complex question now is whether to apply that principle to any particular biblical admonition.

Conservative Christians can do this in regard to transgender rights and needs; they are just very uncomfortable with doing so. Indeed, they probably will eventually adjust their interpretation of the Bible to allow for transgender rights, just as they did for slavery. In the meantime, the two most persuasive rhetorical strategies are to speak up in support of scientific authorities and suggest that these people reinterpret their understandings of biblical passages in light of newer and better information. It is useless to demand that such people abandon their sacred texts. It is much more helpful to suggest that they reinterpret these texts. The Bible never says, anywhere, that everyone is personally created in exactly the form they are to exist for a lifetime. That is an interpretation of texts that can be understood in different ways. Given the facts regarding anomalies of birth, there is a better interpretation that has the virtue of not directly blaming the creator for terrible forms of suffering. This requires a respectful suggestion that conservatives revise their understanding of religious text. In order to do this, interlocutors must show some respect for religious language. Challengers do not have to agree with the conservatives' religious beliefs or their sacred texts to show thoughtful respect for these assumptions that are spiritual sources of meaning, hope, and direction.

## SUGGESTING THE BIBLE DOES OFFER HOPE FOR SEXUAL MINORITIES

Finally, there is one more rhetorical strategy to suggest, which is more challenging to use because it requires a little more knowledge of actual biblical text, and deals not just with how the Bible can be interpreted but requires wading into a debate about biblical content. It is often suggested that the Bible has nothing positive to say about non-traditional sexualities, and that all of what it says about these matters must be reinterpreted or set aside, like the passages regarding slavery, in modern day, but that may not be entirely the case. It is true that the Bible has many negative things to say about alternative sexual lifestyles. However, it is possible the Bible does have at least one very powerful and forward-thinking text, that offers significant hope to the sexually excluded, for a time when "God's perfect will" is better understood. The Old Testament oracle from Isaiah 56:3–5 (RSV):

> Let no foreigner who is bound to the *Lord* say, "The *Lord* will surely exclude me from his people." And let no eunuch complain, "I am only a dry tree."[4] For this is what the *Lord* says: "To the eunuchs who keep my Sabbaths, who choose what pleases me and hold fast to my covenant[5]—to them I will give within my temple and its walls a memorial and a name better than sons and daughters; I will give them an everlasting name that will endure forever."

An ordinary and devout Hebrew would have been shocked to see the Hebrew eunuch promised a beautiful place in the Kingdom of God, because the Old Testament laws had forbidden eunuchs and foreigners from worshipping inside the Hebrew Temple of the Lord (Deuteronomy 23:1). Eunuchs were castrated men, who had been, for that reason alone, set outside the Temple and the right to worship as Hebrews because they were regarded as, by nature, sexually "outside the norm." This way of being in the world set Hebrew eunuchs apart and prevented their inclusion in Temple worship. No matter how much a eunuch longed to worship the Hebrew God, he would never be a fully included part of the tribe, welcome to worship with the ordinary Hebrew men. Even so, the gracious and optimistic promise of Isaiah is that a day would come when even the eunuch would be invited by God himself to be a part of the divine Kingdom. What had been thought to be an eternal principle, the exclusion of the eunuch, Isaiah declared to be a conditional rule that would one day be amended.

Obviously, ritual acceptance of a eunuch is not the same thing as an every-day secular gender reassignment surgery, but it certainly seems to be in the same general category—something set apart from the cisgender-norm. In his book *Trans*forming (2018), Hartke places a great deal of hope in this pas-sage, discussing it at length in the latter part of his book. He says, "through Isaiah God gave me a sense of belonging I couldn't shake. I believed that by declaring those outside the gender binary to be acceptable, God declared me acceptable" (Hartke, 2018, p. 99). A religious conservative might argue that the ancient eunuchs were usually forced into castration, while the transgender person willfully chooses to change his or her gender identity. But Isaiah says nothing about a distinction between eunuchs by choice and forced eunuchs, and when the Deacon Philip baptizes the Ethiopian Eunuch in Acts chapter 8, the question does not come up. The only question seems to be whether the Eunuch wishes to be a part of the Kingdom of God and there are plenty of transgender persons who would join churches with the same enthusiasm if they were allowed to do so. Hartke reports that "half of queer identified adults claim a religious affiliation, and 17 percent consider their faith a very important part of their lives" (Hartke, p. 11).

## CONCLUSION

This chapter seeks to explain how to understand the true motivations of conservative Christians whose attitudes seem increasingly mysterious to a more and more secularized culture. Progressives are usually unaware of what religious conservatives have at stake in these arguments beyond a simplistic "fear of change." This chapter also suggests strategies for a more persuasive communication and engagement with that vocal and influential subculture. Not all conservative Christians can be easily dismissed as simple bigots, haters, or irrational defenders of an outdated social code. Just as often, they are people struggling to remain faithful to the core of their beliefs, trusting in what they perceive to be the authority and truth of their sacred texts. They fear loss of confidence in that authority beyond almost all other concerns.

To communicate with them, this chapter suggests that progressives reason with them through the authority of science and through the language of their texts. Conservative Christians do not want to even see *themselves* as anti-scientific—that is why they sometimes go hunting for their own "alternative facts" through Fox News or the Creation Science Research Center. A steady drumbeat on implications of good scientific truth can work like water over rock, to eventually wear down the strongest resistance to truthful evidence. Add to this a reminder that Christians have adjusted their understanding of Bible verses before, to put the sun in the center of the solar system, and to set enslaved people free. Finally, through this avenue, progressives are able to come back around to claims that the Bible can be a book of hope and love for those who are suffering and excluded. Isaiah's hope for inclusion of the cast aside Eunuch, who longs to be included in the Kingdom of God, is an inspiring jewel within the Hebrew Prophetic tradition. Progressives can stress how the Godly Eunuch suffered for his exclusion and must have rejoiced in this word of hope from one of the greatest prophets. Conservative Christians, faithful to their scripture, can give the same kind of hope to the transgender Christian who wants to be a part of their spiritual family.

It is not a lost cause to enter into spirited dialogue between people who see the world very differently. Interaction between progressives and conservative Christians can get beyond name calling and mutual condemnation, but someone must begin by abandoning prejudiced assumptions about the other. Religious conservatives tend to assume they own the ethical high ground but respectful progressives can lead them to doubt that assumption by treating them more respectfully. Religious conservatives are used to feeling the contempt and condescension of progressive opposition, and vice versa. If progressives can check their contempt at the door and discuss the matter with empathy for what religious people have at stake in the argument, effective dialogue can begin.

## REFERENCES

Alliance of Baptists. "A Clear Voice: Report of the Task Force on Human Sexuality," 1994. The text of this report can be found at https://www.sitemason.com/files/goS LAc/Task%20Force%20on%20Human%20Sexualit y.pdf. Retrieved June 10, 2020.
"Aplasia Cutis Congenita." NIH National Center for Advancing Transitional Sciences/GARD Genetic and Rare Diseases Information Center. https://raredis eases.info.nih.gov/diseases/5835/aplasia-cutis-congenita. Retrieved June 10, 2020.
Association of Welcoming and Affirming Baptists. https://awab.org/. Retrieved June 10, 2020. This is a referral to the homepage of their website.
*Baptist Faith and Message.* The Southern Baptist Convention. https://www.hsbchurc h.com/Misc_Images/Hsbchurch.com_misc_image49318.pdf. Retrieved June 20, 2020.

Barbour, Ian. *Myths, Models and Paradigms*: *A Comparative Study in Science and Religion*. New York: Harper & Row, 1974.

Dias, Elizabeth. *New York Times*. https://www.nytimes.com/2020/06/15/us/lgbtq-s upreme- court-religious-freedom.html. Retrieved June 23, 2020.

Equally Blessed. https://www.glaad.org/blog/catholic-lgbt-families. Retrieved June 23, 2020.

Gilson, Rachel. "Embracing Our Transgender Neighbors on God's Terms: We Should Seek Their Well-Being—But Also Prepare for Strong Disagreement on What That Entails," June 22, 2018. Retrieved June 10, 2020. Review of Austen Hartke, Transforming: The Bible & the Lives of Transgender Christians.

Gourley, Bruce. "Yes, the Civil War Was About Slavery." *Baptists and the American Civil War-In Their Own Words, Civilwarbaptists.com,* December 23, 2010. Web. 27 May 2015. Retrieved June 10, 2020.

Green, Lisa Cannon. "Where Evangelicals Stand on Transgender Morality: LifeWay Research Looks at How Americans Feel About Changing Genders." *Facts & Trends*, July 14, 2016. https://www.christianitytoday.com/news/2016/july/w here-evangelicals-stand-on-transgender-morality-lifeway.html. Retrieved June 10, 2020.

Greenberg, Daniel, with Maxine Najle, PhD, Natalie Jackson, PhD, Oyindamola Bola, Robert P. Jones, PhD "America's Growing Support for Transgender Rights." https://www.prri.org/research/americas-growing-support-for-transgender-rights/ 6/11/19. Retrieved June 10, 2020.

Hartke, Austen. *Transforming: The Bible & the Lives of Transgender Christians*. Louisville, KY: Westminster John Knox Press, 2018.

Henry, Tanya Albert. "AMA Advises U. S. Supreme Court on Transgender Individuals Rights." American Medical Association. https://www.ama-assn.org/ delivering-care/population- care/ama-advises-us-supreme-court-transgender-indi viduals-rights. 7/12/19. Retrieved June 10, 2020.

Horgos, Bonnie. "The Vatican Draws a Line on Gender, and Transgender Catholics Push Back." Religion & Politics: Fit for Polite Company, July 30, 2019. https://re ligionandpolitics.org/2019/07/30/the-vatican-draws-a-line-on-gender-and- trans gender-catholics-push-back/ Retrieved June 4, 2020.

Noll, Mark A. "The Bible and Slavery." In Randall Miller, Harry S. Stout and Charles Reagan Wilson (eds.), *Religion and the American Civil War*. Oxford University Press, 1998.

Rable, George C. *God's Almost Chosen People: A Religious History of the American Civil War*. Chapel Hill, NC: University of North Carolina Press, 2010. Print.

Ramm, Bernard. *Protestant Biblical Interpretation: A Textbook of Hermeneutics*. 1950, 3rd revised edition, Grand Rapids, MI: Baker Book House, 1970 (original 1950).

Roman Catholic Catechism, line 104, https://www.vatican.va/archive/ccc_css/archiv e/catechism/p1s1c2a3.htm Retrieved 6/5/20.

Walker, Andrew T. *God and the Transgender Debate: What Does the Bible Actually Say About Gender Identity*. The Good Book Company 2017, reprinted 2018.

*Chapter 9*

# Transgender and Transracial Identity

## *A Cultural Examination of "Passing"*

### Rachel Friedman and Ashley B. Maxwell

Gender and race are two identities that are often ascribed to biology. While gender is a sociocultural construct, it is often decided based on biological sex (males being XY and females XX). However, cross-culturally, masculinity and femininity vary on a gradient, and in fact, some cultures have what is known as third genders (Hollimon, 2015; Tuvel, 2017). Similarly, race is often assumed to be biological, based on certain features that are visible, such as skin color, eye shape, hair texture, and so on; however, there is no genetic basis for race (Goodman et al., 2019; Gravlee, 2009). Most people assumed to belong to a particular race are more genetically dissimilar than those categorized in different racial groups (Lewontin, 1972). While race is not biological, it is cultural, with well-defined inequalities (Gravlee, 2009). We, as a society, have come to create these cultural identities of gender and race, which begs the question, how fluid are these categories today? This chapter aims to explore how transgender and transracial identities are formed, and the contentious roles they play in society. To do so, we look at two polarizing public figures, Caitlyn Jenner, who is a transwoman, and Rachel Dolezal, a transracial Black woman, and discuss how they constructed their identities through their autobiographies. Second, we dive into how transgender and transracial communities navigate the boundaries of race and gender.

## GENDER AND RACE

Social scientists have a good understanding of how social identities are formed. It is a combination of biology and culture. For example, gender is often ascribed to babies *in utero*, with gender reveal parties that are based on what genetic sex a doctor has announced. Specific color arrangements and ideas about what that child's role should be in the society are assumed before the child is even born. But what about children who are intersex? What is often difficult for people to understand is that children at a fairly young age (around five or six) have a good understanding of how they identify, in terms of race, gender, and sexuality (Connolly, 1998). As the LGBTQ+ community is expanding, we see gender-neutral restrooms become more accepted and prevalent (although it tends to be in certain states/places such as academia). Gendered norms in the United States are beginning to become more fluid and acceptable, although there are still ways to go (Tuvel, 2017).

As with gender, when we construct our racial identities, we are doing so through determined racial groups of American society, which often do not conform to actual ancestral histories (Tuvel, 2017). Thus, social constructs of race are malleable, meaning, they could change based on how society classifies people into racial categories. How then, does one identify their racial membership? Charles Mills (1998) suggests the following five categories:

(1) Self-awareness of ancestry
(2) Public awareness of ancestry
(3) Culture
(4) Experience
(5) Self-identification

As mentioned, children by the age of five or six can have a good understanding of theirs and others' racial typologies (Connolly, 1998). The United States is still a highly racialized society, and some may argue now more than ever. This is most likely where we see differences in the acceptance of transgender and transracial identities. It should be no surprise that passing as a man or a woman, or as a different race, is political and often controversial.

## THEORETICAL FRAMEWORK

What follows is an analysis of Jenner's and Dolezal's desire to transition and pass as part of the larger communities to which they identify; Jenner as a woman and Dolezal as Black. As mentioned, we will apply social identification theory to the actions of Dolezal and Jenner. Thus, their behaviors and actions are examined as they:

(1) Perceive themselves to be more similar to each other (Allen and Wilder, 1975, 1979; Mackie, 1986)—Tajifel and Turner (p. 79)
(2) Are more likely to act cooperatively (Abrams et al., 1990; Back, 1951)

(3) Feel a stronger need to agree with group opinion (Deutsch and Gerard, 1955; Mackie et al., 1992; Wilder, 1990)
(4) Perceive in-group messages to be of higher quality (Brock, 1965; Mackie et al., 1990)
(5) Conform more in both behavior and attitude (French and Raven, 1959; Wilder and Shapiro, 1984).

While Jenner and Dolezal participate in all of these identity conforming behaviors, we would like to focus on the fifth component of *conform[ing] more in both behavior and attitude* for the purpose of this analysis, especially as it relates to transracial adoptions.

## THE POLITICS OF PASSING

Caitlyn Jenner's book, *Call me Caitlyn* and Rachel Dolezal's book, *In Full Color: Finding My Place in a Black and White World* shed light on the various ways people construct their identity in the public eye, and how contentious it can be within the communities with which and with whom they identify. What follows is an analysis of Jenner's and Dolezal's desire to transition and pass as part of the larger communities with which they identify.
According to newsstatesmen.com (2016),

> It's a shame, because, as Rogers Brubaker argues in his pacy and stimulating extended essay *Trans*, it is in the in-betweenness that our binaries break down, whether we are talking about nature *v* nurture (where discoveries in epigenetics are busy dissolving firm oppositions); male and female (those tired categories with which trans politics is playing havoc); or, most interestingly, black *v* white.

Dolezal is interesting because she exemplifies this binary. She was living as a Black woman, engaged in the Black community as the president of the NAACP Spokane, Washington chapter. When people found out that her ancestry was White, they were very upset, which is understandable as the life she portrayed to the Black community was a perceived lie. What is unique to Dolezal's case is that her sense of "passing," is not what has historically been understood as passing through the Black community. She wanted to pass or be seen as Black. When most people of color talk about passing, it is usually as passing for White or Caucasian. So while her life and work as a Black woman were considered to be a lie by most people, she was not trying to pass for the dominant, more privileged White race in America. As Dolezal (2017) points out, "Why would a White person ever want to pass for Black when doing so would involve losing social and economic benefits" (p. 148). We believe her commentary suggests she understood the societal baggage that came with being Black, but still aligned herself with this identity. However, some could argue that she climbed an economic platform through the NAACP and came into a position of power.

The transition of Dolezal's identity as a Black woman comes when she considers herself to be fully accepted by the Black community. Dolezal (2017) writes:

> I wasn't merely "passing" as a Black woman. Passing has existed in the United States as long as White people have oppressed people of color, which is to say for its entire history. Typically, it's been light-skinned Black people who have passed for White in an attempt to accrue the same advantages White people enjoyed: to acquire gainful employment, avoid discrimination, and preclude the possibility of being lynched. . . . My situation was different. Just as a transgender person might be born male but identify as female, I wasn't pretending to be something I wasn't but expressing something I already was. I wasn't passing as Black. I was Black, and there was no going back. (p. 148)

Dolezal embraced blackness in a series of ways dating back to her childhood (in Montana) as well as when she cared for her Black siblings. She says her father Larry (whom she calls Larry, not "dad") adopted children for tax breaks after she and her brother turned eighteen. They supposedly wanted White children, but because of institutional racism, White children are harder to adopt. Thus, he adopted four children of African descent with their favorite being Ezra whose mother was White so he was light-skinned and they called him the "smart one" (Dolezal, 2017, p. 55). Izaiah was their second favorite, again for his lighter skin and being male was a bonus given their religious background. Esther was next in favor followed by Zach, their least favorite because of his "blue Black" color (p. 55). Needless to say, Dolezal took on some of the cultural and parenting roles to help her siblings move forward both in this family and in this world. She often braided her sister's hair (she had to learn through books) so her sister Esther was properly cared for. She cites buying thicker lotion for their skin and good shampoo and conditioner. She also read up on African American history and took to educating her siblings (Dolezal, 2017).

She went to Belhaven University, a Christian college in Mississippi. In college, Dolezal joined an all-Black church in West Jackson and joined the Black Student Association and became the historian even though she showed up to Belhaven "looking like [she'd] just stepped off the set of Little House on the Prairie or escaped from a religious cult" (p. 78). She quickly became an activist trying to recruit more minority students and work on retention. She is also an artist so her body of work centered on Black and African culture. Dolezal made concerted efforts to appear Black. She writes:

> As I got more involved with the BSA, campus activism, and my artwork, the more Afrocentric my appearance became. I started wearing my hair in *Poetic Justice* box braids and sporting dashikis and African-patterned dresses. I thought the patterns and embroidery of these clothes were beautiful. . . . As a result, most people didn't know what to make of me. "So what are you?" I was asked all too often. (Dolezal, 2017, p. 84)

Her responses typically consisted of ramblings about having White parents, Black siblings, and identifying more with Black culture. She eventually stopped telling people about her upbringing and allowed them to assume she was Black (either as an albino Black woman, a light-skinned woman, a mixed-race woman, etc.). One of her Black friends even claimed that Rachel was blacker than she (who was born of African descent) (Dolezal, 2017). If we recall Mills's (1998) categories for determining racial membership, Dolezal could be pushed into the Black racial category (Tuvel, 2017). Her self-identification, exposure to Black culture, and experience living/identifying as an active member of the Black community reaffirm her belief that she is Black in areas that view racial membership this way (aka, the United States) (Tuvel, 2017).

For Caitlyn Jenner, she received more backlash for her political views, than the actual act of being transgender. She was placed on the cover of *Vanity Fair* but it was her lack of understanding of the community she transitioned to that was the issue, not because she transitioned gender. This might suggest that it is more socially acceptable to transition your gender than race. Jenner has a similar, but more polarizing perspective on her identity as she writes:

> Several months later, in a lengthy interview in *Time* magazine in December 2015 after being on the short list for Person of the Year, I was asked a question about image. I gave the following reply: One thing that has always been important to me, and it may seem very self-absorbed or whatever, is first of all your presentation of who you are. I think it's much easier for a trans woman or a trans man who authentically kind of looks and plays the role. So what I call my presentation I try to take that seriously. I think it puts people at ease. If you're out there and, to be honest with you, if you look like a man in a dress, it makes people uncomfortable.

This best and perhaps most problematically explains Jenner's style of conforming in both behavior and attitude. Part of the controversy with Jenner is her inability to understand what the average person experiences in life, especially the typical struggle of a transgender individual. So for her, looking like a woman is important to her identity (as well as making others feel at ease). This is nothing new to the concept of passing but it is also a superficial view of what it means to be a woman. As many people know, she has had to apologize to the trans community on more than one occasion, most recently in August 2017 for her Trump MAGA hat. Without taking political sides, Trump decided to ban transgender people from the military while also rolling back the Obama-era protections for transgender children in schools. Nonetheless, Jenner has had a female identity from a young age questioning all of the sports she played when she was Bruce, questioning all three of her marriages, and so forth. She is also fully aware of how the trans community feels about her. Jenner writes:

> The trans community already has issues with me, and I've only reached my four-month anniversary. They are fabulous, but some can be tough and critical, frustrating and debilitating at times. I am already hearing I am not "representative" of the community. I certainly won't dispute that, although such judgment strikes me as hostile and exclusionary and counterproductive to our collective cause, since much of our fight is to get society to remove such meaningless labels as *representative*. We are all in this together, or at least we should be. (Jenner, 2017, p. 46)

Perhaps this is the nature of trying to pass; but the majority of ways in which Dolezal and Jenner work toward passing for these identities are based in cis-normative stereotypes (i.e., the clothes and makeup for women and the clothes and hair styles for African Americans, and so forth).

Dolezal and Jenner are employing these stereotypes because they are operating under social constructions (i.e., what a woman is like and what Black culture is like). The science of the matter is that Jenner was born male with one Y and one X chromosome and Dolezal was born with pheomelanin, which produces lighter skin. However, we get the chance to define who we are inside and outside of our genetics. Furthermore, the social construction is where each person begins developing an identity; but since these social constructions were created by people, some are problematic (like with what it means to be a man or a woman, Black or White, gay or straight, and so on). Dolezal and Jenner can pass in their respective identities. The problem becomes when and if these individuals lie about their timeline and status.

Dolezal has taught courses at Eastern Washington University called The Black Woman's Struggle. Some women would be pretty upset taking this type of course from her, instead of say an African American history class, because it is not based on her lived experience. She does not belong or qualify to teach what it means to be Black in America since she spent most of her life as a White woman. Tuvel (2017) argues that Dolezal has been racialized as Black in her current life. She goes on to argue that Dolezal has experienced racism and harassment for over ten years, so who or what determines the

"Black experience?" This type of argument can be used in the case of transgender identity. A trans person may not have grown up identifying as another gender, such as Caitlyn, but did so later in life, so should we suggest that a trans person cannot identify as a woman then? (Tuvel, 2017) What might be different in Jenner's case is that at no point in the book did she claim to pass herself off as someone who understands the struggle of women, although after watching a few episodes of her reality show, *Call Me Cait*, she did wish to win a title of "best female pilot." This is a similar problem to that of Dolezal teaching a course on the Black struggle or passing herself off as Black to head up the NAACP. However, Tuvel (2017) argues that there is a difference between someone who identifies as White and pretends to be Black, and those who genuinely identify as Black. The difference is that someone who is pretending often dons a Black identity for a few hours, while the other lives day in and day out as this identity. It is hard to say if Dolezal was putting on a sort of false or temporary identity or not, but it is a perspective to think about because it has parallels to the transgender community. For example, certain adornments or clothes are worn to display identities. Sometimes these may be based on stereotypes but those stereotypes may be based on some realities. There may be ways of speaking, words that are used to confirm one's identity. Perhaps there are actions, both in and out of group, but certainly, in-group can be very telling. And at the core, one's identity, should one feel so strongly to change, is usually based upon a strong internal feeling that one is often born in the "wrong" body. In essence, there are ways of speaking, acting, dressing, and being that may confirm one's identity. These are then, in turn, defined and performed by the individual. This concept is not unique to just race or gender and can thus overlap presenting similarities between Dolezal and Jenner.

Identity is a complicated thing. We are not sure any of us get to tell others how to live in their identities. And because identity typically falls into a system of binaries (gay or straight, Black or White), those who are in between (e.g., bisexual or biracial or nonbinary) often have a harder time defining and explaining who they are and are even unaccepted by the larger communities to which they belong. This becomes more evident in the next section on transracial adoptions.

## TRANSRACIAL ADOPTIONS

Transracial adoptions in the United States show the complexities of racial identity in America. How do children navigate their cultural identities when they realize they are socially classified as different from their parents based on the color of their skin? Patten (2000) interviewed twenty-two transracial adoptees to understand how they formed their racial identities. In one case, a girl name Elisa stated, "and that's where a lot of the anger came from, cause I suddenly was faced with everything I missed out by being with White people, and not knowing who I was or having a cultural identity. I definitely believe that Black kids should be adopted by Black parents" (Patton, 2000, p. 62). Elisa only realized she missed out on understanding Black culture when she went to college and saw different ways of speech, dress, and behavior. She realized that others social expectations of her due to her skin color did not conform to how she was raised, in a White family and community.

Patton (2000) states that transracial adoptions go against normal socialization and enculturation, and some argue, prevent kids from developing the necessary skills to navigate a racially oppressive society. In one case, a Black man discusses his White adoptive parents, and described how his dad went to the "I Had a Dream" march. His father was assaulted by the police, but he states, "but he'll never have walked into a store and be treated like they treat a Black person-watched, you know, handed a bill before you eat-'pay now.'" Black adoptees encounter moments in their lives when they recognize their social standing as an African American, and for some media images are the first line of exposure. These images can project poor, uneducated, drug addicted individuals, which they do not identify as based on their upbringing. This makes it difficult for transracial adoptees to develop a positive self-image regarding their African American identity (Patton, 2000).

This is one of the main arguments against Rachel Dolezal and her claim as being Black. At the end of the day, she can revert to her White ancestry and not have to experience what it is like to be Black in America. She did not grow up Black; at some point in her adult life after taking care of her Black adoptive siblings, she decided to identify more with Black culture. However, she did not have to experience, nor does she have to experience, the conflict of growing up recognizing that popular narratives of being Black in America means that you are not respected, you can be dangerous, poor, and uneducated.

## IMPLICATIONS AND FUTURE RESEARCH

By applying Turner's (1979) Social Identity Theory, we examined how one transgender woman and one transracial woman construct their identity. One of the more obvious and perhaps important aspects of this research is that there are not many theoretical studies of transgender and transracial people. As a result, we know much more about the communicative behaviors of two individuals who identify as transgender and transracial and how these struggles play out in life as with transracial adoptions, for example.

Furthermore, much of one's identity is based on perception, which most closely aligns with the social construction of reality. Thus, perception is learned, culturally determined, consistent, and inaccurate (Berger and Luckmann, 1967). It is fair to say that both Dolezal and Jenner have inaccurate perceptions of themselves, which is perhaps why they are so disliked. Caitlyn has expressed on her show, *Call Me Cait*, now canceled, that many of society's issues are not issues for her. She is wealthy, successful, and comes from privilege. In fact, the *Washington Post* (2015) reported that her trans surgery cost four million dollars. This is unrealistic for most people and as a result, we simply cannot identify. On the other side, Dolezal is highly criticized by the Black community, rightfully so. When this paper was presented at a popular culture conference, one audience member became incredibly angry with Dolezal saying, "she can just stop tanning and take her wig off and she's White again. I can't do that. She wants to claim she's a White minority wanting entrance to Howard, a Historically Black University, yet she sued that same school as a White woman saying she was discriminated against." According to the *Washington Post* (2015),

> Dolezal sued Howard University in 2002 for discriminating against her for being white. She claimed retaliation based on her race, gender, pregnancy and family responsibilities, saying she had been denied teaching positions and scholarship aid. She also complained that some of her artwork had been removed from an exhibition because black students were being favored. A judge, and subsequently an appeals court, found no basis for her claims. (para 3)

It appears that neither Jenner nor Dolezal have gained many fans from the communities in which they have transitioned into.

One implication for future research might be to examine how the full range of communication acts within the transgender and transracial communities. This would likely occur in many ways and in different projects. While Goffman's dramaturgical metaphor helped us understand identity, researchers could more fully examine the communicative interactions that lead to certain gender and roles and racial identities (ethnographies, semiotics, etc., would all be worthwhile research here). In addition, Carbaugh's emphasis on social identification, specifically discourse of identity, takes into account the necessary social and cultural contexts one could also examine. According to Carbaugh (1996), "Each discourse of identity will play upon certain presumed (i.e. cultural) premises about what a person is (and should be), can (and should) do, feel (and should feel), and how that person dwells within nature" (p. 29). This "social identification" is directly related to the "cultural agent" both of which assess identification as an "individual [who] has a self or something inside of himself or herself that is special, unique, yet rather stable across scenes and times (e.g. their personality)" (Carbaugh, 1996, p. 28). There is much to be studied here because while there may be a co-cultural relationship between these two communities, the majority feel that one can transition gender but not race. Comparisons of both communities could yield a better understanding of how certain co-cultures communicate and further identify as individuals and as group members, socially, culturally, and politically.

## REFERENCES

Benjamin, M. (2016). Why Can You Change Gender but Not Race? Retrieved fromh ttps://www.newstatesman.com/politics/feminism/2016/09/why-can-you-change -gender-not-race.

Berger, P. and Luckmann, T. (1967). *The Social Construction of Reality: A Treatise in the Sociology of Knowledge.* Garden City, NY: Doubleday & Company.

Burke, K. (1969). *A Rhetoric of Motives.* Berkeley, CA: University of California Press.

Carbaugh, D. (1996). *Situating Selves: The Communication of Social Identities in American Scenes.* Albany, NY: State University of New York Press.

Connolly, P. (1998). *Racism, Gender Identities and Young Children: Social Relations in a Multi-ethnic, Inner-City Primary School.* New York, NY: Routledge.

Dolezal, R. (2017). *In Full Color: Finding My Place in a Black and White World.* Dallas, TX: BenBella Books.

Goffman, E. (1959). *The Presentation of Self in Everyday Life.* New York, NY: BaDoubleday Dell Publishing Group, Inc.

Goodman, A. H., Moses, Y. T., and Jones. , J. L. (2019). *Race: Are We so Different?* Malden, MA: Wiley-Blackwell.

Gravlee, C. C. (2009). How Race Becomes Biology: Embodiment of Social Inequality. *American Journal of Physical Anthropology 139*(1): 47–57.

Hollimon, S. E. (2015). Third Gender. In *The International Encyclopedia of Human Sexuality,* 1355–1404. New York, NY: John Wiley and Sons, Ltd.

Jenner, C. (2017). *The Secrets of My Life.* New York, NY: Grand Central Publishing.

Lewontin, R.C. (1972). The Apportionment of Human Diversity. In T. Dobzhansky, M. K. Hecht, and W. C. Steere (Eds.), *Evolutionary Biology,* 381–86. New York, NY: Springer.

Mills, C. (1998). *Blackness Visible: Essays on Philosophy and Race.* New York: Cornell University Press.

Morton, T. and Duck, J. (2000). Social Identity and Media Dependency in the GAY Community. *Communication Research, 27*(4), 438–61.

N.A. (2015). *Caitlyn Jenner's $4m Transformation.* Retrieved from https://www.was hingtonpost.com/entertainment/caitlyn-jenners-4m-transformation/2015/06/04/ 0eea065a-0b05-11e5-951e-8e15090d64ae_story.html.

Patten, S. L. (2000). *Birthmarks: Transracial Adoption in Contemporary America.* Albany, NY: New York University Press.

Rymel, T. (2017). Transracial' vs. Transgender: What's the Difference? Retrieved from https://www.huffpost.com/entry/transracial-vs-transgender-whats-the-differe nce_b_58dd5f83e4b0fa4c09598748.

Svrluga, S. (2015, June 15). *Rachel Dolezal Sued Howard for Racial Discrimination. Because She Was White.* Retrieved from https://www.washingtonpost.com./new s/grade- point/wp/2015/06/15/rachel-dolezal-sued-howard-for-racial-discriminati on-because-she-was-white/.

Tajifel, H. and Turner, J. C. (1979). An Integrative Theory of Intergroup Conflict. In W. G. Austin and S. Worchel (eds.), *The Social Psychology of Intergroup Relations,* 33–47. Monterey, CA: Brooks/Cole.

Tuvel, R. (2017). Defense of Transracialism. *Hypatia, 32*(2), 263–78.

*Chapter 10*

# Transition to Neverland

## *Exploring Trans Boyhood through J. M. Barrie's* Peter Pan

Billy Huff

### THE MOST POPULAR TRANS BOY

What if Peter Pan is a trans boy? J. M. Barrie's *Peter Pan* is a text that has survived a proliferation of revisions and traversed numerous genres and media since the first appearance of its protagonist in Barrie's novel *The Little White Bird* in 1902. In fact, according to Neill (2006), the play version of the text has been called "the most written and rewritten play ever" (as cited in McGovock, p. 200). The play is, at the very least, one of the longest running plays on the English stage (Coats, 2004, p. 77). In addition to its narrative, poetic, and artistic (re)inventions, *Peter Pan* has been the subject of many scholarly inquiries. The protagonist of the text, Peter Pan, is subject to a stunning array of symbolic overdeterminations. To some, he is the ultimate embodiment of psychoanalytic *jouissance*, a reminder of that which the subject must sacrifice in order to assume a place in the symbolic order and to grow up (Coats, 2004, p. 77). Others heed *Peter Pan* as an ultimately tragic tale of an asocial "dead boy who never dies" (White and Tarr, 2006, p. viii). Still others attribute the enduring success of the narrative to the adult's nostalgia for a perpetual idealized state of childhood that never actually existed (Rose, 1984). It seems everyone has their own Peter Pan and relates to the figure of Peter Pan and his fantastical Neverland home differently. It is Peter Pan's resistance to symbolic closure that marks him as a figure amenable to queer reflection.

The symbolic resistance evidenced by the overdetermination of Peter Pan can be likened to an emerging body of scholarship in Transgender Studies. There is not one, but a multitude of definitions of trans embodiment and experience. Trans eludes fixity and closure. The potential of trans as a queer theory rests in its critique of static identification within binary structures, and the appeal of trans as a politics arises from its resistance to agonistic structures that rely on fixed identifications and intelligibility within the symbolic. Marking an abject space outside the given antagonisms that typically lead to defensive political reactions and ultimately reify the structures they aim to undermine, I explore Peter Pan and Neverland as promising sites for engaging a particular politics of trans identification.

I describe *my* Peter Pan as a polymorphously perverse boy who signifies resistance to dominant narratives of heteronormativity, and I describe *my* Neverland as a state that exists outside heteronormative conceptions of time and space. *My* Peter Pan embodies the ultimate abject position, defined by Kristeva (1982) as one that "disturbs identity, system, and order" (p. 4). Further, *my* Peter Pan enjoys his status as abject. *My* Peter Pan has a vexed relationship with his own history, and he is not preoccupied with the future, as he is, according to his author, the only child who will never grow up. In addition, *my* Neverland is not a Real place as much as it is an imaginary and symbolic construction born from the coordinates of my own particular desire. Neverland was called "Never Never Never Land" in the original text, which speaks more to an injunction than a proper name. As a self-identified trans boy, I perceive my own transition as one that will never end. There will never be a fixed position within a binary gender system onto which I will finally land, and like *my* Peter Pan, I will forever exist "betwixt-and-between."

Because the subject is both active and passive, and as a symbolic subject, it is constrained by a language that precedes its existence; it is, in the words of Coats (2004), "within the language and images of a specific culture that the subject must both *find* and *create* himself" (p. 4, emphasis in original). It is this type of discovery and invention that lie at the heart of my engagement with *Peter Pan*. So, what is the significance of telling new stories about stories? My occupation of Peter Pan's shadow raises questions about the moralizing impulses of storytelling, the relationship between adolescence and adulthood, queer temporalities, the relationship between gender identity and desire, and perhaps most important, it raises questions about enjoyment and pleasure.

I begin by situating and justifying the autoethnographic method with which I approach Peter Pan as a character and a text in conversation with critical theory and my own story of trans embodiment and experience. I then consider Peter Pan's queer temporality. While a number of scholars consider the potential destabilization of the gender binary wrought by trans existence, few consider questions of temporality that I find central to my own trans experience. I then explore Neverland as a metaphor for a reality that is never uncontaminated by fantasy. Finally, I discuss Peter Pan's relation to enjoyment and pleasure. As I offer *my* reading of *Peter Pan*, I point to the aspects of the narrative that seem particularly ripe for a politically appealing trans identification while striving to remain true to the constantly shifting terrain of Neverland and the promising impossibility of the boy who will never grow up to be a man.

## A TRANS METHOD

In her seminal piece, "The Empire Strikes Back: A Posttranssexual Manifesto," Stone (2006) called on people who are trans to refuse passing, resist medicalized and pathologizing discourses, and tell their own stories. She figured the "transsexual" as a genre and argued that "in the transsexual as text we may find the potential to map the refigured body onto conventional gender discourse and thereby disrupt it, to take advantage of the dissonances created by such a juxtaposition to fragment and reconstitute the elements of gender in new and unexpected geometries" (p. 231). Following Stone's call, Bettcher (2009) offers that "trans politics ought to proceed with the principle that transpeople have *first-person authority* (FPA) over their own gender" (p. 98, emphasis in original). In an effort to add my story as one among many narratives of trans experience that has the capacity to "fragment and reconstitute the elements of gender in new and unexpected geometries" while refusing the temptation to critique the FPA of others, I turn to the method of autoethnography.

According to Ellis, Bochner, and Adams (2011), "Autoethnography is an approach to research and writing that seeks to describe and systematically analyze (graphy) personal experience (auto) in order to understand cultural experience (ethno). This approach challenges canonical ways of doing research and representing others and treats research as a political, socially-just and socially-conscious act" (p. 273). The publication of individual stories of trans experience and identification is perhaps more pressing now than ever. We are currently witnessing a popular mainstreaming of transgender subjectivities in U.S. culture simultaneous with social and institutional threats to trans civil rights and representation. Similar to the normative ideologies of heteronormativity and homonormativity, trans people are met with trans-normativity, a discourse that "deems some trans people's identifications, characteristics, and behaviors as legitimate and prescriptive . . . while others' are marginalized, subordinated, or rendered invisible" (Johnson, 2016, pp. 466–467). Resisting the erasure of trans subjectivities that threaten normative regulatory ideals and have the potential for social and cultural transformation requires that we forge connections between critical theories and the lived and embodied experiences of people who are trans.

Autoethnography and performative writing have long been methods used by feminists of color who understand "the importance of centering theories in the flesh when understanding the experiences of women of color" (Calafell, 2015, p. 13). For, in the words of Madison (1999), "Performance helps me live a truth while theory helps me name it—or maybe it is the other way around. My mind and body are locked together in a nice little divine kind of unity: the theory knows and feels, and the performance feels and unlearns" (p. 109). The autoethnographic method I use in this chapter was inspired in particular by Calafell's (2015) *Monstrosity, Performance, and Race in Contemporary Culture.* Calafell placed her own experience as a woman of color in the academy in conversation with critical theories and cultural texts about monstrosity. This method, in Calafell's words, "allows me to name this space of oppression, connecting media constructed monstrosity with the Otherness experienced in the academic practices of everyday life for many women of color" (p. 13).

The naming of difference and otherwise overlooked spaces of oppression and resistance is not only central to autoethnographic writing, but also central to theorizing a trans method. According to Green (2016):

> A Trans* method requires that we be more attuned to difference rather than sameness, understanding and declaring that our sameness will not protect us. We must move to those uncomfortable places of contradiction and conflict, and in those moments we will develop a more critical and nuanced analysis of the conditions under which we are required to live, named and unnamed. A Trans* method show (sic) us how people become representable as things, categories, and names because it shows us the excess as a perpetual challenge to containment. (p. 79)

Similar to Calafell (2015), I analyze my own experiences through the lens of queer theory together with an oppositional reading of *Peter Pan* to bring attention to notions of temporality, play, and pleasure that challenge transnormative conceptions of gender. Also, consistent with Green's (2016) "Trans* method," I pay particular attention to difference and excess as potentially productive of new representations that challenge the "containment" inherent in mainstreaming and transnormativity.

Due to a lack of public representations of trans subjectivities that resist transnormative ideologies of gender, people who are trans become adept at oppositional readings of popular texts. To an extent, our existence and survival depend on our ability to read ourselves into and against the texts that permeate our culture. Hall (1980) explains that "it is possible for a viewer to understand both the literal and the connotative inflection given by a discourse but to decode it in a *globally* contrary way" (p. 137, emphasis in original).

Further, for Hall, this oppositional reading is inherently political: "One of the most significant political moments . . . is the point when events which are normally signified and decoded in a negotiated way begin to be given an oppositional reading" (p. 137). The oppositional reading of *Peter Pan* I offer in this chapter is also consistent with the political aim of autoethnographic writing. According to Neumann (1996), "One value of autoethnographic texts is that they democratize the representational sphere of culture by locating the particular experiences of individuals in a tension with dominant expressions of discursive power" (p. 189).

Using my own narrative to locate my body within the critical theory and articulate a relation to an oppositional reading of a popular children's story is fitting with queer theory, and the method of autoethnography strikingly fits with the spirit of *Peter Pan*. In "Autoethnography and Queer Theory: Making Possibilities," Jones and Adams (2010) traced the ideological commitments shared by autoethnography and queer theory. They offered:

> Hinging autoethnography and queer theory means making work that *becomes*, like a perpetual horizon, rather than an artifact of experience—making work that acts *as if* rather than says *it is*, recognizing that a (published) text fixes and solidifies experience but that experience is not fixed or solidified; it is always "partial, partisan, and problematic." Such recognition means understanding and embracing, the importance of being tentative, playful, and incomplete, and conceiving of experience as "overdetermined," always in motion, and in need of (perpetual) revision. (p. 143, emphasis in original)

As will become apparent in what follows, the method of autoethnography, queer theory, my own story and political commitments, and the story of Peter Pan and Neverland are all characterized by an *as if* engagement with a reality that is in a playful state of constant becoming.

## PETER PAN: GAY AND INNOCENT AND HEARTLESS

J.M. Barrie's *Peter Pan* (2005) begins, "All children, except one, grow up" (p. 7). Peter Pan, then, serves as the single exception that proves the rule. We must all grow up. Peter explains to Wendy that he ran away the day he was born because he heard his father and mother talking about what he was going to be when he became a man. This confession is rather odd given that a young infant could never actually run away. Nonetheless, Peter Pan maintains a vexed relationship with his history, as he has no long-term memory, and he also does not concern himself with the future, as he rejects the telos of time's progression. He holds tightly to the present moment.

Peter Pan's temporality is appealing to me as a self-identified trans boy. I too hold a vexed relationship with my past. I was socialized as a woman for almost forty years, and while my past years performing and being recognized as a woman will always continue to haunt my present reality, my story is just as difficult to make intelligible to others as the story of the one-day-old runaway. Like Peter Pan, I was born of parents, a therapist and an endocrinologist in my case, who are primarily concerned with who I am and how I will grow up. I was required to tell them that I was always already male, and I had to convince them that I want nothing more than to grow up to be a man, an assumed stable and self-evident position.

When Jas Hook asks Peter Pan who and what he is, Peter Pan responds, "I'm youth, I'm joy . . . I'm a little bird that has broken out of the egg" (Barrie, 2005, p. 135). The narrator translates, "This, of course, was nonsense; but it was proof to the unhappy Hook that Peter did not know in the least who or what he was, which is the very pinnacle of good form" (Barrie, 2005, p. 135). Terms of intelligibility, medical, and psychological regulatory regimes require that I am able to answer the question of who and what I am if I am to be allowed to be "born" at all, and like Peter Pan, this question poses an impossibility. The day of my first testosterone injection friends asked me if I felt more like a man. I responded, "How would I know what a man feels like?" The answer to the riddle of being for all of us is one that can only be provisionally answered retroactively from the position of an assumed stable state of adulthood. Children are asked *ad infinitum* what they desire to become when they grow up. People who are trans, in contrast, are required to know what and who they will be even before their own "birth."

As a young child, I relished in the trappings of young girlhood. I danced ballet and wore sundresses. I curled my hair and longed to wear makeup. I had crushes on boys and dreamed of my wedding. My childhood friends were mainly girls, and I always heeded my mother's warning that "anyone can be a woman, but you have to earn the right to be called a lady." I regretfully never experienced boyhood. The world of Boy Scout badges, skinned knees, and "boys will be boys" was as foreign to me as the womanhood that I was expected to grow into.

Somewhere in my narrative things changed. Like Peter Pan's story, I find the search for origins not only impossible, but also rather uninteresting. I realized that I did not have to act like a "lady." I realized that my most intimate fantasies involve "men" who identify as queer. I stopped dreaming of weddings and babies, and instead, I dedicated myself to a life as a perpetual student. I accepted that I do not like to stay in the same place for long. I rejected the terms that normally define success in the United States. My life is not structured around the accumulation of wealth, owning property, or reproducing new generations. I found enjoyment in marking the canvas of my skin with tattoos and fragmenting my body with piercings, and I began injecting myself with exogenous testosterone.

I am now experiencing many of the biological/chemical sensations and the social-learning of a young adolescent boy in the ever-changing body of a mid-life female. I firmly reject the idea that I will ever grow up to be a man. I exist in a "liminal" state while the world around me seems structured into an array of "befores" and "afters." Those who knew me "before" the transition (marked by many as my first testosterone injection) are uncomfortably confronted with the failures of language to make sense of my being. They try hard to respect my pronouns and name, but innocently mix these male references with the references they used "before." Those who meet me now (at three years into testosterone injections) are not sure, like Jas Hook, what or who I am. I am told that it will just be a matter of time before I will reach an "after," commonly known as passing. This temporality of "befores" and "afters" relies on a heteronormative linear narrative structure bound by a binary model of gender that conceives of my transition as female-to-male (FTM), adolescent transition to adulthood.

Peter Pan represents a liminal figure poised on the edge of a perpetual adolescence, and while all of the other characters in the tale are promised a productive future as grownups, Peter Pan will always hold to the impossible present. Wendy and the lost boys represent a normality constructed around Peter Pan, but Barrie is never able to assimilate him to any normative future (Rose, 1984, p. 36). In fact, Fox (2007) argues that "[in] forgetting the past that determines one's sense of identity, every moment of self-identification becomes an instance of creative potential rather than the recognition of a predetermined subject. Peter's identity is provisional at each given moment: it always contains the potential to be other than it is" (p. 260). "Befores" and "afters" are meaningless to Peter Pan. His status as impossibly present raises interesting questions about the structured temporality of all lives, particularly trans lives.

A number of queer theorists have devoted attention to the figure of the child and the state of childhood. The figure of the child is most often envisioned as a discursive construction that is forced to bear the weight of adult desire and nostalgia and is utilized rhetorically to shore up the failures and lapses in heteronormative narratives. In his controversial polemic, *No Future: Queer Theory and the Death Drive*, Edelman (2000) focused his attack on the figure of the child that he argues grounds all of politics in a social fantasy that he calls reproductive futurism. Because queer practices necessarily threaten the order of reproduction through their constitutive lack of (re)productive value, the queer, according to Edelman, must necessarily inhabit the negative position that simultaneously offers "society" its positive identity. In the words of Edelman (2000):

For politics, however radical the means by which specific constituencies attempt to produce a more desirable social order, remains, at its core, conservative insofar as it works to *affirm* a structure, to *authenticate* social order, which it then intends to transmit to the future in the form of its inner Child. That Child remains the perpetual horizon of every acknowledged politics, the fantasmatic beneficiary of every political intervention. (p. 3)

Edelman continued that the political investment in the child of the future most often comes at the expense of those living in the present, especially those who are queer. While it is not the purpose of this chapter to critique Edelman's position, I will show that there is one image of a child, Peter Pan, who does not necessitate the exclusion of queers in the present. Further, my trans identification with the queer childhood of Peter Pan offers a reconfiguration of the idea of childhood into that which resists political investments in reproductive futurism.

It is clear from literature that explores the topic of queer children that childhood is all about temporality and narrative realization. In "Turning Back: Adolescence, Narrative, and Queer Theory," Gordon (1999) argues that "[t]he meaning of adolescence is always understood to become apparent only in hindsight; it is structured throughout by a foreshadowed denouement, which is the subject's arrival at adulthood" (p. 3). It is due to the foreshadowed denouement of heterosexual adulthood that Gordon warned academics against treating adolescence as "the utopian site of a free-floating 'liminal' exploration of myriad nonbinding identifications and desires" (p. 6). For while children are allowed a certain amount of freedom in gender performativity (i.e., tomboys), this supposed freedom is always shadowed by a normative heterosexuality to be achieved by the time one becomes an adult. But what of the "adult" who returns to liminal childhood identifications that were paradoxically never experienced and also never left behind?

Gordon's warning against the celebration of the liminal experience of childhood, as well as a number of other accounts of childhood sexuality, is bound to a notion of childhood that is strictly tied to a particular age range and stage of life. This notion of childhood as something that is left behind when one's adulthood predicates a once free-floating childhood subject is complicated by the character of Peter Pan and my own trans identification. According to Stockton (2009), "The child is precisely who we are not and in fact, never were. It is the act of adults looking back. It is a ghostly, unreachable fantasy" (p. 5). If the child is not more than an ideological category comprising memory and fantasy, its position, then, becomes available to us all.

While she was not referring specifically to gender transition, Yeoman, in *Now or Neverland: Peter Pan and the Myth of Eternal Youth* (1998), found parallels between the depiction of adolescence in *Peter Pan* and other general life transitions. She argues:

> Understood in the context of his myth . . . the enigmatic Peter Pan forces us to look again at the conflictual dynamics of adolescence, that turbulent period when one is caught between two worlds, and one's whole being seems to hang on the slender thread of the chance remark or decision of the moment, precisely because the dynamics of adolescence reflect those of all periods of transition. If, then, we agree that adolescence is not only a distinct time of life but representative of "an ever-present pattern of transformation," we may see the tensions and conflicts of our teenage years reactivated in any period of change and growth. (p. 170)

My life experience reflects exactly Yoeman's point, and it exemplifies a period of adolescence that is not representative of a "distinct time of life." Regardless of the forty years that place me firmly in the middle of my life, it is apparent that I am "caught between two worlds" in many ways. I am caught without a place in the gender binary; I am caught without a place in language; and I am caught without any kind of stable identity. Recognition depends completely on "the slender thread of the chance remark." Will the cashier at the store refer to me as ma'am or sir? Will the server at the restaurant bring the check to me at the end of the meal? Will a potential hookup on Grindr respond to my profile?

Some, such as Owen (2010), find an "uncanny resemblance between the problem of relationality for someone who is queer and the problem of relationality for someone who is a child" (p. 261). Owen demonstrated this "uncanny resemblance" through engagement with Butler's (2004) comments concerning queer unintelligibility. I will quote Butler at length here:

> To find that you are fundamentally unintelligible (indeed, that the laws of culture and of language find you to be an impossibility) is to find that you have not yet achieved access to the human, to find yourself speaking only and always *as if you were* human, but with the sense that you are not, to find that your language is hollow, that no recognition is forthcoming because the norms by which recognition takes place are not in your favor. (p. 30)

Owen proceeded to replace the word "human" in the above quotation with the word "adult." Hence a child is positioned as one who has not yet achieved access to adulthood and speaks as if they were an adult with the same problems of recognition. While Butler and Owen tackled the problem of recognition as one to be overcome, my identification as a trans boy through the positionality of Peter Pan belies such a hope. Instead, Peter Pan and I revel in speaking *as if* we were human and celebrate in the potentiality of the liminal space this type of speaking births. In regard to Peter Pan, Fox (2007) prized the potential that is opened through the *as if* quality of his engagement with reality. According to Fox, "It is important that an *as if* method of reconceiving reality is understood not to be an indulgence in pretense but rather the practice of actualizing fictions that consequently and incontrovertibly alter reality itself" (p. 260).

Peter Pan's childhood, unlike that of all other children, is not governed by the language of temporality. In fact, many have commented on Barrie's difficulty is fashioning an ending to the text. In the end, Peter Pan continues to summon new generations of children to Neverland *ad infinitum*, or at least "so long as children are gay and innocent and heartless" (Barrie, 2005, p. 159). Hence, no one knows the actual age of Peter Pan. His occupation of perpetual adolescence outstrips generational passing. In his failure to grow up, Peter Pan points to the appeal for trans subjectivity of failure in general. In *The Queer Art of Failure*, Halberstam (2011) articulates failure as a position that "allows us to escape the punishing norms that discipline behavior and manage human development with the goal of delivering us from unruly childhoods to orderly and predictable adulthoods" (p. 3). The failure of recognition, of the ability to speak as an adult or as a human, and the prospect of remaining "fundamentally unintelligible" is inseparable from my trans identity.

Anthropologist Victor Turner discusses liminality as the middle stage in a rite of passage. In "Variations on a Theme of Liminality," Turner (1977) argues that those undergoing the liminal phase "are betwixt and between established states of politico-jural structure. They evade ordinary classification, too, for they are neither this-nor-that, here-nor-there, one-thing-not-the-other" (p. 37). Of course the liminal phase is ordinarily a temporary condition, and liminal subjects undergoing a rite of passage, such as adolescence, are promised a return to a "new, relatively stable, well-defined position in the total society" (Turner, 1982, p. 24). Peter Pan is marked by a never-ending liminality, which places him at odds with normative orders and structures. For liminality is, in the words of Turner, "both more creative and more destructive than the structural norm" (Turner, 1977, p. 47).

The similarities between scholarly accounts of liminality, the adventures of Peter Pan, and my own trans experience are striking. Turner (1982) characterizes liminality as the "blurring and merging of distinctions" (p. 26). Further, those living through a liminal period are "associated with such general oppositions as life and death, male and female, food and excrement, simultaneously, since they are at once dying from or dead to their former status and life, and being born and growing into new ones" (Turner, 1982, p. 26). I suspect that most trans people are acutely aware of the liminal experience in transitioning. My mother grieves that she has lost a daughter. When I teach my courses, I am referred to by students with an intermingling of male and female pronouns just in the course of an hour. I am applauded by the students with whom I work, but I am hated by many others. While in the arduous process of changing my name at my University, I found myself labeled as female in one office and as male in the office directly next door. Normative social and political institutions are structured according to a fixed and static gender/sex binary. My identity, however, eludes these classifications.

The structural threat signified by trans existence echoes the "resistance to narratives of heteronormativity and models of indeterminacy represented by Peter [Pan] as threatening to Victorian heterosexual adulthood" (Wasinger, 2006, p. 217). Peter Pan's perpetual liminal adolescence represents such a threat to notions of heteronormative adulthood that his name is often used in conjunction with a disorder, Peter Pan Syndrome, "often invoqued [sic] by popular psychology to describe a type of personality, *usually male*, characterized by immaturity, irresponsibility, narcissism and manipulativeness" (CERNĂUŢI-GORODEŢCHI, 2012, p. 123, emphasis in original). In regard to the "puer," the archetype most closely related to Peter Pan, Yeoman (1998) explains that "although his spontaneity, creativity and joy were highly valued, the puer tended to receive a largely negative press, mainly because emphasis was placed on the inevitable pathology of one who remains unconsciously identified with the archetype of youth well into adult life, in other words, stuck in stereotypically boyish or adolescent behavior" (p. 17)

Herein resides Peter Pan's appeal as a point of identification for a trans politics. In *In a Queer Time and Place: Transgender Bodies, Subcultural Lives*, Halberstam (2005) hailed "queer time" for its potential to illuminate "a life unscripted by the conventions of family, inheritance, and child rearing" (p. 2). Halberstam (2005) continues that "in Western cultures, we chart the emergence of the adult from the dangerous and unruly period of adolescence as a desired process of maturation, and we create longevity as the most desirable future, applaud the pursuit of a long life (under any circumstances), and pathologize modes of living that show little or no concern with longevity" (p. 4). Amid what seems to Peter Pan as a sure death by drowning in the mermaid's lagoon, the narrator explains, "Next moment he was standing erect on the rock again, with that smile on his face and a drum beating within him. It was saying, 'To die will be an awfully big adventure'" (Barrie, 2005, p. 87). The same spirit drums in me as I consider that becoming a boy also means potentially shortening my life by a decade and also that no one really knows the long-term effects of the chemical I inject into my muscles every two weeks.

Like the pathologization of Peter Pan in the Peter Pan Syndrome, the pathologization of trans people results from what appears to many to be a rejection of the most fundamental and natural "givens" of our existence. Also like Peter Pan, however, my own trans identification points to the constructed nature of all of our bodies, identities, and especially, cultural narratives of progress and maturation. Many have noted that a trans politics that responds defensively to charges of "going against nature" by reifying the categories against which many of us struggle only further marginalizes those who do not find unproblematic identification within normative structures. What is less explored is the challenge to heteronormative narrative structures and temporality that some trans identifications pose. Perhaps a visit to Neverland with Peter Pan can elucidate an alternative politics that does not take constructed categories and narratives for granted and also resists the impulse to cleanse our political demands of their necessary engagement with the structure of fantasy.

## NEVER NEVER NEVER LAND!

Much like our own identifications, which cannot be explained without recourse to the most fundamental fantasies that structure our sense of reality, Peter Pan cannot be understood outside of his Neverland playground. As I stated in the introduction, Neverland was originally called "Never Never Never Land," which is reminiscent of an injunction to never land. In fact, Barrie's Neverland exists only in the mind of each child, and its map is constructed according to each child's fantasies. Peter Pan's Neverland in particular shares a number of features with my own trans experience.

First, much like gender, the terrain of Neverland is not determined in any way by nature. Barrie's (2005) description of Neverland is instructive here:

> Doctors sometimes draw maps of other parts of you, and your own map can become intensely interesting, but catch them trying to draw a map of a child's mind, which is not only confused, but keeps going round all the time. There are zigzag lines on it, just like your temperature on a card, and these are probably roads in the island, for the Neverland is always more or less an island, with astonishing splashes of colour here and there, and coral reefs and rakish-looking craft in the offing, and savages and lonely lairs, and gnomes who are mostly tailors, and caves through which a river runs, and princes with six elder brothers, and a hut fast going to decay, and one very small old lady with a hooked nose. It would be an easy map if that were all, but there is also first day at school, religion, fathers, the round pond, needle-work, murders, hangings, verbs that take the dative, chocolate pudding day, getting into braces, say ninety-nine, three-pence for pulling out your tooth yourself, and so on, and either these are part of the island or they are another map showing through, and it is all rather confusing, especially as nothing will stand still. (p. 11)

The island (more or less) of Neverland is never fixed. Instead, it is populated by undetermined contingency. It is also never separable from the reality of norms and responsibilities, which sometimes find their way into the map and are sometimes a part of another map showing through. The landscape of my trans body changes drastically with every testosterone injection. I use "male" sexual terms for my genitals. What used to be a clitoris I now call my tiny cock. My breasts will be gone this summer. Neverland is pure possibility, and like reality, it never stands still.

Visiting Neverland comes with its own complications. In order to fly to Neverland, a child needs two things. First, the child has to have courage and conviction of belief. Second, the child has to be sprinkled with fairy dust. Trans people must also demonstrate belief that one can take off from the sex they were diagnosed at birth bound for some unknown location. Belief is central to the project of queer world-making, including the construction of the cartography of Neverland. Owen (2010) offers that "if queer describes what is outside those norms, excluded, impossible, then what is queer becomes *possible* only through the practice of believing in it" (p. 260, emphasis in original). This courageous conviction is often accompanied by a desire for the "fairy dust" of hormones. Like the children who venture to Neverland, a person who is trans can only have a vague idea about the treachery and adventure of the journey and what will populate the island of Neverland when they arrive.

Peter Pan's Neverland is always moving and changing. It is primarily invoked as a place of fun and adventure, but it is also a place of danger, murder, and war. In "My Words to Victor Frankenstein above the Village of Chamounix," Stryker (2006) argued for finding points of identification with Frankenstein's monster in much the same way I identify with Peter Pan. She found that the monster's (un)natural construction through medical science shares similar characteristics with her own experience as a trans woman. She called on trans people to refrain from being too quick to reject the insult of "monster." Instead, Stryker advocated identifying with the monster's rage and using it politically to bring attention to the falsity of even the notion of the "natural." While I certainly agree with Stryker's critique, I find Peter Pan and Neverland perhaps more appealing as points of identification because the island valorizes the adventure and play of the journey while never forgetting the danger that also exists there.

Neverland is primarily an island that allows each child to explore their mostly unconscious fantasies. Make-believe is a requirement on Neverland, and, according to *Peter Pan*'s narrator, it is a requirement the lost boys have to negotiate with care for, "If they broke down in their make-believe he [Peter Pan] rapped them on the knuckles" (Barrie, 2005, p. 64). Barrie (2005) narrates that, "The difference between him [Peter Pan] and the other boys at such a time was that they knew it was make-believe, while to him make-believe and true were exactly the same thing. This sometimes troubled them, as when they had to make-believe that they had had their dinners" (p. 64).

Questions of authenticity seem to haunt even my closest relationships. While at times nothing could be more real to me than my partial escape from the category, "woman" (much like Peter Pan's escape from the structuring norms of Victorian England), many people directly or indirectly communicate to me that there is a "make-believe" quality to my identity and my transition. To them, I am still really a woman, and I will never be a real man. While it is tempting to respond to accusations of "make-believe" defensively, it is certain that the political promise of trans subjectivity lies in part in the capacity of illuminating the make-believe quality of all symbolic identifications.

Identities are never fixed on Neverland. The battle with Peter Pan and the lost boys against the "redskins" at Slightly Gulch demonstrates that a child could be anything on Neverland:

> It was a sanguinary affair, and especially interesting as showing one of Peter's peculiarities, which was that in the middle of a fight he would suddenly change sides. At the Gulch, when victory was still in the balance, sometimes leaning this way and sometimes that, he called out, "I'm a redskin to-day; what are you, Tootles?" And Tootles answered, "Redskin; what are you, Nibs?" and Nibs said, "Redskin; what are you, Twin?" and so on; and they were all redskin; and of course this would have ended the fight had not the real redskins, fascinated by Peter's methods, agreed to be lost boys for that once, and so at it they all went again, more fiercely than ever. (Barrie, 2005, p. 73)

The battle that takes place at Slightly Gulch illuminates the liminality of Peter Pan, as well as his orientation toward his identity and the constructed reality of Neverland. In regard to the battle, Fox (2007) argues that "if it is possible to shed essentialized identity and its consequent binary antagonism with alterity, then Peter and the lost boys here afford the reader an understanding of the possibilities for change, of a fictive act that recreates the self as well as, necessarily, that self's relationship to others" (p. 258). Identification for Peter Pan is rife with creative potential and only productive insofar as it opens up the space of play and adventure as infinitely variable.

At other moments in the story, Peter Pan identifies as Wendy, Captain Hook, and a crocodile. His identifications are so convincing that even the lost boys and the pirates are convinced. In order to save Tiger Lilly from the pirates, Peter masquerades as Hook. "'Who are you, stranger, speak?' Hook demanded. 'I am James Hook,' replied the voice, 'captain of the *Jolly Roger*.' 'You are not; you are not,' Hook cried hoarsely . . . Hook tried a more ingratiating manner. 'If you are Hook,' he said almost humbly, 'come tell me, who am I'" (Barrie, 2005, p. 82)? When approaching the final battle on the pirate ship, Peter Pan becomes aware of the sound of the crocodile. "The crocodile! No sooner did Peter remember it than he heard the ticking. At first he thought the sound did come from the crocodile, and he looked behind him swiftly. Then he realized that he was doing it himself" (Barrie, 2005, p. 128). When attempting to rescue Wendy from the pirates, "he whispered to her to conceal herself with the others and himself took her place by the mast, her cloak around him so that he should pass for her" (Barrie, 2005, p. 133). Peter Pan's fluidity and play with identity and embodiment in Neverland is made possible through his understanding of the performative constitution of all identity. His identifications are not bound by biology, or in his case, even by species.

It is worth mentioning that the role of Peter Pan in the stage play is almost always acted by a woman. There are several reasons offered for this choice. One is that the play comes from the Pantomime tradition in which it was common for female roles to be played by males and vice-versa. Others cite that child labor laws prohibited children from sustaining the long hours of rehearsal and performances that the play required. The choice of a woman, then, was more appropriate to play a boy-child than a man. Regardless of the reason, even the instantiation of the play seems to denaturalize gender identity. For one thing, it is certain that a woman is one who will never grow up to be a man. Further, Kavey, in the introduction to *Second Star to the Right: Peter Pan in the Popular Imagination* (2009), describes that "tales of watching Mary Martin dressed as Peter and hearing her say, 'Never gonna be a man, catch me if you can,' and knowing that there might be other girls who would rather dress as boys than marry and raise children" (p. 3). Hence, the form of the play itself works to separate signifiers of age and gender from their usual signifiers.

If Peter Pan is able to playfully assume the identity of a man, a woman, and even an animal on Neverland, how are we to read his sexuality? Many have commented that Peter Pan lacks sexuality. After all, he does not even know what a kiss is:

> She [Wendy] also said she would give him a kiss if he liked, but Peter did not know what she meant, and he held out his hand expectantly. "Surely you know what a kiss is?" she asked, aghast. "I shall know when you give it to me," he replied stiffly, and not to hurt his feelings she gave him a thimble. (Barrie, 2005, p. 27)

Peter does not even seem to understand that he is caught clearly in the center of a love triangle between Wendy, Tiger Lilly, and the jealous, Tinkerbell. When I read *Peter Pan*, however, I find it to be a wholly erotic tale, and I find Peter Pan to be perversely sexual.

## POLYMORPHOUSLY PERVERSE PETER

It has become commonplace in dominant trans narratives to create a strict separation between gender identity and sexual identity. As the seemingly ill-fitting "T" in LGBT, trans people have worked diligently to remind others that lesbian, gay, and bisexual are sexual identities, while transgender stands for gender identity. These identities gesture toward different ontological positions. I always experience erasure through this dominant narrative of trans identification. I cannot think my gender and sexual identities as separate aspects of my being. Because the dominant sexual identity categories (lesbian, gay, bisexual, heterosexual) explain desire strictly in terms of the gender of the person to whom one is attracted within a gender binary system, desires and gender identifications that do not fit within binary gender categories are most often erased.

In "I Went to Bed with My Own Kind Once: The Erasure of Desire in the Name of Identity," Valentine (2006) discussed the problems with conceiving desire strictly in terms of gender and sexual identity categories. He argued that instead of beginning with identity categories, we should focus on desire, especially as it is put into speech, in order to account for desires that elude identity categories. It is my claim that *Peter Pan* is an erotic tale; however, its eroticism is erased by those who search for some form of normative heterosexuality in its pages. My identification as a trans boy, in fact, has as much to do with a desire to play a "boy" to a masculine "daddy" as it does with my temporal identification with adolescence, my refusal of "man" as ending place for my transition, and my disidentification with the category "woman."

I find these same perverse BDSM (Bondage and Discipline, Sadism and Masochism, Dominance and Submission) fantasies played out between Peter Pan and the lost boys and between Peter Pan and Captain Hook in Barrie's novel. Interestingly, I am not the only person who reads *Peter Pan* this way. In hir novel *Lost Boi*, Lowrey (2015) reimagined the setting of *Peter Pan* in a contemporary large urban city. In hir novel, Peter Pan, the lost bois, and Wendy and her siblings are all "bois." According to Noble (2007):

> "Boi" is a term emerging in genderqueer and trans cultures to mark spaces of embodiment outside of the binarized duality of the sexed body as either male or female. The incoherent boi body, replete with flat chest, facial hair, deepened voice, hormonally and sometimes surgically altered but not necessarily anatomically correct genitals, emerges as a new way of embodying gender outside of the rigid binaries of sexual difference. (p. 148)

Regardless of which body claims the boi identity, it is most often characterized as a critique of adult manhood. Levy notes, "It's no coincidence that the word is boi and not some version of man. Men have to deal with responsibilities, money, wives, career, car insurance. Boys just get to have fun and, if they're lucky, sex" (as cited in Abate, 2011, p. 25). In fact, the term actually originated, in part, as the identity for the submissive partner in a gay male BDSM "daddy/boy" dynamic.

In Lowery's (2015) novel, not only are the characters all bois, but they also all participate in BDSM sexuality. The feud between Peter Pan and Captain Hook is conceived as a battle between "old guard" BDSM culture and the newer more open BDSM culture that has emerged since its proliferation on the Internet. In fact, the battle between Pan and Hook is represented as an erotic love story:

> Pan recalled the night many years earlier, when they first battled. [. . .] Pan had gone to the dungeon in search of adventure. He wanted to fly, and the queer at the door pointed him to the man in impeccable leathers with a hook tattooed on his forearm who stood coiling rope beside a package of hooks fresh from the autoclave. Hook put stars of a different kind on Pan's back that night; he took him into the rafters and beyond. Hook hurt Pan, and Pan fell in love, in a way—the closest to love he'd ever gotten. (Lowery, 2015, p. 25)

Lowery's (re)imagining of Peter Pan is not altogether unforeseeable. In addition to Peter Pan's fluidity with identity, it is also clear from Barrie's text that Peter Pan's enjoyment hangs on the assumption of roles, one of the characteristics of BDSM play. There are also numerous references throughout Barrie's novel to BDSM implements, such as a whip called a cat-o-nine-tails. For example, Hook asked the lost boys, "Do you want a touch of the cat before you walk the plank?" (Barrie, 2005, p. 130)

Although Peter Pan seems completely uninterested in a normative relationship with Wendy, he is excited about playing the role of "Daddy" to the lost boys. He is also interested in Wendy playing the role of "Mommy":

> "Peter, what is it?" "I was just thinking," he said, a little scared. "It is only make-believe isn't it, that I am their father?" "Oh yes," Wendy said primly. "You see, he continued apologetically, "it would make me seem so old to be their real father." "But they are ours, Peter, yours and mine." "But not really, Wendy?" he asked anxiously. "Not if you don't wish it," she replied; and she distinctly heard his sigh of relief. "Peter," she asked, trying to speak firmly, "what are your exact feelings to me?" "Those of a devoted son, Wendy." (Barrie, 2005, p. 95)

Wendy makes it obvious that her interests lie in actualizing a normative heterosexual relationship with Peter Pan. Peter is only interested, however, in role-playing the father role to the lost boys and the boy role to Wendy: a queer family indeed.

It was within the BDSM subculture that I came to an awareness of an interest in transitioning. Within BDSM, there is a recognition that sex is performative, and there are few constraints on the roles one can embody. It was also
first within the BDSM subculture that I was able to identify as a boy and also
be recognized as a boy by others (even before I began transitioning in earnest).
Accordingly, Hale (1997) argues that "In sexual-minority communities, such
as queer leather communities, there are rich and subtly nuanced discourses
of gendered pleasure, practice, desire, and subjectivity. These community
discourses sometimes reflect rich and subtly nuanced embodiments of gender
that resist and exceed any simple categorization into female, male, woman,
man, and thus into homosexual, bisexual, or heterosexual" (p. 223). Not only
did I come to an understanding of the possibility of identities that resist binary
categories within the BDSM subculture, but it was also there that I learned
how to resignify my body. Like the openness of the terrain of Neverland, our
bodies are available for resignification in ways unthinkable when we view the
body as biologically determined.

## REMEMBERING NEVERLAND

Like many others, I do not see myself represented in dominant public narratives of trans experience and embodiment that reify the gender binary, seek
normative lives, and separate gender identity from desire. I am also often
overcome with narratives that focus exclusively on loss, pain, and rage. I am
not unaware that my valorization of adventure and play, my ability to exist
and think myself outside of binary categories, and my focus on pleasure are
won in part from my privilege as a white, masculine, middle-class person and
the privilege of my education. The ability to claim and enjoy unintelligibility
is a privilege not open to most. It is also true that alongside my reading of
*Peter Pan* exists a colonial story complete with "redskins" and pirates. While
it seems as though there is an absence, however, of many public trans narratives that offer recognition of my experience, the purpose of this chapter has
been to offer an oppositional queer reading of a text that does reflect my own
identifications and to encourage others to do the same.

Following David Hall, Mallan (2009), in *Gender Dilemmas in Children's
Fiction*, invited readers of children's fiction to become queer agents by
"destabilizing received notions of sexual normality and differential valua-
tions, seeing diverse possibilities for identifications and affiliations, opening
up questions about how to imagine a future of different sexual expressions
and subject positions" (p. 155). Peter Pan and Neverland do not seem so
impossible when approached through my own trans subjectivity. Barrie's

text is a cultural narrative that gestures toward my own imaginings. Kincaid (1992) remarks in regard to Peter Pan that "one of the things that he does not *know* is gender, or maybe it is one of the things we are allowed for a moment not to know" (p. 282).

My version of Peter Pan's story imagines a trans leather boy who will never grow up to be a man. He balks at normative sexuality and refuses the lure of adult responsibility. He holds tightly to the present moment and exists in a perpetual liminal state of constant becoming characteristic of adolescence. His identity is fluid and contingent, as is his Neverland reality. He insists on adventure and pleasure even when he faces sure death. Kavey (2009) says of Peter Pan that he is "always a boy, always attractive, always desired, always living in a self-reflective, constructed reality, he replicates the most appealing aspects of childhood" (p. 10). Peter Pan helps me to make sense of my own impossibility as my occupation of his shadow offers an explanation for his.

It is integral in trans studies to allow for endless variations in self-understanding. My reading of *Peter Pan* is not intended to critique the first-person perspectives of others. I see this as one among many versions of trans experience. It is one, however, that I argue is particularly politically appealing. First, just as Wendy and her brothers are bound by the English Victorian nursery yearning for Neverland, we are all bound by a binary gender system that violently constrains our thoughts, behaviors, and relationships to others. Second, in a society that bases its model of success on secured heteronormativity, wealth accumulation, and growing up, perhaps embracing the liminal experience in transition likened to adolescence can open us up to new temporalities that allow us enjoyment now instead of positioning our success as always something to come. Finally, we might consider that our identities are never uncontaminated by fantasy and desire. While our desires are not determined by our gendered identities, they are also not completely separable. In fact, for many of us, our gendered subjectivity is unthinkable without recourse to our most fundamental fantasies that sustain our pleasure. At the end of *Peter Pan*, Wendy grows up and forgets the way to Neverland. She tells her daughter that "it is only the gay and innocent and heartless who can fly" (Barrie, 2005, p. 154). I call on us all to remember our way to Neverland.

## REFERENCES

Abate, M.A. (2011). When girls will be bois: Female masculinity, genderqueer identity, and millennial LGBTQ culture. In A. Wannamaker (Ed.), *Mediated boyhoods: Boys, teens, and young men in popular media and culture* (pp. 15–36). New York, NY: Peter Lang.

Barrie, J. (2005). *Peter Pan*. New York, NY: Barnes and Noble Classics.

Bettcher, T.M. (2009). Trans identities and first-person authority. In L.J. Shrage (Ed.), *You've changed: Sex reassignment and personal identity* (pp. 98–120). New York, NY: Oxford University Press.

Bruhm, S., and Hurley, N. (2004). *Curiouser: On the queerness of children.* Minneapolis, MN: University of Minneapolis Press.

Butler, J. (2004). *Undoing gender.* New York, NY: Routledge.

Calafell, B.M. (2015). *Monstrosity, performance, and race in contemporary culture.* New York, NY: Peter Lang.

CERNĂUŢI-GORODEŢCHI, M. (2007). Peter Pan: (Why) should he rather be played by a woman? *Philologica Jassyensia,* 3(1), 123–28.

Coats, K. (2004). *Looking glasses and Neverlands: Lacan, desire, and subjectivity in children's literature.* Iowa City, IA: University of Iowa Press.

Edelman, L. (2000). *No future: Queer theory and the death drive.* Durham, NC: Duke University Press.

Ellis, C., Bochner, A. P., and Adams, T. E. (2011). Autoethnography: An overview. *Historical Social Research,* 36(4), 273–90.

Fox, P. (2007). Other maps showing through: The liminal identities of Neverland. *Children's Literature Association Quarterly,* 32(3), 352–68.

Gordon, A. (1999). Turning back adolescence: narrative, and queer theory. *GLQ,* 5(1), 1–24.

Green, K.M. (2016). Troubling the waters: Mobilizing a Trans* analytic. In E.P. Johnson (Ed.), *No tea, no shade: New writings in black queer studies* (pp. 65–82). Durham, NC: Duke University Press.

Halberstam, J. (2005). *In a queer time and place: Transgender bodies, subcultural lives.* New York, NY: New York University Press.

Halberstam, J. (2011). *The queer art of failure.* Durham, NC: Duke University Press.

Hale, C.J. (1997). Leatherdyke boys and their daddies: How to have sex without women or men. *Social Text,* 52(15), 223–36.

Hall, S. (1980). Encoding/decoding. In S. Hall, D. Hobson, A. Love, and P. Willis (Eds.), *Culture, media, language* (pp. 128–38). London: Hutchinson.

Johnson, A.H. (2016). Transnormativity: A new concept and its validation through documentary film about transgender men. *Sociological Inquiry,* 86(4), 465–91.

Jones, S.H., and Adams, T.E. (2010). Autoethnography and queer theory: Making possibilities. In M. Giardina and N.K. Denzin (Eds.), *Qualitative Inquiry and Human Rights* (pp. 136–57). Walnut Creek, CA: Left Coast Press.

Kavey, A.B. (2009). Introduction: From peanut butter jars to the silver screen. In A.B. Kavey and L.D. Friedman (Eds.), *Second star to the right: Peter Pan in the popular imagination* (pp. 1–12). New Brunswick, NJ: Rutgers University Press.

Kincaid, J. (1992). *Child loving.* New York, NY: Routledge.

Kristeva, J. (1982). *Powers of horror.* New York, NY: Columbia University Press.

Lowrey, S. (2015). *Lost boi.* Vancouver, BC: Arsenal Pulp Press.

Madison, D.S. (1999). Performing theory/embodied writing. *Text and Performance Quarterly,* 19(2), 107–24.

Mallan, K. (2009). *Gender dilemmas in children's fiction.* New York, NY: Palgrave Macmillan.

McGovock, K. (2006). The riddle of his being: An exploration of Peter Pan's perpetually altering state. In D.R. White and C.A. Tarr (Eds.), *Peter Pan: In and out of time* (pp. 195–215). Lanham, MD: Scarecrow Press.

Neumann, M. (1996). Collecting ourselves at the end of the century. In C. Ellis, and A.P. Bochner (Eds.), *Composing ethnography: Alternative forms of qualitative writing* (pp. 172–98). Walnut Creek, CA: AltaMira Press.

Noble, B. (2007). Queer as box: Boi spectators and boy culture on Showtime's *Queer as Folk*. In M. L. Johnson (Ed.), *Third wave feminism and television: Jane puts it in a box* (pp. 147–65). London: Palgrave.

Owen, G. (2010). Queer theory wrestles with the 'Real' child: Impossiblity, identity, and language in Jacqueline Rose's *The case of Peter Pan*. *Children's Literature Association Quarterly*, 35(3), 255–73.

Rose, J. (1984). *The case of peter pan, or the impossibility of children's fiction*. London: The MacMillon Press.

Stockton, K.B. (2009). *The queer child, or growing sideways in the twentieth century*. Durham, NC: Duke University Press.

Stone, S. (2006). The empire strikes back: A posttranssexual manifesto. In S. Stryker and S. Whittle (Eds.), *The transgender studies reader* (pp. 221–35). New York, NY: Routledge.

Stryker, S. (2006). My words to Victor Frankenstein above the Village of Chamounix: Performing transgender rage. In S. Stryker and S. Whittle (Eds.), *The transgender studies reader* (pp. 244–56). New York, NY: Routledge.

Turner, V. (1977). Chapter III: Variations on a theme of liminality. In S.F. Moore and B.G. Myerhoff (Eds.), *Secular Ritual* (pp. 36–52). Amsterdam: Van Gorcum Press.

Turner, V. (1982). *From ritual to theatre: The human seriousness of play*. New York, NY: Paj Publications.

Valentine, D. (2006). I went to bed with my own kind once: The erasure of desire in the name of identity. In S. Stryker and S. Whittle (Eds.), *The transgender studies reader* (pp. 244–56). New York, NY: Routledge.

Wasinger, C. Getting Peter's goat: Hybridity, androgyny, and terror in Peter Pan. In D.R. White and C.A. Tarr (Eds.), *Peter Pan: In and out of time* (pp. 217–36). Lanham, MD: Scarecrow Press.

White, D.R., and Tarr, C.A. (2006). *Peter Pan: In and out of time*. Lanham, MD: Scarecrow Press.

Yeoman, A. (1998). *Now or Neverland: Peter Pan and the myth of eternal youth*. Toronto, ON: University of Toronto Press.

*Chapter 11*

# Hijras and the Indian Caste System

## Lucky Issar

Caste operates in the heteronormative world. Since queer bodies blur the male–female distinctions, they are rendered useless in a caste-based society[1] as soon as they are out of the womb. In Indian parlance, such bodies are called *hijra*.[2] In most cases, parents abandon hijra (intersex) babies at birth. The society, at large, does not recognize them; their difference cannot be wished away because it is too visible. Such bodies are pushed away from the caste-oriented world. In this chapter, I examine the role that family, society, and nation play in the formation of hijra bodies.

Because of differences in their physiognomy, they are not included in caste society. Such a child becomes an outsider in the highly gendered domain of Indian household because a hijra child cannot participate in everyday life rituals that prepare children for heterosexual marriage and procreation. The family, if it wants to nurture such a child, finds no support from any quarter. Children born with indeterminate sex are abandoned. Before religion or the sociocultural system intervenes in any concrete way, the families give up such children.

So the hijra groups live among themselves. They earn their livelihoods by prostitution, singing, and dancing at weddings and birth-related ceremonies. They go to bless the newly born babies. They examine the sex of the child and if it cannot be determined, they take the child with them. If the intersex baby remains with the family, such a baby is raised in secrecy.[3] In fact, any child who acts differently from his or her socially assigned gender is ridiculed and mocked. Unlike queer children, the intersex children cannot hide and regulate their bodies; as they grow up their bodies show themselves. It is for this reason that the amount of abuse hijras receive exceeds significantly from what is inflicted on non-hijra sexual minorities such as gays and lesbians. However, a person who joins a hijra group is assumed to be an intersex, regardless of the person's actual gender. All these patterns surface in hijra narratives.[4] Frequently when a hijra child grows up, he leaves his family and joins the hijra community. This leaving home, even though, most of the time, voluntary, is not easy. Furthermore, joining the hijra community comes with its own challenges as hijra communities have their "peculiar" rules[5] and hierarchies; the new entrant has to observe and follow hijra practices in order to be fully integrated. This involves castration if the new member is transgender.[6] Not all hijras are intersex.[7] In fact, most men who become hijras are biologically men, but they identify themselves with the female gender. Meanwhile, the world of caste remains blissfully unaware of the kind of cruelties it unleashes on "unfit bodies." In everyday life, hijras suffer indignities on a daily basis. Many believe that hijras are born as hijras because of their bad *Karma*.[8]

This idea of Karma in connection with caste is used as a powerful tool to maintain caste order. The general public is encouraged to believe in the divine nature of caste. Brahmins—the uppermost and most privileged—and Untouchables—the lowermost and most oppressed—are identified as such due to their Karma. Since the Karmic conception of life is so central to Hinduism, everyone believes in it irrespective of where one stands in the caste hierarchy. The oppressed masses accept their low-caste status as divinely ordained—a consequence of bad Karma. The powerful upper castes use Karmic Philosophy to legitimize their caste-based hegemony. This hegemony based on birth also gives them an eternal edge over the lower castes. A perfect system that keeps the upper caste in a superior position forever, and the lower castes, particularly the Untouchables, eternally to the veritable chambers of horror—with no escape routes—due to the endogamous nature of caste.

Since hijra bodies are not able to perpetuate caste, they are shunned in Hindu society. In order to do anything in India, one has to have a father's name (the right caste), and clearly defined male or female sex. Indian society is hostile to bodies that cannot be identified as male or female. In popular discourse, this hostility toward hijra bodies is seldom linked with caste. Even Indian queer theorists have seemingly ignored the question of caste.[9] Not making this connection is essential for keeping the existing caste hierarchies intact; recognizing the link between caste and sexuality demands a fundamental reconfiguration of society in regard to caste, and by implication, Hinduism. In addition, the perks caste bestows on the upper-caste elites are too enormous to relinquish.

One cannot really talk about India without understanding the Indian caste system, yet most mainstream narratives on India overlook the caste system. Even though caste runs through every artery of Indian social life, it is rarely examined. Its invisibility in everyday life, though, seemingly innocent, is highly strategic. Caste pervades every aspect of life in India. It is in people's names, how they act, how they talk, who they marry, what they do, and so on. It is everywhere, and yet it is not seen. It is a repressive system that exploits a vast number of people, but in all major issue-based discussions in India, caste tends to hide itself (Roy, 2014).

One significant feature of caste is that it functions and strengthens itself not only by controlling and keeping human bodies heteronormative but also by branding bodies as low and high, sacred and profane, touchable and untouchable. Caste borders and the business of naming and categorizing people are regulated primarily by controlling women's bodies. For instance, in Manu's Code of Conduct Manual for Hindus girls are supposed to be in the custody of their fathers when they are children, under the custody of their husbands when married, and under the custody of their sons as widows. Under no circumstance are women allowed to exercise their independence (Olivelle, 2005). Sexual transgressions are relentlessly policed and punished. Hindu religious texts justify punishing sexual transgressions. For instance, if an untouchable man copulates with an upper-caste woman, he is given death sentence (Olivelle, 2005). Additionally, according to the sacred Hindu texts, caste is divine in nature and its observance is mandatory in Indian society. So the society makes sure that caste properties are rigorously observed. Often attempts have been made to eliminate caste, but it has the resilience to renew itself. For instance, although India is a democratic country, caste lurks underneath its democratic institutions.

So this sociocultural obsession with caste, in addition to controlling women's bodies, is reflected in the violence and indifference that Indian society shows toward non-normative bodies such as hijras. In the wake of globalization, many social scientists heralded the disappearance of caste from society but caste, instead of disappearing, has modernized itself (Roy, 2014). For instance, Brahmins—the uppermost caste—constitute less than 5 percent of the Indian population, and yet they hold most of the key powerful, administrative positions; on the other hand, more than 90 percent of menial scavenging is done by *Dalits*—"Untouchables." In contemporary India, modernized democracy and liberalized economy have not altered the caste hierarchies, which means caste not only perseveres and continues, it enforces heteronormativity and discards "unruly" bodies as outcasts.

Caste, in India, is not seen as a contrived, oppressive sociopolitical system because caste ingeniously aligns itself with religion. In dominant sociopolitical discourse, various social issues are discussed but not in connection with caste. For instance, whereas the discussants condemn patriarchy and its various offshoots, they fail to see how deeply patriarchy is entwined with caste and how both reinforce each other.[10] Patriarchy demands that men and women adhere to caste rules. Men and women, when failing to nurture caste, are devalued. Furthermore, society punishes those who are psychologically or physiologically different. Such people have no choice, but to submit to the dominant sexual norms. Historically, in a caste-based society, one has only two possibilities: either curb one's sexuality and submit to the established sexual, sociocultural norms or ignore the caste codes and renounce the world;[11] both are ways to maintain caste order. While heterosexuality is celebrated, encouraged, and supported, the second option, which involves a voluntary renunciation of the world, Indian society tolerates because it does not collide with the caste system. In a tangential way, the practice of renunciation supports the caste system because it has a distinct religious edge.

Indian society imposes—practices—caste in such subtle ways that it gets ossified in the DNA of body politic. One comes into a world already defined by caste. Anyone who fights it is either ostracized or condemned as anti-Indian. Historically, upper-caste reformers have shown a great zeal in uplifting the lower castes, but when their actions are deeply probed, they are found lacking in their commitment toward eradicating caste from Indian society. For instance, one such reformist, anti-caste (upper-caste) association Jat-Pat Todak Mandal wanted Ambedkar, a Dalit (untouchable caste) leader, to deliver an anti-caste speech in May 1936. Realizing that Ambedkar would criticize sacred Hindu texts; they scrapped the conference. However, when such attempts are genuine, caste appears too strong to be dislodged from Indian society. Further in this chapter, I discuss how this resilience of caste in Indian society impacts and perpetuates violence against sexual minorities.

## THE FAMILY AND HIJRA BODY

It all starts with the family. In a highly religious and ritual-based society, caste exerts itself as soon as the child enters the world. The sex of the child determines how the body will be received in the caste-dominated society. For instance, in case of the male child, the rituals are elaborate and celebratory; for the female child, the response is predominantly unwelcoming and even hostile.[12] If the child is of indeterminate sex, the parents and members of the extended family are absolutely clueless as to what to do with such a child. Technically caste is only central to Hindus, but culturally its grip is so strong, that it is practiced across all religions in India.

It is no coincidence that familial hostility toward non-normative people in India is also reflected in literary and visual representations through their erasure. Mainstream Indian English fiction writers have avoided writings about hijras and caste. The Booker Prize-winning Indian author Arundhati Roy is a striking exception in this regard. In her debut novel *The God of Small Things* (1997), Roy addresses the issue of caste. However, in her recent novel *The*

*Ministry of Utmost Happiness* (2017), she takes the reader further into caste society and puts the lives of not only Dalits but also hijras at the center of the novel—a feat few Indian writers ever dared.

In the first half of *The Ministry of Utmost Happiness*, we meet a newborn intersex child in a Muslim family. The mother not only hides this aspect of her child's body from her husband and others, but she also hides it from herself. She encounters an unfamiliar, hostile space, not knowing how to respond to the intersexed body of her child. In the novel, the Muslim mother, Jahanara Begum, feels debilitated, frightened by her own child. This intense reaction reflects her fears, and the grip of mainstream norms (caste) that run through her. Nothing in her immediate environment can mitigate her innumerable fears when faced with the body of an intersex child. She is terrified to discover "nestling underneath of her baby's boy-parts, a small, unformed, but undoubtedly girl-part" (Roy, 2017, p. 7). She contemplates killing herself and her child. The world ceases to make sense to her. Everything in her world has a gender—"all things—carpets, clothes, books, pens, musical instruments. . . . Everything [is] either . . . man or woman. Everything except her baby . . . she knew there was a word for those like him—*Hijra* . . . *Hijra* and *Kinner*. But two words do not make a language" (Roy, 2017, p. 8). Unexpectedly, she comes to inhabit a negative social space.

Even though Jahanara Begum knows nothing about hijras, her fears are visceral. They emerge not only because of the baby's body, she fears that her baby will not be included in the world that is so overwhelmingly codified by caste. Her fears reveal how pervasive caste is. Caste demands her baby be either male or female, and since the baby is neither, Jahanara Begum howls at his "social death." However, she hides the child's "unruly" gender status from everyone—including her husband. She hopes the infant's female part will either heal or fade. Somehow she manages to put off the circumcision ceremony for a few years with a series of inventive excuses, but caste in the benign form of a ritual exerts itself. Eventually "she mustered her courage and told her husband, breaking down and weeping with grief as well as relief that she finally had someone else to share her nightmare with." Her husband, a *hakim*—a doctor of herbal medicine—by profession but a poet by passion, who has a couplet ready for every occasion, "for every illness, every occasion, every mood and every delicate alteration in the political climate" (Roy, 2017, p. 15), is speechless at this revelation.

Both husband and wife panic; the mother has suicidal thoughts, and the father is absolutely flabbergasted. Their extreme fear, toward the body of their own child, is the fear of caste society because the presence of such a child stigmatizes the whole family. Caste not only excludes and rejects the hijra body it seeks to eradicate the hijra body from the family as its presence affects other members of the family. Since most marriages are arranged in

India, people ostracize a family in which a woman has given birth to a hijra baby. Parents avoid marrying their children into such a family because they fear that hijra babies will come out of such unions.

In this case, the child, somehow, escapes the scrutiny of hijra groups at the time of the birth. The mother raises the child as a boy—a tremendous feat in the face of an unreceptive, antagonistic sociocultural environment. The father tries to fix the body of the child through *hakims* and *maulivis*—men who know traditional methods of healing and Islamic laws. As the child grows up, he shows pronounced feminine traits. Other boys make fun of him in school. They make ditties to ridicule him. *He's a She. He's not a He or a She. He's a He and a She. She-He, He-She Hee! Hee! Hee!*(Roy, 2017, p. 12) and this is one of his first real, traumatic encounters with the world outside home. Consequently, he stops going to school. One mother, just on the strength of her will and resilience, cannot save her child from the toxic sociocultural codes that categorize human bodies as profane-sacred, touchable-untouchable, normal-abnormal.

The grown-up child is mocked and teased on account of his body. Soon he realizes he has no place in the family so he leaves home to join a group of hijras. Although this seems like a voluntary act, it is the only possibility left to him. Only in a tangential way does the family push him out (despite challenges, his mother has always shown additional concern toward him). He cannot participate in the family life in any meaningful way because all caste codes implicit in rituals related to living, marrying, and dying, exclude him. He is rendered irrelevant to the family, and by implication, to society. Jahanara Begum tries her best, but raising a child needs the support of the whole society. Trapped in the hijra body, her son is not only rendered casteless, he is made irrelevant as a human being as well.

While regulation of caste affects queer bodies in all sorts of ways, in the case of hijra bodies, the society turns unusually hostile, leaving no room for adjustment or settlement. Hijras are rarely narrated or depicted in mainstream discourse.[13] Only in recent years have some personal narratives of hijras come out in the public domain sharing the horrific stories of humiliation and violence unleashed on them by their own families. Even in death, caste remains relentless and exerts itself by excluding non-normative bodies. Hijras are not allowed to participate in funeral-related ceremonies. One hijra describes his exclusion as thus:

When my father died I did not go to bury him. If I had gone there, the relatives and others would not take part in the burial. The Imam would not conduct the janaza (religious rite). I had very long hair, I used to wear a lot of jewellery and saree, then my relatives told me, "you are wearing gold like women, you should not touch your father's dead body." (Khan et al., 2009, p. 445)

This is just one but significant way to reject a hijra's claim to show grief and touch the dead body of his father. Since everyday life is steeped in (gendered) rituals, hijras are actively reminded of their "impure" hijra status—all this is done in the name of maintaining caste purity.

In Indian society, people are first and foremost moored to their caste identities. Caste affiliation trumps every other identity marker based on language, religion, region, and even nation (Dasgupta, 2014). Therefore, when Indian people witness blatant discrimination toward hijras in daily life, they remain unruffled by it. This indifference is not restricted to hijra bodies; it is reflected in every sphere of public life. Throughout the country, people are profoundly concerned with their own caste communities—any local or national issue is judged depending upon how it relates to their caste interests.[14]

Caste purity is maintained through strict regulation of bodies. The society uses its apparatus to discipline bodies. However, in the case of hijra bodies, control, regulation, and manipulation do not work; these bodies are too few, too unruly to fix. It is easier to discard and strip them of their humanity as soon as they arrive in the world. Most families show their deep-seated prejudice toward intersex children by voluntarily giving them to hijra groups at birth.

## HIJRA AND THE CITY

A cursory glance at Indian cities reveals a few things quickly. People care greatly about the inside of their house, but remain indifferent to the street outside their doorstep. At the core of this mentality, among other things, is caste. Historically and culturally, cleaning of the public places is considered the work of Untouchables and low-caste people. This legacy of caste continues in modern-day India where piles of garbage accumulate unless picked up by the lower caste. The existing social order of a village, town, or city in modern-day, democratic India is based on the older caste lines.

Who can access a city space in India? Schools, places of worship, universities, banks, hospitals, public offices, and courts are run and administered by the upper castes; all menial jobs are done by the lower castes. Caste is deeply embedded in the city space. Men and women, to varying degrees, have access to these spaces, but hijras' access to public places is regulated.[15] In recent years, hijras have been given legal rights. Despite these rights, their everyday life is fraught with danger. The attitudes of the people are not changed by simply changing laws. One hijra describes his work experience:

I have worked in a garment factory for about a year. I could not even go to the toilet, as I was scared that the boys would go there to see me. They always tried to have sex with me. When there was a night shift, the threat was higher. Once my supervisor forced me to have sex with him, and I had no choice but to do it. But when it became public, my job was dismissed, as if it was my fault. (Khan et al., 2009, p. 445)

Therefore, hijra communities prefer to remain private and closed to the larger society. They live in the margins of the city. Their presence on the streets is a spectacle. They are cheered, mocked, hackled, harassed, and assaulted. Their tormentors wrap themselves in caste and unleash a strange civic-minded cruelty against hijra bodies. Hijras are seen as public properties.

One of the ways hijras deal with the collective hostility and indifference of the society is by defying societal norms. Before men abuse them, hijras intimidate them by their vulgar, loud gestures to protect themselves. By performing aggressive, inscrutable gestures, hijras counter the collective street hostility of society. For instance, they clap on streets; only hijras can decode the precise meaning of these claps—*hijra taalis*. These tactics provide them a certain secrecy and a private way of communicating around non-hijras. Even though multiple meanings are embedded in hijra taalis, these are mainly performed as a shield to protect themselves from the harassing public (Hall, 1995).

According to Karmic Philosophy, hijras are born as hijras because of the ills they have committed in their previous lives. It then becomes easier for the society to further demonize them, and see them as abnormal, malevolent, and uncanny, a tactic of caste to exploit, discard hijra bodies by giving their socially orchestrated oppression a divine hue. Everybody is made to believe that wherever one stands in the caste hierarchy is due to one's Karma. Hijras, victimized by caste, accept their wretched condition as the outcome of Karma. It is an easy way to keep things as they are, and this serves the self-interest of upper castes.

In Roy's novel, the hijra child is given a male name, Aftab, at birth which he changes later on and gives himself a female name, Anjum. As an adult, Anjum goes to live with other hijras and when she subsequently has to leave them, she has nowhere to go except a graveyard. The entire social machinery is implicit in pushing her to the margins of the city. Here, there is no external colonizer, and yet hijra bodies are marked and treated as pariahs because of the sociocultural system internal to Indian society.

In a caste-based society, hijras are strategically delinked to the caste because of their physiognomy, which makes it impossible for them to function, participate, and contribute to a heteronormative society. This rupture between caste and hijra body alienates hijras completely, not only resulting in broken connection between hijras and the mainstream society but also nullifying effectively their claims to the citizenry. For instance, the narrator in

Khushwant Singh's novel *Delhi* (1990) comes across a hijra named Bhagmati. He finds her lying bruised in an inebriated state on the street in central Delhi. Further, in the novel, they become friends and lovers. It is an implausible relationship in normal circumstances. However, they establish an intimate bond because both lie outside the caste matrix. One is a privileged, deracinated, upper-caste man, the other a hijra—both outsiders to caste-order and unhinged from any sense of societal decorum.

Only the anglicized narrator could see the humanity of the hijra body because his world is not limited by the trappings of caste. Early on in the novel, the narrator compares Bhagmati with the city of Delhi. He notices that just like the city, Bhagmati is vulgar, coarse, repulsive, and shoddy, but when you know her intimately you see her charm. Also, seeing Delhi and Bhagmati (hijras) through his eyes, the reader is made aware of the remarkable parallels between the history of Delhi and hijras; both have been assaulted, plundered, and exploited by strangers.

Unlike the anglicized narrator and his unusual relationship with Bhagmati, mainstream Indian society seldom interacts with hijras except on specific occasions, such as festivals, birth, or marriage-related ceremonies. Many Indian people consider a blessing from hijras auspicious. Since hijras cannot procreate themselves, many in Indian society believe that hijras are able to bless the fertility of others; a powerful myth the caste-based society uses to create an unbridgeable distance between society and hijras. It is false and insincere because in everyday life, the same society does not interact with hijras. They are not allowed to inhabit any social space, and thus pushed to live an underground life. By branding hijras as wicked as well as spiritually gifted, Indian society dehumanizes them.

Any city in India, both modern and historic, can be seen through the prism of caste. The center of the town is largely inhabited by upper castes: businessmen, teachers, doctors, whereas the periphery is for the Untouchables, with little access to city resources. The Untouchables live not only in inhabitable conditions, but also often in dangerous ones. As India continued to modernize itself on a vast scale particularly after post-globalization, the demography of the town has not changed accordingly. In every urban center, the upper castes take up the upscale neighborhoods and every such neighborhood has a slum attached to it. The slum dwellers—primarily the lower castes—work in the posh residential areas. The hijras navigate both these spaces; the posh neighborhoods as well as the slums, but they do not really belong anywhere. They have to be discreet because any public space can turn against them on a whim. And being casteless and hijra, they have few avenues where they can seek justice. The state and the ordinary people remain completely oblivious to them.

This struggle for space continues as long as they live. In addition, they suffer unbearable pain and humiliations on a daily basis. Unfortunately, struggles for space do not end even after they die. The state and society continue to ignore and harass hijras even after they die. For instance, even dead bodies of hijras are considered inauspicious, and therefore, no one wants to claim them. Their claim to city spaces remains problematic until the end and beyond (Khan et al., 2009).

## VIOLENCE AND THE NATION

Indians are quick to blame the British rule for every ill in modern-day India. The luminaries of the Indian independence movement imagined a democratic nation for all. They sought to render all kinds of differences irrelevant to the national imaginary. However, in order to make the independent nation free from various vices, the reformist leaders went out of their way to impose a certain order on the imagined nation; to give it a uniformity, not realizing they were mostly guided by Victorian ethics. In order to homogenize an extremely diverse country and its people, the upper-caste nation builders used selective narratives from Indian epics in line with the Hindu caste ideology to imagine Indian nation.[16]

For instance, from the vast religious texts, the nation makers took specific male and female figures for its people to emulate. The religious text *Ramayana* was the key to this imaginary. In *Ramayana*, the central figures are Rama and Sita. Rama is the ideal king, who never questions, who submits to his parents' will, and who gives up his own pleasure for the well-being of his family. In short, whatever is individual, personal, and private in him is given up on the altar of family, community, and caste. He is described as *Maryada Purushottam*—the ideal man. Parents secretly want their male children to be like him. Men are admired and valued if they submit to the family. All this insistence on the family is actually an insistence on following caste. However, in the cacophony of morality, this connection is missed or gets buried. Also, just like Rama, his wife, Sita, is the ideal woman, and girls often are raised to be like her. For instance, a girl's childhood and life before marriage do not matter; it is only after marriage that her life begins. Her value is determined by how well she looks after her family. She needs to completely submit to her husband and his family.

The makers of modern India imagined its men and women to be like Rama and Sita. However, in the real world—as opposed to the imagined one—there is an arc of human bodies that does not match the ideal figures of Rama and Sita. Interestingly, while the nation builders remembered Rama and Sita, they conveniently forgot the more complex and challenging figure of, for instance, Krishna, and the other Indian epics that celebrate and acknowledge the full spectrum of human sexuality such as the *Kamasutra* and *Rasas* enshrined in the *Natya Shastra*. Whereas a text like *Kamasutra* explicitly deals with the varied facets of human sexuality, *Rasas* refer to the significance of taste, pleasure, and aesthetics in human life. These texts fully acknowledge the diversity and complexity of human sexuality and desire.

However, the nation builders, in their enthusiasm to build a nation, disregarded the complexity of human bodies by embracing a few selective, heteronormative figures—ignoring the more complex and queer ones—as it suits the nationalist agenda. For instance, Hindu mythology makes references to the notion of queerness;[17] there are stories of men who become women, and women who become men, of men who create children without women, and women who create children without men, and of creatures who are neither this nor that, but a little bit of both. These stories indicate a nuanced understanding of queerness in human life. However, in modern India, it is common to deny the existence of these stories so that patriarchy and caste continue.

Therefore, the ideal nation distances itself from non-normative bodies because these bodies disrupt the national narrative. For instance, hijra bodies cannot be Rama and Sita-like. By their very anatomy, hijras pose danger to the foundations on which Indian nation stands. Whereas hijras are tolerated and seen as sinners paying for their bad Karma committed in previous lives, any voluntary transgression of normative gender lines by the so-called normal men and women is seen as an attack on Indian culture. In order to impose imagined Indianness on a vast population, the nation regulates the bodies to perpetuate and enforce caste. It disregards "unruly" bodies as they blur and threaten the neat binary of man-woman, thereby, posing danger to the existing caste order.

The constant regulation, supervision, and control of bodies is done to maintain caste. The burden of maintaining caste purity squarely falls on the body of a woman. Women have to safeguard their bodies to remain relevant and admirable in society. In addition, caste isolates and maintains its difference from other castes by controlling women's bodies. Even Sita, the paragon of virtue, has to go through *Agni Pariksha*.[18]

If one looks at the figures of Rama and Sita and the democratic nation's image of itself, it is difficult to link these figures to the caste system. However, they are perfect figures for ordinary men and women to emulate. It is through this idealization that the nation "performs" itself. Those who emulate these figures are admired; those who choose not to are branded as anti-Indian. Although Indian constitution provides equal rights to all, prejudice and discrimination toward sexual minorities persist.[19] For instance, the practice of arranged marriage is still the norm in India. Legally, any adult person can marry anyone; however, in practice, this is seldom the case. The norm of arranged marriage and negligible divorce rates indicate society's obsession with caste purity.

However, in the wake of globalization, caste seems to be waning as women are not only getting educated in great numbers, but also are joining the workforce in every sphere that until now was considered a male bastion. However, freedom to educate oneself and to choose a profession does not automatically translate into self-determination. A casual glance at any matrimonial page reveals how prevalent caste is in India, even when it seems to be disappearing from society. Marriage is deemed essential for virtually everyone in India, marking the great watershed in life for the individual. Marriages are arranged within the caste between unrelated young people who may never have met. All these seemingly unconnected, innocent sociocultural practices keep strengthening caste and stigmatizing non-normative—hijras—bodies.

In addition, since the mode of living has changed drastically in all fields because of changes in education, science, and modes of production, caste reinvents itself and emerges in its newer and modernized avatar. Modernization in India has opened up new avenues and a surplus of jobs. Rather than upgrading the lower castes, the more coveted jobs go to upper-caste women. Because of the systematic caste-based oppression of Untouchables, most often it is only the upper-caste men and women who have the required skills to get employment. Whereas policies are made to encourage gender equality in the employment sector by employing (upper-caste) women, these policies, at their core, are ways to maintain age-old caste hierarchies by keeping lower castes, especially the Untouchables, out of the job markets.

Where do hijras stand in this? Nowhere. They are ignored at every stage. The entire civic administration and family play a key role in marginalizing hijras. Whereas in independent India considerable steps have been taken to address the situation of women, and post-1990s, the rights of LGBT communities; no sincere efforts have been made in regard to hijra rights. In 2014, the Indian state recognized hijras as the third gender. In everyday life, despite the law, they suffer massive discrimination in obtaining driving license, identity document, admission in school—all such things that ordinary people take for granted.

Indian state took a laudable step by recognizing the third gender and showing sensitivity toward hijras; however, when seen from the perspective of caste, the recognition of hijras as the third gender seems cosmetic. For instance, the same state does not grant LGBT people the right to live freely and exercise their sexuality.[20] Unlike hijras, sexual minorities function from within the society. They are the arteries through which the caste-based society functions. Allowing these groups the right to their sexuality requires a deep configuration within the society. Indian society is not yet ready for such a drastic change because this would disrupt the existing social hierarchies.[21]

So recognizing hijras as the third gender, and withholding the rights of sexual minorities reveals the twisted psyche of the state. The system that creates hijra bodies continues. Despite constitutional reforms, transgression of sexual norms is still frowned upon. A man wanting to marry another man is branded as anti-Indian culture. Men and Women, in many parts of India, when marrying outside their caste, are punished; there have been cases where their own families had burned them alive to uphold tradition (Krishnan, 2018). These wide ranging practices are ways to keep caste-order in society. For instance, commenting on the recognition of hijras as third gender, one hijra remarks, "see, we have got the gender right. But [it's as if] we've got our hands but we won't be able to do any work. Gender right is there, [but] sexual right is not there. So, are we expected to live a life of an ascetic, lost in meditation?" (Aggarwal, 2017, p. 55) The law's hesitancy to grant "sexual rights," and their implementation when they are selectively given, has its root in the social ontology of caste.

As one studies various forms of oppression, hijras do not surface in the hierarchies of oppressions. They remain at the periphery of social experience; their very mention evokes laughter, ridicule, and disdain. The state focuses on regulating and policing normal bodies to enforce caste; it also deals with dissenting bodies by using force, intimidation, and coercion. In the case of hijra bodies, since their anatomy cannot be fixed, they are demonized as mysterious, wicked, and non-human. They are erased from the national imaginary because they cannot be subsumed by caste.

The modern Indian nation, since its inception in 1947, hails itself as a democratic socialist republic, but its governing sensibilities are caste-oriented and caste-dominated. Therefore, despite the super visibility of hijras in public life, they are not seen. They are put in the category of "non-human." Activist Mohsin Sayeed says that hijras are seen as "diseased," and therefore, they are shunned and forced by society to beg on streets, become prostitutes, and live in ghettos. Unlike the lower castes and Untouchables, hijras are so few in numbers that the practitioners of caste find it easier to abandon them than to deal with them. Furthermore, caste-based violence is not uncommon in India, especially when caste boundaries are transgressed. However, each oppressed or victimized group has its caste to fall back on for support. In this sense, each caste community has a definite stake in the caste system, irrespective of where it is positioned in the caste hierarchy. Even the most vulnerable groups in the caste-grid have support systems they can access. However, in the case of hijras, they have no such safety nets (Gupta, 2017).[22]

In a caste-based society, it is intriguing to see how easily people are led to believe in the irrelevance of hijra bodies. Even the reformers who seek to eliminate oppression and inequality from society disregard hijras. The Indian caste system has led to a deep-seated and pervasive indifference toward hijras. Due to its long history, it is difficult, if not impossible, to dismantle caste. As long as caste prevails in Indian society, it is difficult to anticipate fundamental changes in regard to the rights of hijras.

# NOTES

1. The Indian caste system is a system of social stratification of society based on hereditary division of people into Brahmins (priests), Kshatriyas (warriors), Vaisyas (farmers and merchants), Sudras (laborers and domestic servants). Those who do not fall in the domain of caste are called 'Untouchables'—the most marginalized and exploited people in India.

2. *Hijra* is an umbrella term for eunuchs, intersex or transgender people. They have been part of South Asia's culture for thousands of years. Eunuchs are celebrated in sacred Hindu texts such as *the Mahabharata* and *the Kama Sutra*. They also enjoyed influential positions in the Mughal courts. When the British came to power in India, the community's fortunes changed, with the disgusted colonists passing a law in 1897 classing all eunuchs as criminals.

3. See Kalpana Lajmi's (1997) film, *Darmiyan: In Between.* The film is set in Bombay of 1946. It is a story of an 'effeminate,' intersex child who is raised as a boy by his (actress) mother. The mother disguises the intersex status of her child to protect him from hijra groups as well as from society at large.

4. A number of hijra narratives have been published in recent years: See A. Revathi's *A life in Trans Activism* (2016), Laxminarayan Tripathi's *Me hijra, Me Laxmi* (2015), and A. Revathi's *The Truth About Me: A Hijra Life Story* (2012).

5. Hijras observe death-related ceremonies in secrecy, usually at night. They beat the dead hijra's body with slippers and shoes so that the person does not reborn as hijra again.

6. Castration is common when a transgender person joins the hijra community. Usually such operations are illegally done by other hijras. Consequently many hijras die (Nanda, 1999).

7. There is a widespread belief in India that hijras are born hermaphrodites and are taken away forcibly by the hijra community at birth. It is a myth that persists because the majority of hijras are transgenders. This is also Indian society's clever way not to deal with the multiplicity of non-normative bodies (Nanda, 1999).

8. It is a persistent belief, even among hijras, that they are born as hijras because of their bad karma. For instance, when a hijra person dies, the other hijras pray that the departing soul should not be reborn as a hijra in the next life.

9. The postcolonial theorists (Ranajit Guha, Spivak, Dipesh Chakratabarty) have comprehensively written on the evils of colonialism on India, but they have hardly touched upon the internal Brahmanical colonization of Dalits. More recent theorists (Bhaba, Appadurai) are largely concerned with issues such as globalization, immigration, and hybridity that largely concern upper-caste Indians, and have little bearing on Dalits. The queer theory that focusses on India, too, has ignored the Dalits.

For instance, the word caste has not appeared once in Vanita and Kidwai study(2000). Both queer and postcolonial scholarship in India reflects the concerns of upper castes as it tends to ignore the caste system from which it benefits by oppressing the bulk of Indian population—such as the Dalits. This collective insistence on not dealing with caste makes Indian society hostile toward non-normative bodies such as hijras and (sexual) outcastes.

10. In the Indian context, when issues concerning 'equality,' 'justice,' and 'violence against women and sexual-minorities' are discussed, Indian policy makers exclude the issue of caste on which Indian society is profoundly hinged, and therefore 'inequality' persists in society.

11. Marriages are predominantly arranged in India. People marry within their castes. Men and women who remain single are not respected, especially men. According to Hindu religion, everyone must marry and fulfill one's duty. In such a religious and conservative society, sexual minorities, too, marry as they fear ostracization. However, men and women who renounce the world and become monks are accepted.

12. See, India has 21 million 'unwanted' girls. (2018, January 30). *The Telegraph.* In Roy's novel, the muslim mother gives birth to an intersex child, but she raises her as a boy. She hopes that her child's 'female would part' heal or disappear, which shows her deep-seated wish for a male child. This also shows how Indian society privileges certain bodies over others. These formations of bodies as desirable/undesirable affect non-normative bodies negatively.

13. The Indian film industry is one of the biggest industries in the world. However, Indian films are seldom centered on lower castes such as Untouchables and almost never on hijras—hijras occasionally appear to provide comic relief. These depictions reinforce hijra stereotypes and strengthen society's indifference toward hijras.

14. Sanjay Leela Bhansali's (2018) film, *Padmaavat*, has created a law and order problem in India. Only the Rajputs (the warrior caste) condemned the filmmaker for distorting their history. Rajput men, women, and children led huge demonstrations across India as if their history were more important, or separate from Indian history. This incident showed how caste affiliation supersedes every other local or national concern.

15. Transgenders and visible sexual minorities drop out of mainstream schools at an early age because of the prejudice they face. However, the discrimination toward hijras borders on hostility and contempt, and it continues throughout their lives.

16. The debate between Ambedkar and Gandhi over the (de)merits of the Indian caste system as defended in *the Manusmṛti* brought into question the very idea of Hinduism, and the type of Hinduism that ought to be considered prescriptive in a post-Raj India. In many respects, *the Manusmṛti* lies at the very core of the debate and political activity that brought into being the Republic of India. This debate concerning caste is still relevant in modern-day India (Ambedkar, 2014).

17. Ruth Vanita, "The self is not gendered: Sulabha's debate with King Janaka." *NWSA Journal*, 15.2, Summer 2003, p. 76.

18. A trial by fire of Sita in the Sanskrit epic *Ramayana*. Sita is kept in captivity by the devil Ravana. Rama slays Ravana and saves his wife. Finally, when Rama and Sita come back to their kingdom, a sly washerman cast aspersions on Sita's character.

In order to prove her purity, Sita undergoes a trial by fire—*Agni Pariksha*. This is done to maintain peace and (caste) order in Rama's Kingdom. To this day, this mythical episode guides man-woman relationships in India.

19. Lower castes and Untouchables still do the jobs associated with their caste whereas Brahmins work as teachers, administrators, priests and so forth.

20. See Section 377 and the law: What courts have said about homosexuality over time. (2018, February 5). *Hindustan Times.*

21. After two decades of LGBTI struggle for equal rights, Indian Supreme Court has decriminalized homosexuality on September 6, 2018). This landmark judgement will have a limited reach in a society obsessed with caste. For instance, according to Indian constitution caste-based discrimination is unconstitutional, and yet caste is practiced blatantly.

22. After a long, complicated battle, the supreme court of India has decrimanalized homsexuality on September 6, 2018. Since the Indian caste system still governs everyday life in India, a change in law—though a milestone in Indian LGBTQ history—is not sufficient considering the strength and history of caste in India.

## REFERENCES

Aggarwal, A. (2017). *Hijras and their rights: In mythology and social cultural practices of India* (Master thesis, Utrecht University). Retrieved from https://globalcampus.eiuc.org/bitstream/handle/20.500.11825/304/Aggarwal.pdf?sequence=1&isAllowed=y.

Ambedkar, B.R. (2014). *Annihilation of caste.* London: Verso.

Bhansali, S.L. (Producer and Director). (2018). *Padmaavat* [Motion picture]. International Paramount Pictures.

Dasgupta, R. (2014). *Capital: The eruption of Delhi.* New York: Penguin.

Gupta, B. (2017, November 10). In a polarized world, minorities continue to struggle. *The Independent.* Retrieved from http://theindependent.sg/in-a-polarized-world-minorities- continue-to-struggle/.

Hall, K. (1995). *Hijra hijrin: Language and gender identity* (Doctoral dissertation, University of California, Berkeley). Retrieved from https://www.academia.edu/19614429/Hijra_Hijrin_Language_and_Gender_Identity_1995_192.

India has 21 million 'unwanted' girls. (2018, January 30). *The Telegraph.* Retrieved from https://www.telegraph.co.uk/news/2018/01/30/india-has-21-million-unwanted-girls/.

Khan, S.I., et al. (2009). Living on the extreme margin: social exclusion of the transgender population (hijra) in Bangladesh. *Journal of Health, Population and Nutrition,* 441–451, vol 4.

Nanda, S. (1999). *Neither men nor women: The hijras of India.* New York: Thomson Press Co.

Olivelle, P. (2005). *The law code of Manu.* New York: Oxford University Press.

Pandit, R.V. (Producer), and Lajmi, K. (Director). (1997). *Darmiyan: In between* [Motion picture]. India: Pan Pictures.

Pattanaik, D. (2014). *Shikhandi: And other tales they don't tell you*. Delhi: Penguin Books Ltd.

Roy, A. (1997). *The god of small things* (2nd. ed.). London: Flamingo.

———. (2014). Introduction: The Doctor and the Saint. *Annihilation of caste*, by B.R Ambedkar, 1936, London: Verso, pp. 17–141.

———. (2017). *The ministry of utmost happiness*. New York: Hamish Hamilton.

Sayeed. M. (2015, April 15). Transgender people 'not even considered human.' S.Shams. Retrieved from https://www.dw.com/en/transgender-people-not-even-considered-humans/a-17568119.

Section 377 and the law: What courts have said about homosexuality over time. (2018, February 5). *Hindustan Times*. Retrieved from https://www.hindustantimes .com/india- news/section-377-and-the- law-what-courts-have-said-about-hom osexuality-over-time/story-66xXSTFILnBY o5hE7yNaKL.html.

Singh, K. (1990). *Delhi: A novel*. New York: Penguin Books Ltd.

Vanita, R., and Kidwai, S. (2000). *Same sex love in India: Reading from history and literature*. New York: St.Martin's Press.

## Chapter 12

# A Nonbinary Letter

## *From Camp Epicene*

Mike Perez

Dear Reader—Dear *They, Their, and Them*—

I would like to start this autoethnography "letter" to myself *and* others—for "I am writing for myself and strangers. This is the only way that I can do it," Gertrude Stein said, and I wholeheartedly agree (*Selected Writings*, 1990, p. 261). If strangers can be others *and* ourselves within one frame, it's right to "start as if to start" and inspired by Stein, as she is the butch-femme embodiment of epic inspiration for me and this chapter. I want it to be a correspondence with and for the unruly selves housed inside my endlessly querying frame, questions active for almost fifty-eight years. Speaking of frames, physical, written, or otherwise, I also keep in mind Susan Stryker's reminder that different media iterations and genres are integral to this process, as "the English word 'gender' is derived from *genre*, meaning kind or type" (Stryker, 2008, p. 11). I mix some genres as fluidly as the gender awareness I now embrace beyond binaries, encompassing the voice I write with as well as the voice that thrives in me beyond academia.

Still, here are some useful elucidations from a reliable academic source:

The word *genre* is defined as "Kind; sort; style" and "A particular style or category of works of art; esp. a type of literary work characterized by a particular form, style, or purpose." Both the words gender and genre come from the Anglo-Norman and Middle French, and if you search the etymology for the word genre, the OED links to the etymology for the word gender. (Watkins, OED, 2018)

Gender discovery—or genderqueer identity in search of discovery—is how I can begin, focusing on a word that my academic self snagged on some time ago while re-reading Susan Sontag's canonical essay "Notes On Camp." *Canonical to whom* may become the Russian Nesting Doll game of this chapter, wherein the more one reveals, the more one is left to analyze oneself as microcosm, as miniature; as "moi," "je," or "I" in search of one final subject, hard to discern in its arrived, minutiae state. If Rimbaud was correct when he claimed *Je est un autre*, then have I just been quoting French while blowing academic smoke around my Russian doll, about to open itself in a hall of mirrors, in the style of the film *The Lady From Shanghai*? Which reflection is realest? Is it myself and another at once? And will I appear reflected as a bleach-blond Rita Hayworth in a fun house mirror, accidentally holding a gun on myself? I wish. But who is speaking for whom? And what is that voice even sound like?

*I am an other. I write for myself and strangers.* The nonbinary auditor and writer hears themselves loud and clear in these epigram-slogans; I want you to hear with me as I write what it's like to be "large and contain multitudes" according to Whitman, yet struggle to record the voices that combine to represent a nonbinary life lived assigned to a man's scaffolding, frame, and biology, as a man in noun only, framed to be a man.

## FRAMING (EPI-WHAT?)

The word in question from Sontag inspires the real starting place for this autoethnography. It's not a word I've encountered much in fifty-seven years of being, in order as follows, *a sissy, a queer, a homo, a faggot, a gay cow, a gay man,* and now, *a nonbinary queer gent* (with no relation to Peer Gynt, though this chapter may very well turn out to be the extended pitch of a wandering queer salesman). I've seen "gay" as an adjectival turned into "s/he is a gay" noun. Duality is everything, and nothing, for entering into this chapter, and that camp, by contrived or superficial nature, is less commonly thought of as one integral word hiding in plain sight in "Notes On Camp" and integral to a nonbinary consciousness as more than a serious joke: *epicene.*

As opposed to the brave men and women assigned at birth to the incorrect sex who have fought tirelessly to be binary, accurate, real, the speaker in this chapter learns from genderqueer pioneers and integral moments that direct them beyond binaries to not a third gender awareness so much as a *they* in search of a voice, sometimes male-founded, sometimes female, always nonbinary, and assigned at birth a gender they'll negotiate the rest of their lives. This chapter is the chart and voice for negotiation and navigation, what Kate Bornstein might call "hidden: a gender" (*Gender Outlaw*, p. 198). Good ol' go-to site Dictionary.com (at least for the college students I teach) shows the word *epicene* as already "sissified," and already capable of inspiring a language game "capable of referring to either sex":

epicene

(adjective)

- belonging to, or partaking of the characteristics of, both sexes: *Fashions in clothing are becoming increasingly epicene.*
- flaccid; feeble; weak: *an epicene style of writing.*
- effeminate; unmasculine.
- (of Greek and Latin nouns) of the same gender class regardless of the sex of the being referred to, as Latin *vulpēs* "fox or vixen" is always grammatically feminine.
- *Grammar.* (of a noun or pronoun) capable of referring to either sex, as *attendant, chairperson, Kim, one,* or *they*; having common gender.

(noun)

- a person or thing that is epicene.

(This aligns with being "a gay that is gay," the noun here morphing into an adjective way before gay become flexibly noun and adjective, to being something as opposed to doing something.) I am gay, but have I been, am I, always a gay? No one notified me of the shift in usage. In the daily hazing known as American sixth grade, I just went with what I was called—"gay cow." By others. And these are not always the others meant by *Je est un autre"* or the other-ness I have begun to count and hear inside me as a nonbinary "man" using "man" as a placeholder (at least for today, August 7, 2020, subject to change).

## "MOO"

So what's with that bovine slur in quotation marks? What is with the quotation marks overall? As I was being called a queer cow at fourteen, I was many years away of what Sontag designated on the subject in "Notes On Camp":

10. Camp sees everything in question [or quotation?] marks. It's not a lamp but a "lamp"; not a woman but a "woman." (Sontag, 1964, p. 280)

Here I was being absurdly contained within quotation marks very young. "Gay Cow!" Little did I know the sex I was assigned at birth would fit within quotation marks as well, had always, would always fit inside quotations:

> 11. Camp is the triumph over the epicene style. (The convertibility of "man" and "woman," "person" and "thing.") But all style, that is, artifice, is, ultimately, epicene. Life is not stylish. Neither is nature. (Sontag, 1964, p. 280)

This last quip aligns nicely with the beautician character of Truvy in the play and film *Steel Magnolias* when she says, "There is no such thing as natural beauty" (Harling, 1988, p. 8). That Dolly Parton delivers these lines makes a case for her as a "woman," a construct, a triumph of convertible female, an epicene go-to. Parton is certainly a spokeswoman for a woman under construction for at least forty years: her own home-grown quip about her appearance says it best: "It takes a lot of money to look this cheap." But is she a triumph of the epicene according to Sontag (and more importantly, myself?)? What would a life constructed in popular culture bits assembled as a sequence allow me to understand the binary code I have been working under since I was born and that I now renounce through the fragments shored in this chapter?

As a hard-boiled film noir detective once said, "I want answers, mister!" This is not necessarily the same as evidence—or realness.

## CUE CHERYL LYNN, "GOT TO BE REAL"

Also known as the song playing over the closing credits for *Paris Is Burning* (Livingston, 1990), Ms. Lynn's supple coloratura soprano belts, "What you find . . . what you feel . . . (got) to be real!" Realness, a category that Harlem queens and ball walkers knew the necessity of very well and "delivered every ball" gets complicated when the interior (as opposed to the exterior) construct of visual fabulosity response to *Which self is real?* (a non-academic reaction) is added onto my many nonbinary questions. The question of which one is realest (as both an academic and street question being posed) has to do with both an inner and outer manifestation of realnesses that coalesce. *If they align, I call them mine* is now my "insta-dentity" catch phrase. The problem as I feel it is for a nonbinary person is having to choose one to speak for all at any given moment. This is not the same as schizophrenia!

Thus I want to present myself to you as a suddenly epicene spokesperson, a nonbinary gent who camps but not as he once thought, who sometimes uses the word "man" because they have for almost sixty years. They have recently embraced not nouns, not adjectives, but pronouns as their way to demarcate who they are, all of them inside them, now. No matter which, these questions come with an ever-present, ever-changing soundtrack heard as you try to write yourself into a coherently selved ethnography, with one direction to *Please stand up*! voiced by the game show narrator from *To Tell The Truth*, an old television game show in reruns as I came of awareness, of *popular cultural* awareness, in the late sixties. The format for *To Tell The Truth* was always the same: three contestants assumed and presented one identity that celebrity panelists had to quiz and then choose which person, based on their, shall I daresay proto-verbal autoethnography, was the real person in question, bonafide, certifiable, and matching in both narrative and appearance. The almighty pressure to match! The narrator then bellowed at the end of the quizzing session, "Will the REAL _____ please stand up?" One of the panelists did. My guesses were always wrong, but then I never thought it was a game: just as the smooth, non-gendered game show narrator in my mind would soon and consistently ask me would the real Michael Perez, or Mike Perez, or Michael V. Perez, or Misha P. Kisarli (names I've published under) please stand up—which one, boy or girl? The only answer is *Yes*. *To Tell The Truth* lived on in syndication: however, all questions involving my gender came from the myriad panelists' voices inhabiting my final gender panel, always in repertoried performance.

And this is more than just a game for show.

## WISH I HAD THE YOUTUBES AROUND WHEN . . .

If one cannot build a palpable, human community in isolation, can we build a solo community from the plurality of voices, identities, and genders we contain and have yet to fully let speak? What is their language, and how can they thrive beyond binary codes superimposed upon them since birth?

This is where you say YouTube and social media to the rescue! beyond any analog dialogue. I could have used Victor Lockhart a long time ago—at least fifty years ago, when my epicenely destined self first lived happily in things (more on epicene things later). Sontag's essay was my gateway drug toward questioning the duality of things in a gendered manner, even as she stated that the epicene was unnatural in "Notes On Camp." The book, then, was the genre—the medium—that would unexpectedly deliver the feeling, or perhaps the *felt code*—of non-binariness. What young people questioning themselves today have is a virtual method of revelation in gigabytes that doesn't erase the book method I accessed as much as visualize and personify how a non-binary person appears while a definitional dialogue happens, at once. This is the voice I didn't know I needed, at seven or fifty-seven: the teen activist and author Victor Lockhart posted to Facebook by Tod Perry from www.good.is:

As America limps toward recognizing the rights of transgendered people, there is a growing movement to bring visibility to those who embrace no gender at all. Known as Nonbinary or genderqueer, these individuals aren't specific about the nature of their gender because they choose to live beyond its confines or preferences to remain gender fluid. If that's a bit tough for you to grasp, Victor Lockhart has done a fantastic job at explaining the concept. [. . .] In "Boy of Girl?" Lockhart explains how people can be neither male or female. Our sex is what we've been assigned by our chromosomes, but gender is how we choose to express ourselves. "Gender is what you feel, not what your parts are!" Lockhart says. So when they (most Nonbinary people prefer "they" rather than "he" or "she") is asked "Are you a boy or a girl?" Lockhart always responds, "No." Although that is confusing to most people, by making videos such as the one above, Lockhart can help the average person understand, therefore accept Nonbinary people. And, just as importantly, Nonbinary people can be free to express themselves however they like. (Perry, "Victor Lockhart Explains What It Means To be Nonbinary," GOOD, 2016)

Academic or not, what I want to tell you as a (obviously morphing) thesis is that I no longer identify as gay or a gay first, and that nonbinary has become my first daily truth test to find my voice with, a long time in the making—and in this chapter, I show you how I got there. I want to tell you how popular culture artifacts have carved a path and whetted my desire to identify as nonbinary. These artifacts have become the most potent and resonant evidence I know. How popular culture offers evidence in myriad forms and deliverables—but primarily music, songs, art, essays, television, skin care, shampoos, movies, and eventually online iteration is always the thesis, always the point: that evidence forms the only sequences that forges a sequential "playlist" of sorts as to how and why I am neither male nor female.

Jimmie Manning and Tony E. Adams define what I have been trying to say from my apparently (in terms of appearance) cis-normative queer white male position, though I prefer to say, as an ex-dancer's gesture:

Autoethnography is a research method that foregrounds the researcher's personal experience (auto) as it is embedded within, and informed by, cultural identities and con/texts (ethno) and as it is expressed through writing, performance, or other creative means (graphy). More specifically, it is a method that blends the purposes, techniques, and theories of social research—primarily ethnography—with the purposes, techniques, and theories associated with genres of life writing, especially autobiography, memoir, and personal essay. ("Popular Culture Studies and Autoethnography: An Essay on Method," pp. 188–189)

Above all, in this chapter, I want to honor as I show how I have embodied *epicene*, as the meaning changes within me, has been haplessly and unknowingly superimposed on me, but to own the word as temporal conjugation now—as past, present, and future, noun, adjective, adverb, and verb. The question I never got around to asking about when I first stumbled upon "epicene" in Sontag's canonical essay marks the textual moment I needed further information to define myself as other than a gay man—what lawyers and the legal process call *discovery*—as to the nature of that word Susan Sontag used as synonymous with "camp." Could this be a man in a dress? It's complicated, just by mentioning the garment on certain bodies. Could this be Uncle Miltie (Milton Berle)? RuPaul? RuPaul bitching at Uncle Miltie on the MTV Awards in the early 1990s? Me wearing nail polish on one nail for Sexual Assault Awareness Month? Me for the past fifty-seven years, on or off, being actively sexual or celibate (for the past twelve years—another story indeed)? This is my academic self colliding with the gender *du jour* direct shooter housed by my skin. Sontag might have been focused on the seen thing of a nonbinary appearance—be it person or thing. I want to turn this "equation" inward and also include the nonbinary interior as a mitigating feature of the epicene body, and of my last fifty-seven years.

## "I FEEL LIKE ME"

Let's start at age twelve, in 1975, when I first put a voice to what I was feeling. My mom and I were having dessert together[1] after dinner, or maybe coffee and dessert—drinking coffee was the way I signaled the world that I was mature, already an adult, so I felt. How did the subject come up? Maybe the previous years of being a screeching hyperactive child terrorizing the block with my high-pitched exclamations and early-voguing gestures, all delivered while on half-toe (or "Tippy Toes," as the mean boys of the neighborhood called me—I had discovered ballet class with two sisters, my best friends, and *relevé en demi-pointes* felt like the physical stance from which I could rule the world, or at least our block, at seven years old). The prelude to this gendered revelation was a long time coming, soundtracked by diva albums I bought on my own accord—Queen Aretha, Dusty Springfield, Liza Minnelli, Natalie Cole, The Emotions, and Deniece Williams. Divas started the party, commented on it, and gave it strength. But this is about the cumulative effect of this media and pop culture coming together in a perfect storm identified as Hurricane *Michel*. *Michel* is the name my francophone father called me, always, especially in public—the French male pronunciation of my name that sounded like the American girl name Michelle. Later my father would call me "Mike-*Michel*" together at once, offering a duality of identity both male and female, verbally conjoined.

But that aforementioned coffee is getting cold. My mother and I, sitting together at home, didn't always speak—often we sat together as she thought, usually writing one of the many poems in her head that would become her life's calling and passion—when suddenly, I simply offered, between sips, "Mom, I don't feel like a boy OR a girl—I feel like me!"

Pause.

Pause.

My mom answered, "But you're a boy . . . a MAN!" This was the first time I really considered that word in relation to myself. A man. My destiny—?! Not Tippy Toes. Not screeching and voguing around the block. Not singing the girl part to "Having My Baby" by Paul Anka and Odia Coates. Not lip-synching to "Boogie Woogie Bugle Boy," Mein Herr," or "I Don't Want To Lose Your Love" at my parents' cocktail parties. Not, Not, Not. This was my soul's first nonbinary knot.

This scene dissolves, and fast. I forget what happened next, but I know the subject was changed, as was everything, from then on.

Everything.

[And this scene needs a coda, with its background tune being Sam Smith's "Restart," with "epicenic" vocals that move sublimely from chest baritone voice into falsetto and gender-blurred tonality; to my ears, Smith's vocals on the chorus recall the sublime lilting harmonized coos of gospel/"r & b" of the 1970s trailblazers The Emotions, of "Best Of My Love" fame.] New scene:

I came out to my landlord in early 2020, because I had just realized what I was, thanks to Sam Smith coming out as nonbinary—and if I have anyone to thank for helping my identity coalesce merely by being themselves and being true to their revelatory voice, it's them, Sam Smith, my hero(ine) + 1, at least. I told my landlord and then her husband, to which her husband said, "Wow, you're kinda late in doing this!" I had a moment of what I now know is gender dysphoria, a disengaged feeling of quiet misgendered panic and utter self-effacement— which is exactly what I felt when my mother told me I was a man. Happily, my landlord answered for me and said, "He's not late in doing this—he told his mom when he—sorry, *they*—were 12." This was precisely the timely, life-saving reminder that I needed to hear from someone else, upholding a truth I'd suppressed for so very long and didn't even know I was suppressing. It's my go-to story when asked how I knew I was nonbinary, and how my mom, Sam Smith, and my landlord were the three wise "thems" that made it all coalesce.

## NURSE VS. "NURSE"

If everything fundamental about the misleading word "sex" can be air-quoted in a camp/epicene context, then my earliest trip into gender happened in a bag—in a kit. (Cue Lady Bracknell from Oscar Wilde's *The Importance of Being Earnest* exclaiming in genteel horror "a *HAND*-BAG?!" (Wilde, 1895).)

First, some background. To exclaim "NURSE!" is throwing shade, or what gay and drag queens sometimes yell at other queens or queer folk who need "help," usually a younger, hapless queen still working toward what constitutes as flawless on the outside. As Willam stated on *RuPaul's Drag Race* (Season 6, episode 6, 2015) with facetious deadpan delivery, explaining to younger Lantinx drag performer Kenya Michaels, "Nurses help people" after having read a queen for looking "busted" merely by exclaiming "NURSE!" (My nonbinary consciousness woke and not in need of nursing other than vigilant support toward the healthiest embodiment of "gendered otherness," does not see the drag queen in strictly binary terms.) For me, it's more of a construction that naturally blurs boundaries beyond the status of passing, checked sex box, or looking butch, cis-masculine, girly, or fishy (still an unfortunate example of queen slang).

I had a toy Nurse's Kit around six years old—this would be 1969. I loved that nurse's kit. There's a photo of me with it open as I sit by my grandmother's goldfish pond, me in a little boy Easter suit, with shorts, knee socks, and clip-on bow tie, already uneasy in certain kinds of clothes, in need of a different gender to come to the rescue: "Nurse!" I was ready.

I hear my mother's voice explaining to someone as I played with my kit, "Boys can be nurses, too." Again, this is 1969. I should mention the kit had a vial of candy pills, which I ate all at once. And like that harangued director at a louche Hollywood party in the first version of *A Star Is Born* (1937) bitching to Frederic March's Norman Maine, "I'm no longer a director; I'm a MALE NURSE!" I can relate.

The Take-Away: If genders are born, mine came with a Do-It-Yourself Hasbro Nurse's Kit.


## *TIGER BEAT*, COSMETICS BEAT, GENDER BEAT(EN)

Now it's 1976—and I'm thirteen and always roseate from acne, in need of a cosmetician nurse, in a somewhat ugly age for anyone inhabiting skin, for sure, but my version of gender dysmorphic officially begins here, in my early years as a shamed consumer.

It's Saturday afternoon, and I'm circling a beauty/makeup counter on the first floor (always the first floor) of a department store in a mall in the South (enough said?). I haven't graduated to having sex in the restroom that went by the name of "Men"—also another story, but not the quotation marks my mind always puts around that word when I use a public restroom. On my own and wordlessly, I had questioned where I earned access to by nature, and nature tapped back with *men, male, manly,* all in quotation marks, on doors, or not.

I'm circling that beauty counter because I am, unknowingly, storing parts of myself as compartmentalized departments—parts of me meant to help buy superficial applications outside of the gender I inhabit. Big words. I have none, beyond perhaps what I've heard on a playground in fifth grade (sissy, fairy, twinkle toes, not yet upgraded to "faggot")—and I circle the counters because I want a product I've seen in a teen magazine—*Young 'N Lovin Teen*, *16 Magazine*, or *Tiger Beat*—which is a thick, aromatic cleanser made with honey by Bonne Bell products. I can't remember equations but I know what Bonne Bell is, where I can get it, and what it promises to do for my skin erupted in roseate acne patches. These blips of awareness will become my equations to gender dysphoria *and* the embracing of a nonbinary awareness, from *he* to *they*.

That's a lot to tag onto a product! But I have always believed in the comfort of products to both saturate and wash away my strange gendered pangs of not belonging inside the skin I sell myself from every day, from a young age. While I'm circling that beauty counter, a teen magazine I could've used will say what I felt but couldn't articulate except in the purchase of a new shampoo bottle, joining the dozens of bottles lining my shower's window ledge (hands off for the rest of my family). More on that row later, but for now, take it away, *Teen Vogue* online. In 2018, Suzannah Weiss neatly states what I wouldn't—and couldn't—hear for years:

Nonbinary sex educator and therapist Aida Manduley, MSW defines a *nonbinary person* as "someone who does not identify as a man or a woman, or solely as one of those two genders." It's often used as "an umbrella term for other identities that fall outside the man / woman dichotomy and may be more specific," they add. "However this person identifies their gender, it does not neatly follow the binary of man and woman."

That definition's pretty broad because being nonbinary means different things to different people. To me, it means that I reject the whole concept of gender. Growing up, I never felt people were wrong when they called me a woman, but it felt like a label imposed on me rather than one that fit. Then, in college, I learned about nonbinary identity, and that did fit. Sure, I have likes and dislikes that some might label "feminine" or "masculine," but I don't feel any need to label them that way. The gender binary has made me feel pigeonholed, and I don't want to identify with it. (Weiss, *Teen Vogue*, 2018)

How media for teens has advanced! But I understand feeling pigeonholed now, and then—especially when the older maven lady clerk of the Bonne Bell counter—all I remember is a pursed, over-lined mouth more like a stained anemone saying, "What do you want, son? These are all women's products (with a sweeping arm gesture)—ALL OF THESE PRODUCTS are for women!"

I didn't get my bottle of Bonne Belle cleanser. That time. I kept trying, always circling the counter at first, looking for an ally, a lady ally, preferably a younger clerk, who would just laugh a little when I asked if they had the cleanser I'd seen in that dog-eared hard copy of *Teen Vogue*. How empowered

I would feel when I left the counter with a bag of cleanser, or astringent, or eye crème, or moisturizer, or even—this was the ultimate victory—a tube of lip gloss, preferably flavored with 7Up or Dr. Pepper, and going by the name of Bonne Bell Lip Smackers.

## LIP SMACKERS ON A TRAIN

Not to be confused with the Alfred Hitchcock film starring sexy-but-scary Robert Walker pitted against sexy-but-safer Farley Granger—why choose?!—this scenario is me at twelve traveling with my uncle, a long-distance railway train conductor. They still existed. He had secured me a sleeper berth for a trip to Columbia, South Carolina while he punched tickets and walked from railway car to railway car, in a smart conductor's cap and a wicked silver hole puncher. If I knew, I would tell you why I was there. But Vincent (my uncle), the stalwart, good-humored epitome of a nice guy who did a great impersonation of a normal man his whole life, had decided that his young sissy of a nephew might enjoy going with him on his weekend gig—from Jacksonville, FL, where he lived, and where I'm on summer vacation, to Columbia, overnight, with a day layover, and back. I go, excited to collect my skin care and beauty toiletries into a small zippered bag I'd bought just for the occasion. Beauty travels!

Once on the train and in the berth (or my heart's epicene compartment?), I lift up the window blind immediately and start applying lip gloss in profile, pretending that I'm looking at the reflection of my mouth in my compact's mirror. I start applying the lip gloss—the Lip Smacker—diligently to my lower lip and with more rhythmic, uncommon diligence than Joan Crawford's fingers opening a bottle of ketchup. An ostentatious *swipe, swipe*—I look up and out of my window at a man sauntering by—I knew that walk already, and wanted it not in the msovies on a silver screen but live, in person, and walking toward me, because of me. Already beauty expectation, sex, and gender were becoming a matter of projecting my private inner cinema to a real-life version in hopeful CinemaScope.

Separated by only glass, the man was moving, watching me.

HE waited a beat, then broke into a grin of nodded acknowledgment. There was no ridicule—the man acknowledged without definition other than me at my "tween-'epicene-ic'" and ripest. I've been waiting forty years for that sauntering grin to get me again and not walk on by. There I was—a girl?—a boy?—only clearly linked to my budding physical ambiguities by a thin sweet tube of lip gloss, Dr. Pepper flavored. Not for the last time, product linked and cinched my interior and exterior engendered making-up. And I

would make myself up (I mean my gender) endlessly, waiting and hoping for
one to take, to let me saunter, and not under glass.

Funny I should say that just now: for under glass is how I first found men
desirable—but wait: didn't girls like boys? Was I really a girl deep down?
(Thank Goddess we get to choose to extract desire from gender today.) At
six, all I had was a man behind glass on a screen to light the way. I'll offer
this section in a *genre-fluid* manner, switching to an "autoethnography poem"
from a prose essay format, perhaps in the spirit of Susan Stryker's reminder
of how gender dovetails nicely with genre:


## TEN ORBITAL STEPS TO BEING QUEER

### (Close-Up on Keir Dullea from *2001: A Space Odyssey*)[2]

1
It isn't because of the music,
the tympani pounding with
horrid authority, screeching apes
or that huge damn flying bone.

2
The cinematic learning of tools.
The flesh of the being-torn.
Is movie violence violence? I'm 6.
I checked out until . . . That face!

3
Here is a helmeted face surrounded
with squiggly colored lights—ecstatic
blues, golds, reds, whites, greens—like
visible motion marks from melting crayons.

4
Odyssey this: I didn't know the name
of Keir Dullea: a needed beacon

that the first sight of his Cinema-
Scoped face would light—and lit.

5
I was a wick and didn't know it, how
can you know what leads you to desire's

straining keg embedded in your brain
(and elsewhere)?—his was a face that filled

a window screen for the first time you're
stunned with, glimpse a religion, a curving
Cinerama window framing him from mouth

to brow, okay, that *simian* brow, I guess
the apes in this movie could claim escape
from the hairier planet of themselves.

5.5
I saw:

      a gloss that masked a mask for outer space;
      a close-up on a screen twelve times my size;
      a face of chiseled turbulence, well-suited
      to hold the shaken gaze of his blue eyes;—

      his shaken close-up, stirring me to—what?

6
I'm only 6. Weren't we in the spacecraft taking us,
the passive audience, to that planet aped

with buried liberties? No: that was last year, '68,
the first in a sequence of films that terrorized

my young new boy, unselved by new attractions.

7
Keir Dullea played the astronaut
that played and re-played my tingling view.

His suited face I wanted to unmask
I could fit, the screen was big, big, big.

His face could launch a million spaceships.
I thought Keir was Dean Jones from "Herbie

The Love Bug." But why was he so serious
now and in space, floating, talking back

to an unseen, droning analog? Every nonbinary child begins in anonymous analog.

8
From my seat in the theater's fifth row
(I could count but couldn't be counted

yet) the projection, God the projection,
I'm still in that huge cushy seat,

head tilted towards the relentless *yes,*
*but no,* an untouchable, masculine vision.

I had to go to the bathroom,
the darkness swelled, I held it,

wondering when my body would be released
to be more than a shameful function

as new words balanced on my tongue:
*man, boy, me; no, sissy; men are beautiful,*

all confused with hunger. Suddenly,
my lap was warm and wet as I stared up.

9
No "upward" got as high as me, June 1969—

this astronaut would let me touch
his helmet, saw me in the dark,

still gazing at his helmeted face,
—above all, saw *me* seeing him.

No gaze could hold a candle
to its squinted expectations,

so monolithic but what the hell
was a monolith you peed for as

you're gobbling candy kisses,
hoping he would come to clean you up

as the screen dissolved like seeing
the taste of slowly moistened licorice.

Lights came on. I'd taken one small
buoyant step—towards men, for men.

10
So this was the start of searching for homo
*homo sapiens*, outside of cinema's (mis-)
leading men, harder than simian obelisks,

removing their helmets and suits, revealing
the rigidness of their well-trained systems,
such relentless standards as our frames would take off
together, grinding and grounded in earthbound flight.

## CHARLTON HESTON'S LOINCLOTH VS. STEVE MCQUEEN (MORE HELMETED MEN)

Here are more small gendered steps: Charlton Heston in a loincloth in the aforementioned *Planet Of The Apes*, sweaty, always, already a proponent of concealed weapons. And screaming at what's left of the Statue of Liberty, buried on the beach. I'm only five here and already wondering where exactly that beach was off-screen, allowing me to start a new united state of loin-clothed, angry men, where I could make them happy.

The year 1971 brought another helmeted man on screen: Steven McQueen in *Le Mans*. As I have told a race car enthusiast friend, being taken to this movie may have been one parent's attempt for me to start "manning up." I think watching men go in oblong circles might have been an attempt to make me a purveyor of manly things. Another sweaty grimacing dirty-blond blue-eyed man in a helmet? It backfired.

## BACK TO "MICKE" (WITH OR WITHOUT QUOTATION MARKS)

Early epicene-ery: no camp delivery intended:

From fostered, gendered liberty, free of statues and statutes, comes my voice saying, assuredly: "Micke. That's how I spell it—M-i-c-k-e," I said to a lovely lady as I manned our garage sale in 1976. The lady was writing a check for my (never-used) bicycle and asked to whom she should make the check out to. (Cue a Robert Plant voice belting, "Does anyone remember CHECKS?!") As I saw it, the lady was simply buying a second-hand mobile stairway that moved forward and horizontally, and—heaven was mine and immobile!—she had referred to me as "she" when she used our phone to check with her husband on buying the bike. I was thrilled inside—my pudgy boy-boob body looked anything but masculine, and my daily triumvirate of braces, glasses, and blow-dried winged hair only settled the issue: my frame held nothing masculine, nothing sporty, nothing bicycle-friendly. Yes!

The lady left, promising she'd come back for the bicke (I meant "bike"). I didn't see her when she did—I was asleep, taking a victory map, and my father gave the lady her bike. I didn't need to know if she called me "she" to my Dad, nor the very awkward moment when he corrected her. Did he correct her? The moral of this story is, *There's nothing like a vehicle unmanned.*

## MY FIRST TRANSMEDIA?
## MISS CHRISTINE JORGENSON

Mom's turn, again: at the mall in 1976, I ask her, "Mom, who is Christine Jorgensen?" after I had come across a copy of her autobiography at the Waldenbooks store in the mall. She paused (this was actually less painstaking for her than when I asked her where babies came from), and said, with a frown, and I paraphrase, "Oh THAT was this sick guy who cut off his penis and wanted to be a girl." That's where the memory ends—FAST fade to black—but I remember well how my mother stressed the word "cut." This may have been the start of the Fast-Food Woman Syndrome for me—that becoming a woman was synonymous to a procedure, a violent one apparently, and that a woman would be delivered as a result of one snippet of a moment. And above all, Christine Jorgensen was a "THAT." Her autobiography had a photo section where a newspaper headline was shown with the following lead phrase: "It's A Girl, By George!" Even then, I got it, way too fast—I might turn out to be that *it* my mom and I talked about.

## THOSE CONCERTS

I liked Bette Midler, Liza Minnelli, and Labelle (the group) when I was twelve. No one told me to listen to them—you would have thought that I had a bachelor uncle who spotted the sissy in me and guided me toward gay male musical icons, but these artists were popular from 1972–1975 on the radio, or at least for Liza, in a popular musical film. In my room, I lip synched endlessly to these women's voices, assuming their pronouns, their phrasings, and their melismatic vocal calisthenics. When Bette Midler came in concert to Atlanta in 1974, my mom bought tickets for her (advertised on the radio) and she and I went—on a school night!

This was the beginning of genderqueer—or really, gender**k, as that word really describes better the impact I felt of seeing the following: a row of tall, multicolored, hirsute men leaning in to their reflections in the men's room mirror to apply . . . mascara. Small wands swiping up and out; then the men standing back to gauge the effect, smiling, more like grimacing, at their reflection. I forgot to go to the bathroom and went to find my mom, saying, "Mom! They're putting on makeup!" more as commentary than confusion.

## LA BELLE OF THE GENDER BALL

At the Labelle concert in 1975—actually, at both, as my mother and I went to see them when they came to Atlanta in the spring and then again in the fall of 1975—the audience came ready—spangled jumpsuits with feather boas and rhinestones, fully-made-up faces, and lame and silver outfits. It was as if a minor planet of intergalactic funkadelic amazons had descended upon the Atlantic Civic Center to strut and yell at the stage as the three women who comprised the group Labelle sang for the fiercest, grooviest two hours I had ever witnessed. Who was this pudgy white suburban boy naturally in love with the safety he felt from strong women? (*Why did he not feel safe in the first place?* is a question still searching for an answer.) Labelle's image had transformed from doo-wop girl group glam to, by 1975, layered, bedazzling space children coming of age courtesy of hot-glue-gun artisans, and courtesy of the far-out early-to-mid-1970s stylings of divine fashion designer Larry LeGaspi.[3] "Star Wars throws a ball and creates a house for its shimmery lunar suited gospel songbirds"—this may begin to say what I saw that night, and with butch and femme strengths combined in the group's lyrics and growly, ebullient alto all provided by Nona Hendryx, I was given a pass to touch the velcroed plasticized hem of three women in gender wonderland—Sarah Dash removed her lamé epauletted jacket with a snapped flourish to reveal a bustier of silver-bullet breast plates, to which the crowd—male and female—went WILD. My mother dropped her purse and yelled "Fabulous!"

> More unknown quotations: I'd never seen a "fabulous."
> And this, to me, became a benevolent, nonbinary reveal.

## ROBERT REED / MEDICAL CENTER

In 1975 on an episode of *Medical Center* entitled "The Fourth Sex," I (twelve years old) watched Robert Reed, a/k/a Mike Brady, the father of the Brady Bunch, turn overnight into a woman, from a man named Pat to a woman named Pat. See how easy that is? Therein lies the problem.

At least it was a two-part episode, and okay, aired a week apart. The effect of this temporal collapsing of a process that I thought took place, well, in a snip, *pace* Christine Jorgensen and my conversation with my mom—was for me a transmedia fail with the unspoken titles of "Lady In A Day," "Insta-Woman," or "Fast-Food Lady du Jour." The episode talked a lot—Reed's character espousing variants of "I've waited for this moment" and "I've always felt this way"—and while I had to wait a whole week to watch Brady Bunch Dad prepped for an operation that took a few hours in the episodes, Reed "became" a woman with a soft but not lower voice, a strawberry blonde matronly wig, a draped lowing chiffon scarf and a skirt/blouse ensemble worthy of Lane Bryant, plus tasteful low heels (my budding gaze was close by nature, baby), all on display as Pat The Woman walks hurriedly in a slow fade toward a cab taking her to (presumably) some new-locale-for-transgender-women-town for cancelled-miniseries parents. I remember looking at Reed's costume and specifically his makeup and lurching, sissified gait and thinking I could do better than that!"[4]

I attribute this episode to the aforementioned "InstaWoman-Fast-Food-Lady-In-A-Day" delusion that I—and many others—held, thanks to Erroneous Transmedia, where obviously no one trans seemed to have been consulted: from Lou Reed's narrative that Holly Woodlawn shaved her legs and poof!—"he" became "she" in "Walk On The Wild Side," to Nona Hendryx's seminal proto-trap sleaze-tempo anthem "Transformation" which directs us to "cash a check / change your sex," featured on her second solo album from the group she wrote and performed with, my beloved Labelle.[5] It took being schooled (not their job!) by a transwoman for me to notice that you don't enter a hospital overnight and leave a woman; that razors often came in contact with transwomen in non-cosmetic processes; and that the check casher on the corner was not the first and primary stop for transgender realization. As a non-binary boy watching the Brady dad transition like magic, I somehow equated transgender realization with magic, procedures, and money, not to mention a quick shave not to be hirsute. I knew I felt drawn to what was then called a sex-change, but I was confused: why didn't the Brady Bunch dad change his voice when, after almost two hours, he became a woman?

## SWEET 16 / GENDERING PRODUCTS
### *BOYS IN THE BAND*

Based on the expectations of my collective beauty aids purchases, I have always wanted to know what it feels like for a girl as applied to my exterior—my hair and skin. Products allowed me gender freedom, choice, fragrance, moisture, softness, volume, very important for a Hir/Unheard. When I first saw the movie *The Boys In The Band* in an Atlanta classic film repertory house in 1979, another "film-engendering event" from a parent that backfired. In this case, it was not to make a man of me so much as make a straight man out of me who was alerted to the dangers of homosexuality depicted in the film. I loved the film, though the anger and reading scared me. Integral to my awareness though as nonbinary was the character of Michael's bathroom—filled and stacked with beauty products arranged in haphazardly fabulous display, like a gay man's tiny Stonehenge of current historic grooming. Michael was my cosmetic twin, both dependent and re-assured by the amount and exhibition of his purchases that broke the beauty barrier in terms of intended gender. This was power to me, a ceremony engendered daily by liberal application and reassuring glance at the tiers of products. I have replicated this bathroom anywhere I've lived.

*The Boys In The Band*'s Michael has a hilarious exchange in his bathroom that probably I only find germane and funny—he unpacks the new products he has bought for his buddy Donald to share for the weekend, and then pulls out a can of hairspray marketed for men and bought for the somewhat-butcher Donald. Michael reads the name of the hairspray dramatically: *Control*. He laughs and says, "Well it's still hair spray—no matter if they call it "Balls"!" (*The Boys In The Band*, Cowley, p. 24) Crowley makes fun of gender fear via cosmetic usage and appearance—indeed, the hairspray was intended to keep things manly, controlled, while (in Michael's view) "manning up." And this is the only time I will refer to that particular facet of male genitalia. Today.

## THE NONBINARY SALESPERSON AT THE ULTA IN YULEE, FLORIDA

Today I went to buy some Clinique products, my favorite product line once I was taller than the top of the cosmetics counter in any department store and not afraid to be there or called out as dude lost in a beauty counter maze. I used to buy only the regular Clinique, then the Clinique for Men, then all of the above, to heck with the gender: it all worked, no matter for whom. I picked up some scrub crème and a bar of soap for combination skin (that bar in that signature sleek green sliding Clinique soap dish seems to have graced the background of my bathrooms since age fifteen). A female salesperson asked me if I needed any help; I didn't—I knew where what I wanted was. I went to the counter to purchase my stash, then looked up—I tend to grab and buy when I am in a beauty counter venue, probably because I still hold the key to gender shaming not to a bathroom but to a virtual cosmetic counter in my mind where I'm turned away and told to be a boy—to man up and take "control." I looked up at the salesperson ringing me up and was delighted to see that they were a gender-fluid person in full makeup, naturally bridging the gap or line between their gender performance with an emphasis on artfully applied product. I smiled at them, they smiled back, we shared something that the conquest of beauty inspired but was achieved in the way two nonbinary people recognize and celebrate themselves and their right to be open, out, painted, and groomed for the gods, or maybe just your rearview mirror before you get out to start your shift as you choose to be, without commentary. I could feel the kid in me circling beauty counters finally belly up to the beauty bar and be honored and noticed for good by one of their own.

## CAPOTE (OR "NONBINARY" AS GENRE-BLENDING FROM A WHITE CIS-GAY MAN OF POWER AND PROSAIC PRIVILEGE)

Truman Capote had a peripatetic, poetic, and chic history of wit, adapting himself—his works, that is—into no less than six genres by the time he was thirty, at work on one new genre that would purportedly combine the detail and drive of non-fiction with the "technique" of fiction. The "non-fiction novel" *In Cold Blood* was the hit of 1966, spawning, over thirty years, three feature films, one mini-series, several exhumed bodies, two hangmen's nooses, and a wild party with Capote at its helm in 1966 at The Plaza in New York City to celebrate his gender-blending achievement. What is striking is that Capote sensed that genre supremacy and mixing—or remixing—allowed him a more active application, a more apt opportunity to use his colors, true or otherwise, ironically fulfilling his name, *Tru*-man.

What I am calling genre fluidity may not have begun here, in Capote's non-fiction novel, but it did and does for me—I would argue that this example of an epicene "man" may have made the most visible case for genre fluidity, and did so because of his own "nature" (and here, as usual, I'm freely using Sontag-ian air quotes). Gender-blending while genre-bending? Yes.

Casting the real Capote in 1975's Neil Simon comedy *Murder By Death* with such heavy hitters as Maggie Smith, David Niven, Peter Sellers, and Elsa Lanchester might have merely been wish fulfillment of someone in the film's production chain saying "We need a Truman Capote type!" after seeing Capote throw shade and wreak havoc on many a talk show in the early to mid-seventies, apparently under the influence. Indeed, Simon's comedy got their Capote type—and I got a life-long litmus test for the performance of Capote "realness" that will probably never cease. The droll, "over it" dazzle of the performance would gradually affect me over time; the approach, or slant, of it needed more time to reveal a fully accurate impact.

This was a nonbinary man presenting, as the joke in the film stresses more than once, a female—as every person on the other end of this fictional Capote answers "Yes, Ma'am" to his unmistakable slur of an adenoidal high-pitched drawl. I argue the voice itself works as a swaggering "Foghorn Leghorn" on estrogen and with a cold, or maybe just as a girly-boy-other blaring foghorn, period. This was my first awareness of what nonbinary sounds like, unapologetically itself, and tonally beyond the male-female sonic scale, camp, perhaps, but more clearly epicene. That voice would be the key to unlocking Capote—for Philip Seymour Hoffman in *Capote* and for Toby Jones in *Infamous*—and it's more than a caricature—that voice will always be there for me as a guide to my nonbinary soundness.

Thus the real question for me may not be, "Do I Sound Gay?" but "Do I Sound Nonbinary—or Epicene?"

## APOLOGIA PRO VITA SUA (DRAG QUEEN EDITION)

As previously stated, I've been watching drag for a long time, blurring my expectations of what drag means and expects me to expect. Women in different stages or presentations of transitioning have always been a part of any cast I have watched and enjoyed—to the point where the controversy over transwomen being eligible to compete on *RuPaul's Drag Race* seemed really reductive and missing the point and the heritage I've enjoyed and supported since I was sneaking into the Sweet Gum Head show bar at age seventeen in Atlanta, Georgia in 1980. The distinction can't be made for everyone, surely, but no distinction in terms of performing drag was ever imposed—and frankly, it seemed a private issue (none of our business) and an attempt to colonize a queer body and have them deliver certain rigid expectations of gender. Queer bodies that opted for surgical procedures both were and weren't drag queens, but the stages (and tips) they earned allowed them to maintain the prominent part they have always played in the evolution of drag.

Presenting as female off-stage, in other words, was, again, none of our business.

I need to say their names, names as I came of age on stages and in stages (and sometimes with my mom in the audience with me!) in Atlanta, then a formidable hub for drag show bars and performers, not necessarily transwomen, but all drag artists, regardless, that showed me from 1979 to 1998 the art of heroic, glamorous illusion able to play with binaries and genders, ya'll: Tiffany Ariegus, Chena Black, Lily White, Lisa King, Rachel Welles, Yetteva Antoinette, Tina DeVore, Lani LaToke, LuLu, Amber Richards, Taisha Wallace, Roski Fernandez, Charlie Brown, Bertha Butts, and Satyn

DeVille. There's always a place in my mind where they walk in perfected gender synchronization.

There is a kindred space that drag performers deliver as they perform that a nonbinary audience member can recognize, exult, and thank: the way gender is synched, sculpted, snatched, and beat (as in "beat your mug") to allow freedom of gender expression. This gendered synchronization developed along with the skills and craft of making-up and costuming allows a nonbinary person to identify which the choices, the synchronization above all, or taking a recorded voice and owning it physically. Above all, the nonbinary person recognizes a multiplicity of genders being performed, even if one is being suppressed to allow another visual delivery "space to do all they intend to," to quote the emcee Junior Labeija from *Paris Is Burning*, another place and space where drag performers and women (with no need to designate necessarily as trans—they *are* women, no matter what their gender assignment at birth is, or was). Space to do all you intend to—in this chapter, "You better werk!"

## H(E)ARD OUTINGS

Hear me out: I have always seen gender as fluid just as I have always seen different performers in various stages of cis-feminine realization present as the women they are, even as they dress, paint, and corset themselves into said cis-femininity as performance, career, or trip to the mailbox with curlers in. I grew up understanding that some drag performers were surgically enhanced, and that other performers created the illusion for two shows a night as well but may or may not have aligned to either gender when they left the show bar. They were women for a moment and shared a stage with women of stages— defined by themselves for themselves and the gender they inhabited, with or without surgical milestones. They were to be "heard" in or out of drag; what became a common denominator that could "speak" for any performer was their ability to lip sync effectively and create an illusion that was real for the length of the song they were performing.

THUS my lurching nonbinary continuum includes what I've already dubbed as Women for a Moment versus Women in Stages as the exhibitors of gender construction and performance, with lip sync skills a common denominator for any presenting as cis-feminine while covertly as male or as female at their core of their very being, rag or no drag, naked or not. If RuPaul is correct that we're all born naked and the rest is drag, then we are also born in response to intersexed "anomalies" and the rest is gendered drag, a constant performance. No: there is no rest for the rest, not male today nor female, inhabiting the purple, black, and yellow shades their nonbinary flag displays for them, the right flag for the sissified boy who always mentally tucks himself, especially when he is made to take a bath at a relative's house, tucking himself (where he is still a *him*, a hymn to a gender disguised by skin); he doesn't yet know he is more than his genitals, more than a sign for a place to pee, as his home has no such restrictions. All our homes have no such restrictions!

This is the boy I write to now, who is thrilled to be "they" and "them" and no longer fears a relative's probing hands to create his identity as always relative to abuse. That relative's hand in the bathroom after their bath had a voice, not male, that scanned the surface of his pre-pubescent tuck, saying gleefully, tauntingly, "Where is IT?"

This is when all genitals became ITs, forever more, to the kid.

This is where all of my nonbinary skin became of age—through abuses, in spite of, beyond a relative touch. This is where the words *body* and *safety* changed. For good-not-good.

## DRAG TO THE RESCUE, AGAIN

For me coming of age, drag is what negotiated the place between functional genders—the epicene place beyond binaries. Drag allows us to perform gender visibly—or distort it altogether into a true epicene performance. Performativity is integral to understanding the need for drag—and to situate a deliverance of gender that is founded in and refers back to a nonbinary origin and constancy of shifting, delivering cis-normative gender roles and compositions at the same time as a gender that is queered, third, perhaps, but more often the navigation of cis-visuals and performances into a *hir*, a "you are *hir/here*,"[6] a location in transit bearing motion marks by nature, constantly tectonic and eruptive of foundations, unsettling and building at once to a third place that is truly queer in its unacknowledged normalcy.

At times I feel that "nonbinary" is active within binary expectations, seeking elsewhere, physical or otherwise, that both define and free our natures, sexual and otherwise—the wisdom of the "Other" that is not just about getting laid, but can be about the obligatory liberties to be productive against the obligations of reproductive freedoms (and constraints).

So now, the good real work begins: a locus, a start, a once upon, a genesis: because I started my woke life as a sissy, one might as well start there, with a ready toy nurse's kit, and no need for alarm or a shot other than a verbal snapshot. There will be drag queens, always: there always have been and will be, on the front lines of our consciousness and amorphous genders liberated for the ultimate liberated status, self-definition.

I started this book project as a cis-normative gay male who morphed into a nonbinary unsplit infinitive, an active otherwise, a verb(al) version of myself that adds sexuality into the mix but is not governed by it, especially as an inevitable box to check on any document. No one asks if you are LGTBQIA+, much less "S" or "+," to get a job. Who assumes "S" or "+," in this case "+" = nonbinary, without engaging the other acronyms as effacements, others, or thirds—in degrees? No matter how many degrees I earned, my gender never graduates.

But graduate school showed me how to unpack a quote that feels gutturally right, if shown through smoky mirrors, my "educated" mind's dry ice, bouncing back from the surfaces of known things:

> But when we consider the essence of technology, then we consider enframing as a destining of revealing. In this way, we are already sojourning within the open space of destining, a destining that in no way confines us to a stultified compulsion to push on blindly with technology or, what comes to the same thing, to rebel helplessly against it and curse it as the work of the evil. Quite to the contrary, when we once open ourselves expressly to the essence of technology, we find ourselves unexpectedly taken into a freeing claim. (Heidegger, *The Question Concerning Technology*, pp. 25–26)

Toward a "freeing claim," or an enframing—technically, physically, spiritually, and mentally—that holds and reveals not a "genitalia event" but instead what I hear as more of a passage toward an *essence chorale*, is what Janet Mock beautifully addresses in her 2014 bestselling memoir *Redefining Realness*:

> People often describe the journey of transsexual people as a passage through the sexes, from manhood to womanhood, from male to female, from boy to girl. That simplifies a complicated journey of self-discovery that goes way beyond gender and genitalia. My passage was an evolution to from me to closer-to-me-ness. It's a journey of self-revelation. . . . I sought something grander than the changing of genitalia. I was seeking reconciliation with myself. (Mock, 2014, p. 227)

Here, what I appreciate as autoethnographic transmedia, then, extends into a Heideggerian scenario that illuminates Mock's essence in this paragraph. This is an example of what I call transmedia thriving beyond the code of binaries, violence, and rigidity, translating gender not as a second language but fluently, fluidly, as a continuum that cross- references itself and works gloriously in and out of order—especially captured by the morphing iterations and deliverables of technology, the screens we inhabit and glimpse iterations of ourselves in, the digital pages we draft, the voice we search for, find, and reconcile, the peripatetic essence we synthesize in Heideggerian fashion.

Perhaps when I hear such a thick but gorgeous quote by Heidegger regarding technology and how I feel transmedia always helps to create my digital selves and synthesize them into a melodic yet often dissonant chorus, then maybe the academic part of me can wed the basic sissy still scared to come out to understand beyond the shape-shifting memory of daily abuses,

fast-food gendered transition expectations, and the rigid binaries sometimes dismissed as camp but ever-present in all of us. For me, a nonbinary *hir* understands finally the red spot on the map of anywhere indicating You Are Here, starting where your feet are—and replacing it, finally, flexibly, and inclusively "othered" beyond mere thirds as elsewhere aligned, indeed, at last, you are H-I-R, you're here, hear, *hir*—and, in terms of gender, more will be revealed, not once, but infinitely. Sometimes my body knew before I did the contradictory places where gender was quizzed, merely by what a soul inhabits, by the queer theater of inhabiting binary—and nonbinary—appearance:

(LOCATING PRONOUNS) MY BREASTS[7]
débuted in freshman gym class:
"Look at him: he needs a BRA!"—last
picked for volleyball, first abused.
I learned to stand with folded arms.
      Armor can be soft.

*Pudge, curve, flab, love handles, girth* . . .
Words brought sex to my virgin frame.
How could they see through my shirt?
That, around my heart, I'd pass for *girl*?

At 8 I drew an ad for a men's clothing store
(I was in love with *The Gap*) named
Male Man. I thought I was clever: I knew

that *male* was a message of sorts to a boy
that wouldn't dress for a gender already
announced by his chest in the first place

*[folds arms]*. Male man, what was the message?
Late one night I drew a circle around
my breasts with red magic marker.

Not a real circle but dashes, like welts.
This was where nothing could hurt me.
It really meant *In here, nothing's felt.*

Then I learned to dance and be a man
who partners women; my pecs knew
the difference faster than I did: dancing
with women made men masculine

(on stage). *Lift* became a noun. No U.K.
elevator, this: a human bench press, under
lights. If you support her, your chest benefits.
A *she* could be lifted, but never a *he*.

Flash-forward through blurry nocturnal
mouths at work on my nipples, by the men that
meant *gay*—or 'down-low' husbands who,
zipping up in the park afterwards, tweaked

my nip, and winked. Exit, stage left. Left
hand, ringed finger, making a tiny wave of
a flare, or flipping me off, in the moonlight,
through post-coital night and foliage:
clandestine green, a glimmer, then black.

Back in the day when *marriage* meant
women and men. For me, no husbands;
just tweaks. A measure for heat, or hotness,
at least. One twink called them *breasticles*.

They'd started to sag a bit by then—33? or 4?
At 36, trying to strut with topless women
in the Gay Pride Atlanta Dyke March. Girl!

Chants and percussion and freed breasts,
oh my. My shirt stayed on. At the beach it
stayed on. And then there was medication.

Don't look now: they're back: a side effect
called *gynecomastia*. From 'g-y-n' back to gym . . .
full circle? The bully gets the last word? No:

Meds grant cleavage now, what side does a
side effect take? Both, for me: to the right
*and* left of my dogged chest's hairy crease,
where the circle's still dashed, a restless sac

hangs with a tiny virtual pup inside, one
on each side. If a colleague pats my arm
in passing, my tit-tails wag, not like Jello.

These boys are tied-up dogs. You do not
call them *the girls*. Good boys: a loyal heart
softly guards what every hardness engenders.

Just don't look back at that boy at the volleyball
net, crying mid-smile as balls whizz by his face.
This is just physical education, don't ask him

to uncross his arms: no one told him this wasn't
dodgeball, he's waiting to be struck by his
truer sex, and for the hygiene quiz next period,

delivered with a testy glance from his butch
lady P.E. teacher to tell him (choose one):

that a) he can be queer for good, that b)
his body is queer and good, that c) his
breasts deserve better names and clothes
than t-shirts and gym shorts and *homo*.

Now look back: the bully who yelled
*He needs a bra* has his arms folded, too—
can't you see his circle through his shirt?

My message to him is *One day we'll love
outside the broken lines where skin
and sex do not choose teams to test
     their body's best disguises.*

*In this crimson circle's where you'll
feel your queerest GPS: trust:
no matter where you go, you're* hir.

So when is the body a successful disguise? How is it different for a nonbinary person, other than the expectations of butch vs. femme, embodied,
viewed—or synthesized without commentary, lived, housed, presented as is,
without modification other than that which the person in their respective body

feels enables their soul's clarity, beyond the reference of heteronormative cis-edits a checked sex box can inculcate?

Kate Bornstein ruminates to these effects much more comprehensively than I can:

> When I was first writing in [their autobiography] Gender Outlaw, transgender was an umbrella term, totally and completely. This is another big change. There were transsexuals, transvestites, street fairies, there were drag queens, there were drag kings, there were butch women and sissy men, and they all banded together under "transgender."
>
> Nowadays, transgender is defined by and large in the mainstream world—the "regular" world, as you phrased it—as men or women who have transitioned out of another gender. They're men and women, and they've transitioned. That's fine! That's a valid identity, and an important identity to acknowledge in our world. Everyone else I mentioned—drag queens, drag kings, dandies, transvestites, cross-dressers etc.—they really fall under that Q. Remember, we could laugh and giggle about transsexuals up until basically 2014—we were laughing, and asking people what their genitals were like, and all that. Now we can't, and what's replaced transsexual as an umbrella term is "trans"—I like that, it's fine. "Non-binary" [*sic*] and "genderqueer" are the straight and queer versions of someone's who's messing around with not being a man or a woman. *And now, nonbinary and genderqueer have replaced transsexual as who it seems safe to laugh at* (italics mine).
>
> So I think the next huge change in terms of sexuality and gender in terms of welcoming unpredictability is the embracing of non-binary. Queer, and straight. Faggot, gay man. Dyke, lesbian. Pansexual, bisexual. Tranny, transgender. Genderqueer, non-binary. As soon as we can start welcoming the unpredictability, that's going to change everything. (Blunt, *Signature*, 2016)[8]

Not surprisingly as I consider her now, but serendipitously for sure at first, Bornstein would play a foundational part in the forming of my nonbinary awareness and solidarity.

## THE BOOKSTORE READING (IN MORE WAYS THAN ONE)

I started this autoethnography mired in words in search of an identity beyond the dualities we absorb every day; I want to end on a moment that really has become the locus place for my nonbinary awareness. Visiting my folks in Miami in 1995, I stumbled upon the *flaneur* paradise of Collins Avenue and a book store with alluring sale carts lining the entrance. My mother and I went in immediately—I bought (tellingly) the poet James Merrill's autobiography, *A Different Person*, from the sale carts, and a copy of his *Selected Poems*. These genres, read together, would let me know who he really was. Soon it became evident that a reading of some kind was about to take place in the main area of the bookstore, as employees were opening and lining up folder chairs in front of a podium. I looked up at a flyer next to the cash register— (does anyone remember cash?!)—and saw Kate Bornstein's name next to the image of her book, *Gender Outlaw*. My mom and I decided to stay for a while; we sat in the back while most of the rows filled up.

Except the first.

The first row stayed empty up until the moment when Bornstein entered the room, fabulous, glamorous, androgynous, and engaging. They immediately said, "Doesn't anyone want to sit in the front row?" And then to herself, softly, "They never want to sit in the front row at first."

They were right: we were gender cowards.

Eventually, a gaggle of late queens descended upon the first-row seats and became the welcome chorus that responded to Bornstein's reading with requisite gay phrases of encouragement—*yes, girl, tell it, sister, work*. Bornstein seemed to enjoy their commentary. Language empowered the moment from one iteration of genderqueerness or affiliation to another—and thus the almighty important bridge was forged, from sub-category of queerdom to another, still forming, amorphous. I want to go back and have the chance to inhabit the front row again, where I belong, not necessarily gay first, but learning from the truest outlaw that ever intimidated a row of gender-gripped folks to be other than just in the front row by choice.

For we're all in need of inhabiting that row at our own good fearless pace, welcoming the dichotomies we've inherited and turning them into the narrative that guides us to our most realized selves, no matter the boxes or sexes we check, no matter how many morphing nouns we've carried until the day we let go of back row codification and engender the path— both forward and backward—to our realest, freest selves. Cue Sylvester, fabulous gender artiste and disco queen vocal *ballerina assoluta*, in his epicene-finest falsetto, sings "You make me feel / mi-igh-ty *real*."[9] (Sylvester, "You Make Me Feel (Mighty Real)," 1978) This is the voice that is still there, will always be there, nursing me, guiding me to genderqueer discovery, a disco/very space where fluidity is upheld, choices are made that do not hinder but empower, where the music's in you, and you're still real HOT! (I'm miming Sylvester's emphasis on this word in his song) after a night of dancing. Hear: you are about to be touched, figuratively or literally by the person of your choice that gets you without too much explanation, to solidify what realness means, sounds like, feels like, looks like, is—to you.

And, as gender blends in genres, here is where our selves, beyond any required dichotomous shape, can coalesce and thrive within the act of being read and re-read, again and again, like the map of your life re-assembling behind you as you forge your best epicene hybrid path, to a new unity beyond either/or, and always located forward. This is what I did for my 2020 summer vacation that wasn't, except for gender confirmation as the third, or other, or worthy—ready to come out and come home from camp's inhabited, natural, epicenic scenery. This has been my letter of transition, for myself and strangers. Let it engender one well-multi-tracked harmonic voice more often than not that moves us—forward. I'll be there with you, not only male, not only female, but the *me* we've always been. Together, we will inhabit the front row, the virtual public place where we nurse our realest genders.

## NOTES

1. That I don't remember where my brother and father were for this particular *kaffeklatch* shows that I really wasn't paying attention to the smaller *or* bigger picture of the men in my family. Not a surprise.

2. This poem is for Mark Doty, my former mentor at the University of Houston; the beautiful phrase "relentless standard" I use at the end of the poem is his.

3. Please see https://www.instagram.com/gofreemoonstone/ to do justice to LeGaspi's influential and far-out designs for LaBelle, Grace Jones, and other purveyors of 70's musical genderqueer-couture.

4. See for yourself: https://www.youtube.com/watch?time_continue=365&v=Z4JHvizrxr4&feature=emb_logo.

5. I should mention that Hendryx is a primary gender hero reference and monster musician to me; her glorious fluidly butch-femme image and solo album trajectory play a huge part in my nonbinary coming-of-age. I'm sure the ironic dichotomy in the lyrics I've quoted here are more about cause-effect wordplay than reductiveness of any transgender process.

6. See my poem to this effect, "My Breasts" later in the chapter.

7. This poem is a response-*homage* to J.D. McLatchey's poem "My Mammogram."

8. See http://www.signature-reads.com/2016/12/interview-gender-outlaw-kate-bornstein-explains-why-lgbt-demands-the-q/.

9. This is the voice that needs no introduction and that probably launched a million gender ripples through the viewers of this particular show: see him here with the "Two Tons Of Fun," Martha Wash and Izora Rhodes, making the "American Bandstand" TV show kids go berserk: https://www.youtube.com/watch?v=nz9CPABNMWo. I'm sure I saw this back in 1978 on a Saturday afternoon, stuck in the Atlanta suburbs, loving and *feeling* Sylvester and his music as epicene years before the word retroactively showed me how to feel "mighty real."

# REFERENCES

Bornstein, Kate. (1994). *Gender Outlaw*. New York, NY: Pantheon.

Belli, Willam. (2014). Episode 6, "Nurse." *RuPaul's Drag Race*. Season 4. World of Wonder, producers Fenton Baily and Randy Barberato.

Blunt, Thompson. (2020). "Interview: Gender Outlaw Kate Bornstein Explains Why LGTB Demands The 'Q. XX Judgement." Digital magazine.

Charles, RuPaul. (1992). "Supermodel (You Better Work)." On *Supermodel of the World*. CD. New York: Tommy Boy.

Crowley, Mart. (2018). *The Boys In The Band. Samuel French Acting Edition*. New York: Samuel French Ltd.

Harling, Robert. (1988). *Steel Magnolias*. New York: Dramatists Play Service Inc.

Heidegger, Martin. (2013). *The Question Concerrning Technology*. New York: Harper Perennial Reissue.

Hendryx, Nona. (1983). "Transformations." On *Nona [vinyl recording]*. New York: RCA Records.

Livingston, Jennie. (1990). "Paris Is Burning." DVD. New York: Miramax.

Lynn, Cheryl, David Foster and David Paich. (1979). "Got to Be Real." On *Cheryl Lynn*. Columbia Records.

Manning, Jimmie and Tony E. Adams. "Popular Culture Studies and Autoethnography: An Essay on Method," pp. 188–89.

Mock, Janet. (2014). *Redefining Realness*. New York, NY: Atria.

Perry, Tod. (2016). "Victor Lockhart Explains What It Is Like To Be Nonbinary." GOOD, https://www.good.is/articles/non-binary-explained.

Smith, Sam and Zane Lowe. (2005). "Restart." On *In the Lonely Hour* [CD, deluxe edition]. Capitol Records. (https://www.youtube.com/watch?v=JqRJpiQdamc).

Sontag. Susan. (1990). "Notes on Camp." *Against Interpretation and Other Essays*. New York: Picador.

Stryker, Susan. (2017). *Transgender History*. New York, NY: Seal Press.

Warrick, Tip and Sylvester James. (1978). "You Make Me Feel (Mighty Real)." [Recorded by Sylvester]. On *Step II* [vinyl recording]. San Francisco, CA: Fantasy).

Watkins, Susan. (2019). "Gender and Ganre: Students, Researchers, and the OED." Oxford English Dictionary online.

Weiss, Susannah. (2018). "Nine Things People Get Wrong About Being Nonbinary." *Teen Vogue*, May 2018. Retreived from https://amp.flipboard.com/@TeenVogue/9-things-people-get-wrong-about-being-non-binary/f-1ebaded3b8%2Fteenvogue.com.

# Index

# About the Contributors

**Traci Abbott** is assistant professor in the English and Media Studies Department at Bentley University in Waltham, Massachusetts. She holds a PhD in English language and literature from the University of Maryland College Park and focuses on gender and sexual identity in American literature and culture. Her works have been published in *Women's Studies*, *The Southern Quarterly*, *The Journal of American Culture*, and elsewhere, and she serves on the editorial review board for *Queer Studies in Media & Popular Culture*. Currently, she is working on a book monograph, *Transformation: The Transgender Narrative in Popular Visual Media*, which examines transgender presentations in U.S. televisual fictional narratives.

**Rachel Friedman** is associate professor of aviation administration at California State University, Los Angeles. Her research varies between rhetoric and cultural studies and aviation. She has worked on projects ranging from flight data monitoring systems to rhetorical analyses of prominent female political figures. Her works have been published by Lexington Books, McFarland Books, *Advancing Women in Leadership*, *The Cross-Cultural Communication Journal*, and *Communication Teacher*, among others. Dr. Friedman also manages several aviation publications for private jet and turboprop owners. While aircraft is her current passion, her roots in communication studies and the fight for fairness and equality is what drove her to take on *Beyond Binaries*.

**Billy Huff** (PhD, Georgia State University) is a lecturer of communication at the University of Illinois at Urbana-Champaign and a research associate with the Unit for Institutional Change and Social Justice at the University of the Free State in Bloemfontein, South Africa.

**Lucky Issar** is a literature graduate with a degree in education. Currently, he is working on his PhD in Berlin, Germany. He is interested in Indian English fiction, gender studies, queer theory, and Dalit studies. He has contributed books reviews, fiction, and academic essays to various publications. His most recent essay is, "Hidden in Plain Sight: Caste and Sexuality in Khaled Hosseini's *The Kite Runner*" in *Critical Insights The Kite Runner*, edited by Nicolas Samuel Tredell (2020).

**John C. Lamothe** is associate professor of humanities and communication at Embry-Riddle Aeronautical University in Daytona Beach, Florida. He is coeditor of *Athletes Breaking Bad: Essays on Transgressive Sports Figures* and has written and spoken widely about a variety of issues related to sports and culture.

**Finn Lefevre** is a dramaturg, applied theatre facilitator, and educator. They currently serve as a visiting lecturer at the University of Massachusetts Department of Theater, and as a founding member of the queer and trans performance collective Queer & Now (wearequeerandnow.com). They have previously taught in the Department of Theater and Dance at Keene State College, and the Ethnic and Gender Studies Department at Westfield State University. They facilitate workshops in "Theatre of the Oppressed and Cops in the Head," story circles, and trans and queer performance (www.finnlefevre.com).

**Ashley B. Maxwell** is a lecturer of anthropology at Washburn University in Topeka, Kansas. She is a broadly trained biological anthropologist with experience in both bioarchaeological and forensic contexts. Her research is interdisciplinary and takes a biocultural focus, which includes understanding how age and gender influence migration, diet, and health. Dr. Maxwell is also involved in forensic anthropological casework, research, and has multiple publications in the field. Her four-field anthropological background provides a holistic approach to topics such as gender and race, which drove her to contribute to *Beyond Binaries*.

**G. M. Mozer** holds a PhD in English literature from the University of Miami. Their research examines intersectional and interdisciplinary transgender cultural production. Their book project, *Writing Transgender: Speculative and Real*, examines the intersections of narrative and transgender studies across literary genres. They teach writing and literature courses that emphasize multicultural LGBTQ+ literature and media studies.

**Jacob Muriel** is a PhD candidate in English at Northeastern University and former reviewer for *The Comics Journal*. He has published and presented multiple papers on comics.

**Mike Perez** earned an MA in creative writing from Florida State University and an MFA from the University of Houston. His father was an aviation expert and his mother is the acclaimed poet Nola Perez—thus Mike considers his current occupation as a professor at Embry-Riddle Aeronautical University to be merely Kismet (and DNA) fulfillment. His poems have been published in *GLASS, Bloom, Crab Orchard Review, Route Seven Review, Oscilloscope Lit Mag, Beyond Queer Words, Bangalore Review, The Journal of Florida Studies*, and at winningwriters.com as a finalist for their annual War Poetry Contest. Book chapters have appeared recently or are forthcoming in *The Susan Sontag Anthology, Queer /Adaptations, The Power of Makeup*, and *Essays on Billie Holiday*, an anthology for which he also was lead editor.

**Peter Piatkowski** is a UK-based writer who is originally from the United States. He has written for a variety of publications, both online and in print, and maintains a blog on cinema, *A Seat in the Aisle*. His interests include film, literature, television, popular culture, music, and food writing. Along with writing, Peter has also taught for the City Colleges of Chicago for a number of years. He graduated from the University of Illinois, Chicago with a BA in English, later earning his MA in English literature from DePaul University, and an MFA in creative writing from Roosevelt University. He has seen his works published in *The Daily Harold, Feminist Review, Bright Wall/Dark Room, Fashion X Film, Off the Rocks*, and *A View from Here*.

**J. Michael Ryan** is assistant professor of sociology at Nazarbayev University. He is the editor of multiple volumes including *Trans Lives in a Globalizing World: Rights, Identities, and Politics* (2020), *Gender in the Middle East and North Africa: Contemporary Issues and Challenges* (with Helen Rizzo, 2020), and *Core Concepts in Sociology* (2019).

**Jim Shoopman**, PhD, is associate professor of humanities and communication at Embry-Riddle Aeronautical University in Daytona Beach, where he specializes in comparative religions, ethics, and Holocaust studies. Dr. Shoopman has formerly served as a clergyman associated with the Cooperative Baptist Fellowship and the Alliance of Baptists, two progressive Baptist communities of faith in the South.

www.ingramcontent.com/pod-product-compliance
Lightning Source LLC
Chambersburg PA
CBHW022310280326
41932CB00010B/1054